Tourism

How effective management makes the difference

Roger Doswell

Butterworth-Heinemann
Linacre House, Jordan Hill, Oxford OX2 8DP
225 Wildwood Avenue, Woburn, MA 01801-2041
A division of Reed Educational and Professional Publishing Ltd

A member of the Reed Elsevier plc group

OXFORD   BOSTON   JOHANNESBURG
MELBOURNE   NEW DELHI   SINGAPORE

First published 1997
Reprinted 1998

British Library Cataloguing in Publication Data
Doswell, Roger
    Tourism: how effective management makes the difference
    1. Tourist trade – Management
    I.   Title
    338.4´7´91´068

ISBN 0 7506 2272 5

Typeset by David Gregson Associates, Beccles, Suffolk
Printed in Great Britain by Biddles Ltd, Guildford and King's Lynn

Contents

Preface

No single organization runs the tourism sector. Tourism is not really an industry or a sector in itself. It is an economic activity that runs through society involving many different sectors. The tourism sector comes together only loosely, pushed forwards by market forces, controlled by a regulatory framework, and governed by general economic conditions.

What a government tourism administration (GTA) should do, for no one else can do it, is to guide the development of the sector through planning, organizing, directing, coordinating and monitoring its various activities. This helps the private sector by building up all the pieces into a whole. The GTA does not manage in any direct sense, but in an indirect, indicative way.

It should, however, manage with a certain lightness of touch, setting directions, providing support and creating the right conditions. It assists the sector, within the particular political and institutional framework, to work together and to set and achieve certain objectives. This book looks at how this management process can be made more effective.

The term 'government tourism administration' (GTA) has been used in preference to 'national tourism organization' (NTO). NTO seems to owe its origin to the early government organizations which acted nationally, and concentrated principally on advertising and promotion. However, the government's involvement in tourism is more extensive than marketing alone covering, as it does, an overall management function. It is also not only national, but involves the management of the sector at regional and local levels. GTA is a term which describes more adequately this wider role.

Management in the private sector relates to the management of a particular type of tourism enterprise, e.g. a hotel, tour operator, travel agency, or tourist attraction. The GTA's management of the sector as a whole is of central importance to the private sector, since it helps to set the conditions in which all tourism development takes place.

This is not an argument for wide-ranging government intervention in tourism. A GTA, and the effective management of the sector, may protect it from unnecessary intervention.

The old-fashioned approach to tourism planning as a one-off plan owes its origin to architectural project-oriented physical planning. Tourism planning is ongoing and incremental by nature, and a part of management. One-off tourism development plans, executed and updated every now and then, should give way to an integrated and continuing management process.

The book is divided into three parts. Part One looks at the characteristics of the tourism sector and the organization and responsibilities of a GTA. Part Two examines the various influences on the public administration of tourism, its economic, environmental and cultural impacts, some of the major development issues, and key aspects in its management and planning. Part Three includes an examination of a sound management approach to each area. It deals with managing the GTA, regulation and research, marketing, product development, human resources development and public awareness. Each chapter in Part Three finishes with a comprehensive list of objectives, results and activities. Taken together these comprise a comprehensive overview of a sectoral management approach.

The three parts of the book represent first what is to be managed, second the influences on the management process, and last exactly what to plan and manage.

The book is aimed at both students and tourism professionals. It can serve as a comprehensive text in courses with a particular focus on sectoral management. It can also provide valuable assistance to anyone concerned with the planning and management of tourism.

One needs to hold in constant view the full picture of the tourism sector. Where it is, how it is developing, where it is going. This is the frame of reference to which one returns again and again. At the same time, there has to be familiarity with the detailed situations; for example, the planning of a new tourist information office, the rehabilitation of an historic site, the development of a new resort, or the extension of an airport runway.

The tourism professional moves constantly between the two viewpoints, the faraway strategic view and the close-up tactical view. The faraway view enables the framing of policy and long term objectives. The close-up view considers the immediate implementation issues and problem-solving viewpoint; getting the details right and knowing that day-to-day operations are functioning as they should.

This need to build up over time a truly comprehensive overview was echoed by Marcel Proust. He noted that the discovery in life is 'to see the universe through the eyes of another, of a hundred others, to see the hundred universes that each of them sees, that each of them is . . .'

Tourism can always develop badly or well. The choice exists whatever the country, whatever the culture. Tourism professionals can mobilize society in such a way as to make it aware of the issues, the decisions and the stakes. They do whatever is necessary to bring tourism to the forefront, to get it recognized, studied, funded and, where justified, prioritized.

The complexity of tourism often creates a confusing and contradictory picture. Roland Barthes claimed 'to live to the full the contradiction of my time'. Inevitably we are all forced to grapple with such contradiction.

Each discipline has its own preferred vocabulary, yet different disciplines often share the same concepts. They simply express them with a varying focus, often using different words and terms. I have chosen the terms which I prefer, and have then tried to use them consistently.

Ideas, particularly of an abstract kind, can be communicated in many different ways. Understanding the underlying concept matters more than the particular words used. Sometimes we need to see through the words to get at the idea. We need to see that different authors may be saying the same thing but in a different fashion. We need to achieve a common understanding of ideas regardless of how they are expressed.

The management by objectives breakdown used in the last part of the book is similar to the approach used by the United Nations Development Programme and other technical assistance agencies. It sets objectives and expresses their achievement through a series of measurable results, supported by checklists of all the necessary activities.

These days it is common to find the indiscriminate use of sources and direct quotations when they contribute little or nothing to the text. The number of references cited is not necessarily indicative of the depth of argument.

Sources and direct quotations may indicate how and where authors have built on the previous work of others. They help to establish the foundations for the new work. They may also help to illustrate and corroborate the findings and arguments presented. And they may indicate how the work represents a logical continuation in adding to existing viewpoints. Finally, they may be used simply to conjure up the imagery to reinforce a particular idea.

In this book I have tried not to clutter the text with frequent references to other books on tourism or articles from learned journals. As a result I have finished up using few references. At the end of the book, however, a bibliography of 100 useful titles has been included.

I am grateful to Rik Medlik for his comments on the first draft of the book. I am also grateful to Brian O'Shaughnessy for reading the second draft. The following people were also kind enough to read and comment on various chapters when first drafted: David Bowden, Ed Krowitz, Fred Lawson, Philip Nailon and Neil Taylor.

Roger Doswell

Part One
The Background to
Tourism Management

1 Tourism – definitions, concepts and policies

This chapter introduces the history of tourism, and analyses the underlying reasons for the sector's rapid growth. It goes on to discuss definitions of the sector, its structure and its division into three different levels. It looks at tourism in the context of national planning, and then examines tourism statistics and internationally recognized concepts and definitions. It discusses some of tourism's distinctive aspects: spontaneity; remembrance; the tourism patrimony; the matching of product components; product perishability; carrying capacity; product changeability; the competition for space; the fixity of operating costs; and the seasonality of demand. It then goes on to describe how to structure the tourism planning process, and concludes with an example of a typical tourism policy statement.

The history of tourism

Wide-scale temporary travel away from home is a relatively new phenomenon. In the past few people enjoyed leisure time. For ordinary people any time off was usually for religious reasons. For holy days – hence the word holidays. Early travel was often confined to pilgrimages. Later, as the spas developed, people travelled for health. With the Age of Reason, they started travelling for culture. As a result the famous Grand Tour became popular.

As the social and economic development of countries accelerated (principally in Europe and North America), so wage levels and working conditions improved. Gradually people were given more time off. At the same time forms of transport improved and it became faster and cheaper to get to places. England's industrial revolution led to many of these changes. Railways, in the nineteenth century, opened up now famous seaside resorts such as Blackpool and Brighton.

With the railways came large and palatial hotels. In Canada, for example, the new coast-to-coast railway system prompted the building of such famous hotels as Banff Springs and Chateau Lake Louise in the Rockies.

During the first half of this century, the moneyed classes started to travel more widely. The advent of air transport opened up more of the world and stimulated tourism growth. However, the opportunities for holiday making for ordinary people were still limited in scope. For most people, in developing countries, the chances to travel are still limited.

Tourism exploded in the developed countries after the Second World War. Prosperity, more discretionary income, cheaper and better transport, and more time off, brought new marketing opportunities. Tour operators started up and responded to the demand. The 'package' tour developed along with charter air transport. Mass international tourism surged. The great sprawling urban developments of the Mediterranean coastline began to take shape. Other parts of the world started to follow these same patterns of development.

Holidays continue to lengthen while transportation systems develop and become cheaper in real terms. More countries become relatively prosperous, starting to generate substantial flows of outbound tourists. Domestic tourism also expands and many people now take more than one holiday.

New destinations continue to emerge and tourism has become the world's largest industry. The World Travel and Tourism Council estimates that, in 1994, it generated US$3.4 trillion in revenues, created 204 million jobs (one in every nine), and accounted for just over 10 per cent of world gross domestic product (WTTC, 1994).

The growth of tourism

According to the World Tourism Organisation's (WTO) forecast of trends to the year 2000 and beyond, there will be close to 650 million international tourist arrivals by the turn of the century. By comparison, the population of the world in the year 1000 was only 500 million.

International tourism rose to 500 million arrivals in 1993, despite a world economic recession. International tourism receipts rose to US$304 billion. These receipts represented 8 per cent of total merchandise exports and 30 per cent of exports of services. Tourism ranked first among world exports of goods and services, ahead of oil, motor vehicles and electronic equipment. According to WTO forecasts, world tourist arrivals will increase by 3.8 per cent a year taking the 1990s as a whole, and slightly above 3.5 per cent a year in the first decade of the 21st century (WTO, 1994).

In 1993 almost 90 per cent of the world's travellers did not cross an international frontier. Domestic tourism, the WTO estimates, probably represents between 80 and 90 per cent of total world tourist demand. It points out that in the USA over one billion trips are made away from home each year.

Two major factors have tended to characterize international tourism. First, most of it has been both generated and received by developed countries — the better off going to visit the better off. In 1960 over 96 per cent of world arrivals were in Europe and the Americas. In 1993 the figure was still very high at about 80 per cent.

Second, most tourism has been concentrated within the immediate regions of the developed countries. Generally the closer countries are to each other, the more movement there is between them. Intraregional tourism is still the major driving force in tourism growth.

The travel account

Earnings from international tourism represent an invisible export; they are the result of selling the country's tourism product to tourists from abroad. Expenditures on tourism are the opposite. They represent an invisible import; one's residents are buying a tourism product elsewhere.

What is earned and what is spent are reconciled in the country's travel account. Countries in the north tend to have a negative balance. Countries to the south, accessible from major markets, are likely to have a positive balance.

It is not strictly fair to compare tourism earnings and expenditures in this way. If a country reports a deficit, it may appear that it is not managing its tourism well. The reverse may be true. It could be doing exceptionally well with only a few resources.

Defining tourism

In March 1993 the United Nations Statistical Commission adopted a set of recommendations on tourism statistics prepared by the World Tourism Organisation (WTO).

Tourism is defined as comprising 'the activities of persons travelling to and staying in places outside their usual environment for not more than one consecutive year for leisure, business and other purposes'.

This definition is oriented to the demand for travel. Tourism definitions tend to favour either a supply or a demand focus. The supply-sided definitions describe the product offered to tourists – what the tourists experience. The demand-sided definitions focus on the behaviour of tourists and what they need and seek.

Tourism is not so much a sector in itself as a multi-sectoral economic activity. This is why economists find it so hard to categorize and governments so complex to coordinate. It is difficult to delimit tourism in its totality and, because of this, it is an activity difficult to both define and manage.

Tourism should be seen as the interaction between supply and demand; the development of a product to meet a need. It is this interaction which introduces economic, environmental, sociocultural and other effects.

There are many ways of looking at the tourism experience. One is to divide it into three stages:

● What happens before leaving home. Studying the publicity. Choosing the destination. Making the purchase.

- What happens on the way there and back. The journey. Departing and arriving.
- What happens once there. The quality of the whole experience. Memories and satisfactions. Dissatisfactions.

The three levels of tourism

From the supply side then, the tourism sector is made up of all those services and features which come together to comprise the experience enjoyed by a tourist. As illustrated in Figure 1.1, it can be viewed in terms of three levels.

The *first level* includes the role of government in terms of tourism policy and planning, and the establishment of the framework within which the sector must operate. This covers the economic, environmental and social goals at all levels of government, and the corresponding system of controls. These include physical planning controls, licensing controls, labour controls, and fiscal and transportation controls. Involved in the development and management of this framework is the government tourism administration (GTA) with its principal departments such as marketing, product development, regulation and control, human resources development, public awareness and research.

The *second level* covers the front line organizations concerned with tourism development and operations. These include the hotels, other accommodation facilities, catering and related services, the cultural,

First level	Tourism policy and strategy framework; the Government Tourism Administration (GTA)	
Second level	Hotels, accommodation, catering, attraction, transportation	Coordinating and consultative mechanisms
Third level	Network of supporting services	

Figure 1.1   The tourism sector's three levels

historical and scenic attractions, and the entertainment and recreational centres and facilities. They also include the travel trade and its various services, and transportation including air, road, sea and rail services.

The *third level* includes the whole range of ancillary support services and organizations, which are in both the public and private sectors. They include the police, post office, customs and immigration, consumer association services, the media, the retail trade, banks, churches, universities and colleges, trade unions, and all institutes and associations with some activities which bear on tourism.

Coordinating and consultative mechanisms linking these three levels are provided by committees, councils, working groups and task forces which involve public sector bodies and agencies, or private sector organizations or associations, or a combination of the two. They try to create the necessary collaboration and consultation for the harmonious development and operation of the sector.

National planning

Any tourism sector must be placed in the context of national, social and economic development. This is shown in Figure 1.2.

Tourism can contribute significantly to economic development. It often represents an important option for countries to pursue, but has to be assessed against alternative economic opportunities. All the various areas in Figure 1.2, both economic and social, may compete for scarce resources.

Tourism statistics

The definitions in this section follow WTO recommendations (WTO, 1993). Tourism takes three forms:

- Domestic tourism involves 'residents of the given country travelling only within this country'.
- Inbound tourism involves 'non-residents travelling in the given country'.
- Outbound tourism involves 'residents travelling in another country'.

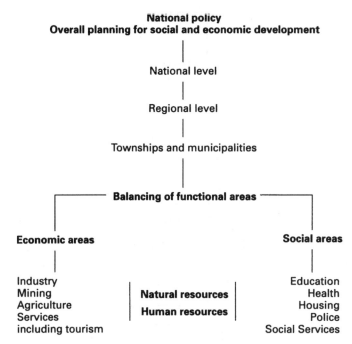

Figure 1.2   Tourism and national development

These three forms of tourism, as described by the WTO, are shown in Figure 1.3.

As will be noted the term 'internal tourism' comprises domestic tourism and inbound tourism.

'National tourism' comprises domestic tourism and outbound tourism.

'International tourism' comprises inbound and outbound tourism.

All types of travellers engaged in tourism are described as visitors. The term 'visitor' represents the concept underlying the whole system of tourism statistics, and is illustrated in Figure 1.4.

Following on from this the term 'international visitors', for statistical purposes, means, 'persons who travel to a country other than that in which they have their usual residence but outside their usual environment for a period not exceeding twelve months and whose main purpose of visit is other than the exercise of an activity remunerated from within the country visited.'

International visitors include:

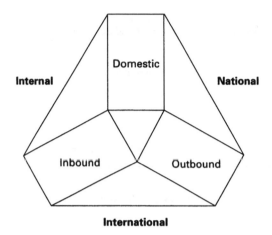

Figure 1.3   Forms of tourism (demand side). *Source*: WTO

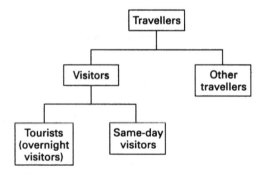

Figure 1.4   Definition of visitors. *Source*: WTO

Tourists (overnight visitors)

A visitor who stays at least one night in the country visited, in either private or commercial accommodation.

Same-day visitors

A visitor who does not spend the night in the country visited. This includes cruise ship passengers, even though the ship may pass one or more nights in the harbour. Similarly it would not include train passengers if they are accommodated on the train.

In classifying the origin of visitors, it is important to count them according to their country of residence rather than by nationality. Each country of destination should develop a classification system of its important centres, cities and resorts, in order to report the main distribution of tourism.

The following categories of traveller are not included in tourism statistics:

Border workers
Temporary immigrants
Permanent immigrants
Nomads
Transit passengers
Refugees
Members of the armed forces
Representation of consulates
Diplomats

The purposes of a visit for either inbound, outbound or domestic tourism, are as follows:

Leisure, recreation and holidays
Visiting friends and relatives
Business and professional
Health treatment
Religion/pilgrimages
Other

Figure 1.5 shows the classification of international visitors in diagrammatic form.

Domestic visitors describes persons residing in a country who travel to a place within the country, outside their usual environment, for a period not exceeding twelve months and whose main purpose of visit is other than the exercise of an activity remunerated from within the place visited. In a similar way to international visitors, domestic visitors can be classified as tourists (overnight visitors) and same-day visitors.

WTO classifies the means of transport as follows:

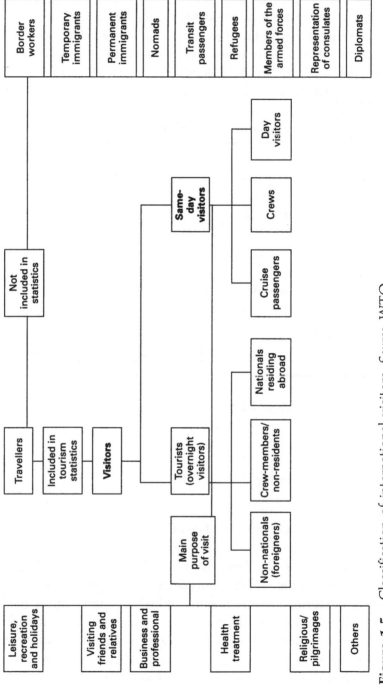

Figure 1.5 Classification of international visitors. *Source:* WTO

Air

Scheduled flights
Non-scheduled flights
Other services

Waterway

Passenger lines and ferries
Cruise
Other

Land

Railway
Motor coach or bus and other public road transport
Private vehicles (capacity up to eight persons)
Vehicle rental
Other means of land transport

WTO classifies tourism accommodation as follows:

Hotels and similar establishments
Specialized establishments
  Health establishments
  Work and holiday camps
  Public means of transport
  Conference centres
Other collective establishments
  Holiday dwellings
  Tourist camp sites
  Other collective establishments
Private tourism accommodation
  Owned dwellings
  Rented rooms in family houses
  Dwellings rented from private individuals or professional
    agencies
  Accommodation provided without charge by relatives or
    friends
  Other private accommodation

Tourism expenditure is defined by WTO as: 'the total consumption expenditure made by a visitor for and during his/her trip and stay at the destination'.

For inbound tourism, international tourism receipts are defined as 'expenditure of international inbound visitors including their payments to national carriers for international transport'.

It is recommended that international fare receipts be classified separately. These are defined more precisely as 'any payment made to carriers registered in the compiling country of sums owed by non-resident visitors whether or not travelling to that country.

For outbound tourism, international tourism expenditure is defined as 'expenditure of outbound visitors in other countries including their payments to foreign carriers for international transport'.

It is recommended that international fare expenditure also be classified separately. It is defined more precisely as 'any payment made to carriers registered abroad by any person resident in the compiling country'.

The WTO working together with the United Nations Statistical Division, supported by organizations such as the WTTC, have worked towards a more comprehensive statistical representation of tourism. This should result in a travel and tourism satellite account. The grouping together of tourism-related activities in a more complete way, will allow for improved sectoral analyses. This will provide better information on tourism's contributions to social and economic development.

Distinctive aspects of tourism

Three immediately striking aspects of tourism are:

- Mostly it is not seen or tried out before it is purchased.
- It is consumed where it is produced.
- The place and the people, where it is produced, are a part of the product and tourism therefore involves many sections of society.

These three aspects help to give tourism its unique character. The people living and working in a particular destination do not just produce a product, many of them become a part of it.

Tourism has other distinctive aspects related to either demand or supply, although some do tend to be shared by other service sectors.

Taken together, therefore, there are the ten aspects which tend to make tourism different.

Spontaneity
Remembrance
Tourism patrimony
Matching — the interdependence of product components
Perishability
Carrying capacity
Changeability
Competition for space
Fixity of operating costs
Seasonality of demand

Spontaneity

The product is given a spontaneous characteristic, because of the intangible aspects of service. No guest experience is exactly the same. The way people are greeted will vary. So will the way they are served and treated.

This makes the control of quality difficult. In manufacturing, by comparison, the product can be standardized and controlled easily.

Even in hotels and restaurants, for example, one can standardize a steak. One can specify from which part of the animal it must be cut, that it should weigh 200 grams and be three centimetres thick. However, a smile cannot be standardized; one cannot specify its width, length or any of its other characteristics.

People cannot be ordered to smile. People tend to smile if they are happy and enjoying themselves, and because the job gives them satisfaction. It is not possible to run a tourism enterprise successfully if the staff show unhappiness.

In a hotel two guests might get up in the morning after an early morning call from the operator; this makes one contact with the staff.

They then call room service and order a continental breakfast; this is two contacts. They call housekeeping to say they have some laundry to send; three contacts. The room attendant comes and collects the laundry; four contacts. The room service waiter arrives with the breakfast; five contacts. Somebody then arrives to check the room's mini bar; six contacts. The guests go downstairs and leave their key at the desk; seven contacts. They go to the newsstand and buy a paper; eight contacts. They then go to the information desk to ask what's on at the theatre that evening; this makes nine contacts. They then ask for a taxi to go somewhere; and this makes ten contacts.

This is a total of ten contacts with the staff even before leaving the hotel in the morning. If this same hotel had 200 guests who behaved similarly, this would make a total of 2000 staff/guest contacts even at the very start of the day.

It is evident that it would be impossible to monitor the quality of all of these 2000 contacts. Staff themselves have to take responsibility for the quality of their contacts with guests. Only a well trained and well motivated staff will do this competently and consistently. In tourism, therefore, there are special needs in terms of personnel management, human relations and training.

Remembrance

Tourism is about enriching people's lives. While many parts of a person's life will fade away into a blur, holidays and journeys tend to live on in the memory. When people are asked to talk about their lives, they will tend to talk about only the happiest and the saddest moments. Holidays and travel are usually among the happiest of recollections.

When people go on holiday they are already looking forward to creating memories. Tourism offers an escape, the indulgence of fantasies and realization of dreams. The promises of the tourist brochures often become realities. Once people have the leisure time and the discretionary income to take advantage of tourism, their lives are changed in a major way.

Tourism patrimony

Certain features — mountains, lakes, forests, beaches, etc., an agreeable climate, cities, towns and villages, a rich cultural heritage and many cultural and historical sites — create the essential conditions for a successful tourism product. These natural and cultural resources, together with climate, comprise the country's tourism patrimony.

If a country possesses only a few such positive features, its tourism opportunities may be limited. It will be forced to rely on newly created features.

A country's tourism possibilities are like those of young women competing in a beauty contest. If they have not inherited the right characteristics — are not born with the right degree of natural beauty — their chances of success are limited.

Matching space

Tourism is about matching. The development of a successful tourism product depends on the matching of quality levels and capacities, to meet the needs of different markets. For example, the matching of airline seats to airport capacities and hotel rooms. The matching of cars to roads, of buses to the number of airport arrivals, or buses to sightseers, of hotel rooms to restaurant seats, of square metres of beach to sunbathers, of golfers to golf courses, dancers to dance floor space, theatre seats to theatregoers and so on.

The adequate matching of complementary capacities, of maintaining balance and harmony through the complete range of services and facilities to be provided, is a major consideration.

Perishability

The tourism product is perishable because it cannot be stored. If an airline or bus seat, or a hotel room or a restaurant seat, or even a deck chair on a beach goes empty on a particular day — it is lost, gone! — it perishes. It can be sold again on another day, but the chance to sell it on that particular day is lost.

Space for rent is perishable. Each day it remains unsold, it loses revenue. Other commodities can be kept and sold later. The use of space cannot.

Selling something which is perishable creates additional pressures. One has only to visit a supermarket just before it closes for the weekend to realize this. Perishability creates particular marketing and sales needs.

Carrying capacity

It is said that a certain Spanish tourism expert, asked how to judge the optimum carrying capacity of a given tourism destination, replied, 'When there's no more room for anybody else'. This is, of course, far too simple an answer.

The carrying capacity of an area, attraction or facility is reached when further visitors would damage the environment, or lower the enjoyment of everybody else to below an acceptable level.

The concept of carrying capacity is of great importance, and further reference will be made to it in later chapters. As tourism grows, so will the pressure exerted on tourist facilities and attractions.

It is mostly a question of both measurement and judgement. Of what the attraction or place can withstand without threat of damage or deterioration. And what the market will accept in terms of crowds and queues.

Changeability

Most products are conceived at a certain point in time and remain basically the same. A new tourism destination, however, grows over a number of years. As it succeeds in the market place, so it is expanded and developed further. As a result it can change enormously.

A destination may even double, triple or quadruple or more in size. New hotels and other facilities are added, more employment is created, the population grows and urbanization increases. Anybody visiting the same new holiday destination some five to ten years later, will testify to this process of transformation.

Until the carrying capacity is reached, and there is no more room or possibility for further growth and expansion, a destination often continues to change. Just the increasing number of people using the product change it.

It may take 20 to 30 years to develop a destination to this point. This characteristic is sometimes confused with the concept of product life cycles, discussed in Chapter 3.

Competition for space

Tourism competes with the local population for space, for example, space for the construction of hotels and other types of tourism facility. And space in terms of the services, for example, space on the buses, in the shops, at the post office, and on the golf course.

Land use for tourism may often compete with alternative economic opportunities. In many cases, however, tourism may provide the most environmentally attractive option. In many Latin countries tourism is called the industry without chimneys, emphasizing its clean and environmentally positive aspects.

Tourism facilities may also compete for land best left undeveloped as open space for public enjoyment.

Fixity of operating costs

As in other businesses, tourism profits must be planned and costs budgeted accordingly. Costs are normally fixed, semi-fixed and variable.

Fixed costs do not vary according to the volume of business, for example, rental charges for the hire of equipment.

Semi-fixed costs vary partly, for example, electricity.

And some costs are entirely variable, for example the cost of food and beverages.

The costs of the tourism product are largely fixed. For example the costs of providing an airport or hotel, staffed, equipped and waiting to receive tourists, are incurred regardless of how many tourists arrive. If fewer tourists than expected come, many of the costs remain the same.

There are also many fixed costs in the operation of a museum and other tourist attractions. Even a municipality, in the range of services which it provides, has a high level of fixed costs.

The fixed costs in tourism make it critical to maintain a sufficiently high volume of visitors.

Seasonality of demand

In most countries the tourism sector suffers from seasonal fluctuations in demand. This creates a lack of continuity in operation. Consistency in quality levels is hard to achieve, and cash flows and incomes become interrupted.

Seasonality affects many things, for example, the flow of supplies, employment, energy consumption and community services. Some hotels and other facilities may even be mothballed and closed for a number of months.

Seasonality is caused by changing climatic conditions, traditional holiday making habits, and institutional patterns in holiday breaks particularly those of schools and other educational establishments.

However, destinations enjoying a demand from different geographical areas can take advantage of complementary holiday patterns. The Caribbean exploits the winter market from North America, and also attracts Europeans during their traditional summer break. It has been able to develop and sustain almost a year round demand.

Other tropical destinations such as South East Asia have been able to exploit demand from the two hemispheres. Bali, for example, attracts both the European and Australian and New Zealand markets. It exploits winter and summer demand from both areas of the world.

A traditional summer resort such as Banff Springs in Canada, was able to develop a substantial skiing market in winter. Traditional ski resorts in Europe have succeeded in developing as summer mountain resorts.

The Mediterranean resorts have been able to develop a winter market consisting mainly of retired people from northern Europe. Reduced prices have persuaded large numbers of older people to escape the north's harsh winter weather.

Usually tourism is seasonal; most destinations have low, shoulder and high seasons. They all seek new ways of overcoming seasonality.

Structuring the tourism planning process

There are countless ways of using words like plans, tactics, strategy, programmes, policy, tasks, activities, objectives, goals, targets.

Terms need to be clearly defined to communicate exactly what is meant, and they should be used in a consistent way.

Figure 1.6 illustrates a clear way of defining the steps in the planning function or process.

The various terms used, interrelated in this manner, make an easy and logical way of approaching planning. Together they represent a simple, straightforward and workable structure for the planning function.

Policy can be defined as an overall set of guidelines. Policy points the way.

The strategies, guided by the policy, will specify the actions to implement the policy.

These actions are expressed as objectives. Each objective will have results which can be expressed in measurable terms.

A number of activities will have to be undertaken to achieve these results.

Resources will then need to be allocated and responsibilities assigned. A budget will list the costs.

The following explains each of these steps more clearly:

Policy

Policy is the same thing to a government as values are to an individual. It provides guidelines for subsequent action. This chapter concludes with a typical national tourism policy statement. It serves as a useful checklist.

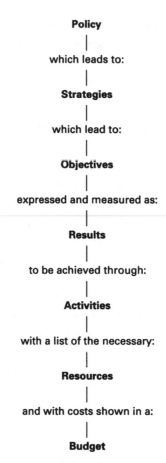

Policy

|

which leads to:

|

Strategies

|

which lead to:

|

Objectives

|

expressed and measured as:

|

Results

|

to be achieved through:

|

Activities

|

with a list of the necessary:

|

Resources

|

and with costs shown in a:

|

Budget

Figure 1.6   The structure of the planning process

Strategies

The term strategy has a military origin. A strategy may be designed to win a particular battle with a minimum loss of men and materials. It sets out the series of actions chosen to try and do this.

Strategies therefore show how to pinpoint objectives. For example, a strategy might propose making tourism the leading foreign exchange earner.

Objectives

An objective is something to achieve. For example, it might be to establish a tourism planning framework and finalize a tourism product development plan.

Results

Results indicate specific changes in status, condition, numbers, or behaviour. These are achievements or outcomes. They should be measurable and expressed in quantifiable, or otherwise verifiable, terms. Results might include a product development plan with the numbers of new hotels and resorts, and the total number of new rooms.

Activities

Usually there are a series of activities to be undertaken in a logical sequence. Actvities spell out all the steps needed to achieve the above results.

Activities are interrelated, and many are also interdependent; the execution of one activity may depend upon the completion of another.

Resources

The various resources required will be listed and specified. For example, it is insufficient to say that a tourism development specialist is needed. A detailed job specification will be prepared, as well as a job description listing the precise duties and responsibilities.

It is not sufficient to say that a computer is needed; the piece of equipment and the system, of which it forms a part, should be specified.

Budget

A budget will show the costs of the necessary resources. As with any budget the various costs listed should be as accurate as possible.

Checklist – a national tourism policy

Policy statements tend to sound self important. This tends to be unavoidable. They are needed, as already noted, to provide guidelines for the rest of the planning process. A national tourism policy might read as follows:

- To develop tourism in a balanced and sustainable manner in harmony with the country's economic and social goals, and according to the national priorities as set from time to time.
- In particular, to create employment, to generate income, foreign exchange earnings and government revenues, and to stimulate regional development.
- To encourage local entrepreneurship, with linkages established to stimulate the economic growth of other sectors.
- At the same time, to seek foreign investment when it contributes towards the country's tourism development plan and conforms with the regulations and controls established.
- To use tourism to conserve the uniqueness of the country's heritage, its history, its culture, and way of life.
- To also use tourism to stimulate the expression of all forms of contemporary culture, through a wide range of events, festivals and other activities.
- To develop tourism to help to conserve and protect the physical environment, enhancing the use of sites and attractions.
- To develop tourism facilities only in areas judged appropriate, in accordance with zoning and land use controls.
- To permit tourism infrastructure, facilities, services and attractions to be enjoyed by the resident population and visitors alike. In this way, to ensure that the development of tourism contributes to the quality of life of local residents as well as visitors.
- To keep various components of the tourism product in balance in both quality and capacity. For example, infrastructure and the environment, accommodation and transportation, attractions and services etc.
- To develop strategies to attract only the quantity and types of visitors able to contribute most readily to the values outlined in this statement of policy.

- In this context, to establish any necessary controls over the quality of the tourism product.
- To promote the development of appropriate training facilities and programmes, to both maximize employment opportunities and achieve the desired standards of quality.
- To coordinate all public and private sector agencies, organizations and interests, involved with tourism.
- To keep the general public informed about the growth of tourism, explaining its development and its contribution to the country's social and economic well being.
- To also explain to the general public how it can help and support the development of both international and domestic tourism.

This example gives a very clear and typical picture of the general nature and style of a policy statement. Subsequent tourism development should follow the policies closely.

References

WTO (1993) *Recommendations on Tourism Statistics.*
WTO (1994) *Tourism Market Trends.*
WTTC (1994) *Travel and Tourism — Progress and Priorities.*

2 Tourism demand

This chapter defines the marketing concept and the difference between marketing, promoting and selling. It indicates that people travel either by obligation or for pleasure. The pleasure category of leisure, recreation and holidays is then explored, breaking it down into mainstream tourism, special interest tourism and alternative tourism. The chapter goes on to discuss whether tourism is supply or demand led. It then explains different levels of demand, and the concept of price elasticity of demand. Structuring the demand for tourism is discussed, and the chapter moves on to explain various approaches to market segmentation. The chapter concludes with visitor surveys and market information systems.

The marketing concept

The marketing concept can be expressed very simply as the matching of the product with the needs and desires of the market. People should be offered what they want to buy.

One must also develop the right product at an acceptable price. Potential buyers have to be told that this has been done. Then they have to see the product in the right way, and they have to be stimulated to buy it. Finally its purchase has to be made as easy as possible.

These elements are known as the marketing mix, and are further discussed in the next chapter.

The key to successful marketing lies in understanding the market and creating the products to satisfy its needs.

To know what people want requires the analysis of two types of data:

Who are the people who travel? – what are their characteristics? e.g. social class and profile, age, sex, marital status.

Second, what are the motivations of these different groups? – what do they want? – what are they looking for? – why are they travelling?

It is important for the GTA, in collaboration with the private sector, to adopt a complete marketing role. Apart from promotion it should play a key part in product development. It should also act as the catalyst in the formulation of the destination's marketing strategy. And it should also monitor the effectiveness of sales programmes, lending its support as necessary.

The term marketing is best understood in a wide context embracing market research, product development, promotion and sales.

Why people travel

People travel for two reasons:

● by obligation
  – having to go somewhere on business, or feeling an obligation for religious reasons, or for reasons of family or friendship, or for medical reasons.
● for pleasure
  – choosing to go somewhere for pleasure – the pleasure, for example, of rest, adventure, escape, discovery, excitement, sport or romance, or any other pleasure seeking motivations. These may differ from person to person. Taken altogether they comprise leisure tourism.

In Chapter 1 the purposes of travel were listed according to the WTO. They were: leisure, recreation and holiday; visiting friends and relatives; business and professional; health treatment; religion/pilgrimages; and other.

Travel for leisure is central to our understanding of tourism. It is linked to the growth in leisure which has accompanied social and economic progress. It is a major contributor to contemporary culture,

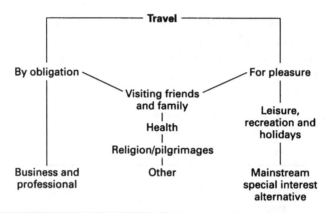

Figure 2.1   Why people travel

a part of any modern concept of individual freedom of expression, and the subject of intensive and competitive international market forces.

Travel for leisure as a broad category can be broken down into mainstream tourism, special interest tourism and alternative tourism.

Figure 2.1 illustrates the reasons why people travel.

Mainstream tourism

Although the overall market may become more diverse, its mainstream changes little. This solid major market segment, by far the largest, is made up of people looking for rest and recreation.

They want comfortable holiday hotels and other types of smart tourist accommodation on a beach or elsewhere. Many may prefer to be in a resort complex offering a full range of shopping, recreation, restaurants, entertainment and other facilities and services.

This is the traditional holiday market which changes only according to contemporary fashions, tastes and values.

It can be segmented mainly on the basis of nationality, social class, spending power and age (stage of life).

Special interest tourism

The following are examples of special interest markets.

- Nature tourism – in all of its specialized forms (popularly included under the description ecotourism)
- Trekking
- Fishing
- Cultural interest in various specialized forms (e.g. related history, art, literature or archeology)
- Photography
- Deep sea diving
- White water rafting
- River cruising
- Adventure tourism – based on camping expeditions
- Game watching
- Youth tourism – outdoors and adventure

These markets are formed through the common special interest possessed by the people who make them up. It is this interest – this motivation – which is more important than other characteristics e.g. age, cultural background, etc.

A passion for archery, or photography, or ornithology, or deep sea diving, or military history or archaeology, may unite a highly heterogeneous group of people with otherwise dissimilar backgrounds and characteristics.

Another market may be composed of naturalists. These may be people with a passion for such subjects as ornithology, etymology or botany. In a similar way, hobbyists can be divided into a wide range of segments, for example pastimes like painting, photography or ceramics.

Another segment of the market may be looking for soft adventure. This kind of holiday will capture excitement and thrills, while providing a certain level of security and comfort, for example a safari staying at comfortable game lodges or a canoeing trip, again with good food and comfortable accommodation.

Hard adventure is quite different. It will have elements of hardship and apparent risk to go with the thrills. Another segment may be composed of the sports enthusiasts eager, for example, for new golfing, tennis or fishing experiences.

Alternative tourism

It can be questioned whether alternative tourism should exist as a separate category at all, or whether it should just be included as another special interest segment.

Tourism marketers tend to talk about the new traveller. The new traveller is described as better educated, more culturally aware, more environmentally and culturally sensitive, and more curious and analytical.

Such people are looking for an alternative to the mainstream trends of the large mass tourism markets. They do not want large, modern hotels constructed and equipped according to international norms. Alternative tourism is usually based on small locally owned accommodation units, very much a part of the local community and reflecting local values and ways of life.

Alternative tourism seeks to feature and protect local culture, and to involve the community in such ways that local people benefit fully. It is a tourism which aims to be better assimilated and more supportive of local needs and aspirations.

Alternative tourism promotes local cuisine, the use of local materials and handicrafts, and the development of a whole range of other participating tourism services, e.g. local folkloric performances, trekking, handicrafts demonstrations, and cultural and recreational activities. It also fosters the creation and development of tourism enterprises operated and owned by local people.

Is tourism demand or supply led?

In business travel, or visiting friends or relatives, or going on pilgrimages, or for health reasons, or for conventions, the traveller's destination tends to be pre-selected by the purpose of his or her journey: going to New York on business, going to Lourdes on pilgrimage, going to Florida to see one's mother, going to Singapore to participate in a convention, or to Zurich for a particular medical treatment.

As already noted, these kinds of travel tend to be motivated by a sense of obligation. This obligatory travel is obviously driven by demand. The number of pilgrims is generated by the strength of a particular religion. There is a correlation between business traffic, economic growth, trade and commercial activity. Visiting friends and relatives is related to the ethnic ties between communities in different countries.

By contrast, travellers motivated by pleasure are free to choose their destination. There is no obligation to visit a particular place, except perhaps for people who may own a holiday home there. It is a question of choice. People choose the destination which, they believe, will best meet their needs. One can go anywhere. In this sense tourism is supply led. It is the destination with the most attractive product which draws the visitors.

Obviously, unless a destination possesses the natural, scenic and cultural attractions, it is difficult to create a demand. In this sense tourism is always supply led. A place has to be attractive to even consider developing leisure tourism.

For a destination to be demand led – given that it has the right natural and other attractions – requires a marketing approach. This means the complete analysis of all marketing opportunities, and the selection of certain markets. It means the development of an appropriate product to satisfy these markets, with the pursuit of particular types of tourist.

However, the capacity must then exist (in both resources and professional knowledge and skills) to create and operate facilities of the required category and standard to satisfy these tourists.

Sometimes marketing strategies are chosen which are not workable, given the level of local skills and know-how.

It can be seen that tourism is led by both supply and demand – by both the product and its markets. Figure 2.2 shows the influences of supply and demand on product development.

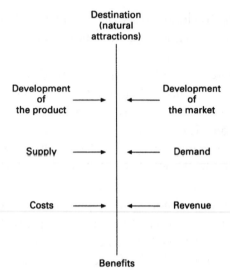

Figure 2.2   The relationship of supply and demand

Levels of demand

One can talk of four levels of demand – basic, displacement, created and future as illustrated in Figure 2.3.

The basic demand is an existing demand which is not being completely satisfied, for example, there is a demand to stay in a destination but there are still too few hotels.

Displacement demand occurs when people are persuaded to stop using one product in favour of another product which better fulfils their needs, for example, new and better hotels are opened in one destination and displace demand from other destinations.

Created demand is when the creation of a new product creates a demand which did not exist before, for example, new hotels in a certain destination create a completely new demand.

Future demand will be brought about by future changes and developments, for example, by increases in standards of living, by economic growth, increases in population, and by a general growth in tourism. Future demand eventually becomes a part of the basic demand.

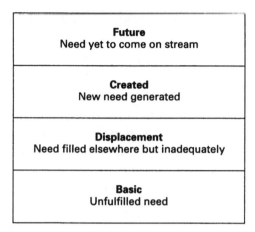

Figure 2.3   Levels of demand

These levels of demand are well illustrated, for example, by the countries of South East Asia. The basic level of demand has tended to exceed the supply of the right kinds of facilities. Rapid regional growth has brought future demand on stream at a steady rate. As countries have added facilities, so they have displaced demand from other destinations. And they have created demand – particularly from short haul tourism within the region.

Total demand consists of different groups of people, with different preferences, tastes and spending power. There may be lots of different market segments each seeking a particular product with distinctive characteristics.

Demand has to be analysed and the market for a destination segmented accordingly. The product should then be developed to meet the various needs of these segments. This means that the product will be segmented in a matching way.

Each product segment may have distinctive characteristics and pricing to match fully the needs of its corresponding market segment.

Elasticity of demand

Sometimes when prices are lowered it results in people buying more.

Sometimes it has little effect. When the sales of an item are very sensitive to any changes in price, demand is said to be price elastic. When sales are insensitive and demand remains the same, it is price inelastic.

Even small changes in price may result in a substantial effect on demand (elasticity), while quite large changes may have little effect (inelasticity). Leisure travel of the popular mainstream type tends to be price elastic. In contrast, business travel – people must travel regardless of cost – tends to be price inelastic.

The price elasticity in relation to marginal costing and the need to fill up empty space at the last minute, is an important factor. When prices are greatly reduced to encourage last minute travel, the market tends to respond quickly.

However, price is also linked to the image of a product. The value attached to a product, its prestige and desirability, may depend largely on how much one has to pay for it. Price as related to the image is discussed in Chapter 3.

Marginal cost is the cost of producing one more unit or as is the case in tourism, of accommodating or serving one more visitor. If the cost is low it may be tempting to cut prices to fill up space – on aeroplanes and in hotels. Such a strategy takes advantage of the price elasticity of demand. However, it may also cheapen the product, undermine the image, and antagonize people who have paid full price. These considerations are discussed in Chapter 4.

Structuring the demand for tourism

Countries market a tourism product according to its diversity. The product may subdivide into many different places and experiences. Separately these may attract both large and small markets – domestic and international.

When confronted with this complexity of products and markets, there is a need to try and structure them in a sensible way.

Large countries have a very diverse tourism product indeed

appealing to a huge spectrum of market segments, one can almost say a continuum of segments, for example, countries such as France or Italy.

However, to make sense of large countries they may have to be broken down into regions, areas, counties, provinces, cities, towns and resorts. Each one has first to be studied separately. They are then all brought together and viewed as a whole.

The product is differentiated according to market segments. And markets are segmented according to the entire range of products offered. This is how supply and demand are matched.

Each market segment has to be well understood and analysed according to its characteristics. As noted, product segments are discussed in the next chapter.

Market segmentation

Each market segment represents people with different characteristics and needs. Segments then sub-segment and sub-segment on down according to these criteria. For example:

- Nationality or place of cultural origin, and gender
- Stage of life
- Social grade
- Psychographics
- Motivation and interests
- Mode of travel/distance travelled

This is illustrated in Figure 2.4. If one was selling clothes people's physical characteristics would matter. Are people tall or short, fat or thin? If it was shoes, do they have big or small feet, and what shape are their feet? If it was golf gloves how many are left handed or right handed. How big or small are their hands?

Markets can be segmented in any way, using any criteria, that make sense in identifying the characteristics and patterns of consumer behaviour and needs.

For example, American women, single, between 30 and 40 years old,

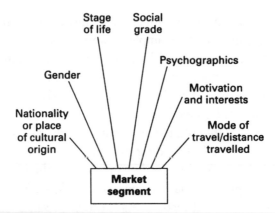

Figure 2.4   Market segmentation

in the professional group, successful, innovating individuals, who play tennis and golf. A particular resort specializing in these two games might target this market segment.

There are three basic reasons for segmenting markets:

- to develop the product to satisfy specific needs
- to identify where and how to sell the product
- to judge if and how to mix different segments together (as noted people who use the tourism product become a part of it).

The following describes typical sets of criteria in the segmentation of markets.

Nationality and gender

The concept of a common culture – people of the same nationality sharing the same behavioural and other characteristics – will be discussed in Chapter 9. It is obviously important for a resort to know whether visitors are, for example, Japanese, French or Italian. Each nationality has its own language and many distinctive preferences and patterns of behaviour.

A particular resort or hotel has to judge the extent to which it can mix nationalities. Few studies have been done which can assist operators in this decision. Operators go by experience. They know that if they exceed 50 per cent of resort or hotel capacity for one nationality alone, say Japanese, it may be difficult for other nationalities to blend in.

Many consider that 50 per cent is already too high. It is sometimes held that once 50 percent is exceeded it is better to aim at 100 per cent for the one nationality. Doing this however, makes the resort dependent on one market only. This has obvious dangers.

Similarly there may be dangers in mixing sub cultures from the same country. There has to be a good understanding of the ways in which groups of people differ and how well they will mix together. People from different regions, with variations in educational and cultural levels and incomes, may not go well together. It may depend on the precise proportions and the nature of the holiday.

Gender is also an important variable. Men and women may have some different travel preferences and needs. These have to be identified.

According to each nationality and market, people may also have a different order of priority in the way in which they choose to spend their disposable income.

Stage of life

An important criterion in the segmentation of markets is found in people's life cycle. The following is a typical breakdown based on the period of life reached and the likely travel preferences.

Teenagers	Mostly single, not yet in employment, dependent on parents, little disposable income. Adventure and discovery travel, action and fun packed.
Single in employment	The bachelor stage, young, single (plenty of disposable income). Still adventure and discovery travel, action and fun packed. But with more sophistication.
Newly married	Young, no children – little disposable income available.

	Family type holidays at an integrated resort.
Family and babies	Youngest child under six – little disposable income.
	Still a family type holiday often with repeat holidays to the same resort.
Family with young children	Youngest child over six – start to be a little better off.
	Still at a resort but more diversified holidays, doing more things.
The broken marriage	Divorced, single parents or just remarried, still with dependent children and little disposable income.
	Short breaks, modest holidays, resort destinations.
Family with older children	Getting older and still married or married again, children still dependent.
	Parents possibly holidaying alone. Diversified holidays; perhaps multi destination, likely to pursue special interests.
Alone again	Older and married, children have left home (much wealthier than before).
	A variety of diversified holidays e.g. cruises and tours – and still pursuing special interests.
Survivors/widows and widowers	Single again and alone (still relatively wealthy).
	Travelling on tour in groups or clubs – often for special interest.

These stages of life give a broad indication only. There are many exceptions; for example, people who choose not to get married or not to have children. Such people are likely to be better off financially.

There are various similar approaches to the classification of the stages of life as, for example, by Kotler (Kotler, 1984).

Age exercises many other influences on a person's motivations. Needs and tastes will change at each stage of life. Young single people want to do different things to older married couples with children, and elderly people will have developed altogether different preferences.

Social Grade Groupings

The following breakdown, from the Institute of Practitioners in Advertising, is now used as the Social Grade Profile of the UK's National Readership Survey sample and serves as an example of social grade grouping.

		% of the population
A	Administrative or professional	3.1
B	Middle management	16.8
C1	Supervisory	26.7
C2	Skilled manual	24.7
D	Semi/unskilled	16.3
E	Casual workers/lowest grade	12.4

The basis of this social grading was originally based on the Head of Household concept, but this has now been changed to Chief Income Earners. This has had the effect of shifting the social class profile more up market (National Readership Surveys, 1993).

People's incomes help to indicate the price they may be able and willing to pay for a particular product. Some groups, however, may be willing to pay different proportions of their discretionary income for travel. Pricing policy may be developed accordingly. Generally, however, one does not segment markets according to price level; one prices according to each market segment. The marketing mix as a whole is formulated to target particular segments.

In most countries there are numerous sources of demographic data characterizing segments of society according to criteria such as age, sex, occupation, educational level, income and place of residence. Alone these data allow for crude segmentation only, representing an inflexible way of categorizing society. Marketing specialists have tried to identify more complete ways of explaining consumer behaviour, and have used psychographics. This is a technique which relates personality to social values and lifestyles.

Psychographics

Different psychographic profiles may describe inward and outward looking people, adventurers and play-it-safers, leaders and followers and so on.

Some of the thinking described may be useful to apply. It may also be based on studies with some validity, and it may increase understanding of the particular appeal of various tourist experiences.

Sometimes, however, the concepts tend to be too glib and fail to recognize all the complexities of human behaviour. People categorized according to one particular profile, may suddenly demonstrate a range of behavioural inconsistencies. They do not always behave as they are supposed to behave.

The main examples of the psychographic approach are:

● Stanford Research's Values and Lifestyles Programme (VALS).
  These are four value groups divided into nine life-style categories – Survivors, Sustainers, Belongers, Emulators, Achievers, I-am-Me, Experiential, Societally Conscious and Integrated.
● Yankelovich Clancy Shulman's Monitor.
  These are seven lifestyle categories – Self-explorer, Social Resister, Experimentalist, Conspicuous consumer, Belonger, Survivor and Aimless.

Both these approaches have been widely used internationally. In the United Kingdom, Young and Rubicam's 4Cs – Cross Cultural Consumer Classification reflects the VALS approach. It uses the following categories and groups.

Three basic categories:

> Survivors
> Internal values
> External values

These make up seven different groups:

Innovators ⎫
Reformers ⎬ Internal values

Succeeders ⎫
Aspirers ⎬ External values
Mainstreamers ⎭

Struggling poor ⎫ Survivors
Resigned poor ⎭

Beth Salmon covers these various systems in her short guide *Psychographics and Lifestyles* (Salmon, 1989). She points out that they have many common threads. 'The major inner-directed/outer-directed axis always seems to be present; the 4Cs "succeeders" and "reformers" seem to bear more than a passing resemblance to Monitor's "conspicuous consumers" and "self explorers".'

She indicates that most systems have some sort of mass market moral majority at their core. Whether they call them belongers or mainstreamers is not of crucial importance.

In tourism, as noted, it is this mainstream demand which sustains most destinations.

Motivation and interests

Travel motivations and interests were discussed earlier in the chapter. They can be summarized as: leisure, recreation and holiday; visiting friends and relatives; business and professional; health treatment; religion/pilgrimages; and other. Linked to motivations and interests are peoples' needs and preferences. What do they like and what don't they like? What particular product features are they looking for?

Mode of transport/distance travelled

People will choose to travel by air, sea, rail or road, and they will travel independently – alone or with family or friends – or in groups.

Access can usually be described as follows:

- Long haul access by air – 6000 kilometres or more – usually more than about seven hours flying time.
- Medium haul access by air – between 3000 and 6000 kilometres – from about four hours flying time up to about six to seven hours.

- Short haul access by air — under 3000 kilometers or up to about three to four hours flying time. This will usually include the major regional markets.
- Access by train — mostly national or intraregional.
- Access by road — also mostly national or intraregional from neighbouring countries.
- Access by sea — mainly from neighbouring and other countries in the region. This does not include cruise ships.

Tourists can be differentiated according to the mode of transport chosen, the distance travelled and whether they are travelling independently or in a group.

The complexity of human behaviour

The various means of categorizing tourists illustrate the complexity of human behaviour. People share the common characteristics of the species. Beyond this, however, they appear to be infinitely variable. As noted, some of the differences originate in their genetic make-up and sex, some in the major cultural influences that play upon them, some in their age and marital status, some in their previous education and experience, some in their economic and social status, some in their spiritual and inner life, some in their simple likes and dislikes, their interests and passions, and some in a variety of other ways.

It is important to keep analysing demand. To be sensitive to every clue about behaviour, and to never stop asking questions. One needs a constant flow of market information; keeping track of people, of who exactly they are, and what exactly they want and need.

Some of the psychographic ways of classifying tourists may seem, at times, to be too superficial or fanciful. However, they are still helpful in the review and discussion of tourist behaviour and in shaping future research projects.

Successful segmentation, enabling clearly defined marketing targets, is assisted by interconnecting various kinds of data and criteria. As data is built up — age, nationality, gender, occupation, income, motivations and interests, needs and preferences, lifestyles, stage of life, etc. — the picture formed becomes clearer and sharper and more particularized.

Visitor surveys

Visitor surveys are conducted to supplement the market information obtained from routine tourism statistics. In designing a survey questionnaire, the following points should be noted:

- The purpose should be explained and people thanked for their participation.
- The meaning of questions should be clear and free of any ambiguity.
- It has to be easy to understand and complete.
- It should be well laid out, organized into clear sections, printed in large clear typeface — allowing plenty of space to write answers and comments.
- It should be presented in a logical sequence.
- Questions should not lead the respondent, i.e. suggest or imply an expected answer.

The length of a questionnaire depends partly on the time people have to complete it. It also depends on people's goodwill and the time they are prepared to spend.

If tour groups are being asked, they will generally spend some time in the departure lounge before their return journey. They may have to sit and wait for as long as 30 minutes — given that last minute or duty free shopping has been completed. This may be the ideal time to complete a questionnaire.

Ideally each questionnaire should be collected and checked by a survey assistant. Any part not filled out or not clear can be clarified immediately with the respondent.

The design of the questionnaire will also depend on the survey methodology and the size of the sample. As noted, the questionnaire has to permit the collection of accurate and useful feedback. But it must also facilitate the subsequent correlation and analysis of the data.

The more extensive the comments and assessments made by respondents, the harder this is. But it is often worth the effort. It will provide more complete answers about the respondents.

- Not only who they are and what they do
- But also where they stayed
- How long they stayed
- What they did
- Where they went
- How much they spent
- And what they liked or didn't like and why.

It is this last assessment which is essential in improving and developing the product.

There are usually no other reliable sources for data on tourist expenditures. Banks and currency exchange agencies can give some data on foreign exchange earnings but not enough to build up an accurate and complete picture.

Surveys can help identify and define market segments. Knowledge has to be built up on each market segment, to provide information on how to develop the product and how to promote and sell more effectively.

When segments are lumped together the value of a visitor survey is seriously diminished. However, it may not be practical to define and isolate segments in too detailed a way.

The sampling method used can take account of a number of the major variables, for example, seasonality and time of the year, the nationality of visitors, age, and whether travelling independently or in a group. With mainstream leisure tourism there may be quite pronounced differences between people of different nationalities/ cultures. And there will obviously be major differences between age groups.

Some market segments can be determined by the reason for travel; for example, it is easy to identify and survey separately business and official travellers and visiting friends and family traffic.

Special interest visitors and people coming for health reasons can easily be surveyed separately since they will normally be found together in their related centres. It is also easy to identify backpackers and to keep them apart in a separate survey category.

If possible it is always best to separate different nationalities.

Sampling has to be done in such a way that results are representative of the total number of people (the universe) under study. The likely error – or deviation – in survey results also has to be calculated. A random sample means that everybody in the universe under study has an equal chance of being included. If the sample is to be structured according to particular groups, a stratified random sample may be used. Generally the more visitors surveyed, the more reliable the results.

Surveys where people themselves choose whether to respond or not, such as guest comment cards in hotels, do not arrive at a reliable sample. Respondents are self-selected and therefore not sufficiently representative.

Market information systems

A market information system, also to be discussed in later chapters, is essential. It is a system established to study market characteristics and trends. The results of desk research and data collection, the analysis of tourism statistics, and the findings from visitor surveys, will feed into this system.

There are many published sources of data, for example, the results of country-specific studies and analyses of particular market segments. These are often prepared and published by specialized research companies. The travel trade press should also be followed closely to monitor various trends and new developments.

It is possible to subscribe to a clippings service which will identify and clip all press items of particular interest.

Through its statistics, surveys, and market information system, a GTA can be expected, in close collaboration with the private sector, to follow all marketing trends. It should be able to keep in focus the various characteristics of its markets and visitors.

However, a GTA would not normally be involved with research of a psychographic nature. This might be carried out by advertising agencies, tour operators or even large hotel companies. These various enterprises will be interested to establish a correlation between choice of holidays, destinations and facilities and particular lifestyles and profiles.

Such studies may help to give a clearer idea of who buys what and why, enabling promotional and sales efforts to be better directed. Motivational research of this kind is often carried out through group discussions and in-depth interviewing.

Where research is carried out by private sector interests, they should be encouraged to share the results with the GTA. While marketing information may give companies a competitive advantage, the GTA represents the interests of the sector as a whole. One should try to reconcile any conflict between these two sets of needs.

Household surveys are conducted in many countries to establish consumption patterns and trends. Some surveys concentrate on travel and tourism, for example, the United Kingdom Tourism Survey organized by the four UK national tourism boards. Useful surveys may also be conducted by consumer groups.

References

Kotler, P. (1984) *Marketing Management: Analysis, Planning and Control*, 5th edn, Prentice Hall International.

National Readership Surveys (1993) Bulletin No. 28, 26.11.93.

Salmon, B. (1989) *Psychographics and Lifestyles, A Short Guide*, Institute of Practitioners in Advertising.

3 The tourism product

This chapter explains the marketing mix and the components of the tourism product. It discusses the concept of the destination, the image and the price. It then describes the product life cycle and its possible application to tourism. It goes on to examine product feasibility covering marketing, operational and financial criteria. It then describes the transportation component of tourism covering air, sea and waterways, rail and roads. Various development concepts are then discussed including staging points/areas, the cluster concept and resort complexes. Also included are the concepts of people seeking other people and the street itself as a part of the tourism product. The various facilities and services are then summarized and the chapter concludes with some project feasibility checklists; one from the government viewpoint and one from the private sector viewpoint.

The marketing mix

The marketing mix, illustrated in Figure 3.1, includes the following components:

- The *product* includes both the tangible and intangible components.
- The *price range.*
- The *promotion* includes all marketing, promotional and sales activities with the exception of the image. This is such a decisive factor in tourism that it is listed separately.
- The *image* therefore is separate from the product and promotion although influenced by them. It is the way people see the product, what it suggests and means to them.
- *Distribution* (the sales network − where the product can be purchased) includes all channels and sales coverage. It embraces the ease of purchase, particularly concerning the overall sales and

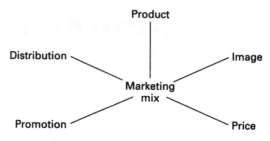

Figure 3.1   The marketing mix

distribution network, and includes coverage in terms of tour operators and sales and retail outlets. Distribution therefore covers travel trade relationships (tour operators, wholesalers, retailers).

These relationships are flexible and vary according to particular markets. They are dealt with more fully in Chapter 4.

Components of the tourism product

Figure 3.2 illustrates that the tourism product divides between resources which already exist and cannot be duplicated, and components which can be created.

The tourism product at the destination comprises all those attractions, facilities, and services used or visited during a stay. It also comprises everything that happens to visitors; everything they experience.

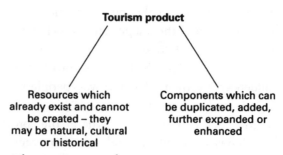

Figure 3.2   The tourism product

Natural resources, such as beautiful lakes or mountains, cannot be duplicated, and climatic conditions cannot be changed. A destination either has an agreeable climate and bountiful natural resources or it does not.

Similarly, authentic cultural and historical features cannot be duplicated; for example, in France the 'Mona Lisa' by Leonardo Da Vinci, the Palace of Versailles, Notre Dame, and Balzac's House. Like many other cultural and historical attractions they already exist. They are part of the heritage which France is able to offer. They cannot be duplicated or replaced as such. Similarly, it would be impossible to duplicate monuments such as the Taj Mahal in India, Angkor Wat in Cambodia or Borobodur in Indonesia.

Tourism infrastructure and superstructure, of course, can be created.

Infrastructure includes the road network, airports, the supply of water, electricity, drainage and sewerage systems, etc. It provides the base for the superstructure.

Superstructure includes hotels, accommodation units, restaurants and the whole range of tourist installations and services.

A destination with natural and cultural attractions and an agreeable climate then needs both infrastructure and superstructure. There has to be access to get there. New hotels need power and water. Roads have to be built and harbours expanded. Sites have to be opened up. Drainage, waste disposal systems and other services need to be provided. Various tourism facilities and services have to be developed.

A beautiful lake needs access. A road has to be built to it, and its use (even for sightseeing) requires careful planning. Cultural heritage alone is not enough. A collection of paintings and sculpture needs a museum to house and display it. The Louvre without the Mona Lisa would not be the same, but arguably neither would the Mona Lisa without the Louvre.

As illustrated in Figure 3.3, the tourism product consists of both tangible and intangible components. The natural, cultural and historical resources, infrastructure and superstructure are tangible. They can be evaluated, measured and subjected to specific standards of provision. The intangible aspects cannot. They come together to form the atmosphere of a place and its feeling of welcome and friendliness.

The intangible elements can be said to give the tourist product its

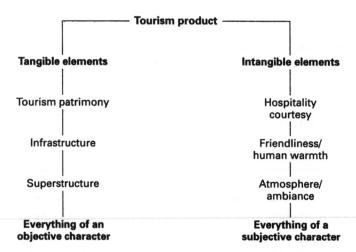

Figure 3.3   The tourism product

life, colour and excitement. All of the tangible aspects, however good, cannot guarantee satisfaction. The way tourists are treated and how they feel, influence decisively their overall reaction to a place.

Each successive event or situation which the tourist experiences should be in harmony. It should contribute to an overall feeling of well being and enjoyment. This tourism harmony will determine how well the total product is accepted. Harmony also means the matching of quality and capacity between complementary tourism facilities and services, as discussed in Chapter 1. There has to be enough of each component in each category.

Transportation to get to a destination is sometimes defined as a part of the product. Sometimes it is not. Whatever the case, it must be treated as a major part of tourism.

Destinations

The concept of the destination needs to be treated with caution. It is not necessarily the country, or even the town or area, which is the destination or object of the holiday.

The destination may be an integrated, well-appointed resort, offering a complete experience. Where this resort is found may be secondary.

A town, area, or island may also act as the destination rather than the country. People appear to visit Varadero rather than Cuba. People, without doubt, visit Bali and not Indonesia. People also think of Phuket, rather than Thailand, as their destination, or Ibiza rather than Spain.

Similarly, the theme of a holiday (its special interest), may also be more important than the place or country. Cross-country skiing as a purpose, for example, may replace the destination in importance. It may be incidental that it happens to be Norway where it is particularly good or challenging. The same may apply to diving in the Bahamas, or a safari in Kenya.

The outstanding quality and fame of a golf course may be much more important than the country or area where it is located.

For tennis fans the destination may be the Wimbledon championships and not a holiday in London or Britain.

In analysing the tourism product, the interrelationships of destinations and motivations should be clearly interpreted.

Image

The image of a destination is the way in which it projects itself, and the way in which it is viewed by its markets.

As noted above, some particular places or activities tend to forge a separate image from the countries where they are located. In other cases, however, it is the image of the country itself which is predominant.

Image is an overall idea; the associations which a place has; its identity; what people think about it. If the image is positive, people may visit; if it is negative they stay away. The image builds up over the years, it is a product of history, of cultural influences, and also of myth and legend. It is also influenced by political viewpoints, by current affairs and international relationships.

The image of a place changes, of course, from market to market. The image of France in Japan is different from France in Italy. It may not be less positive but it will differ. For example, Ireland appears to have a positive image in the United States on which it easy to build. South Africa, during its apartheid period, had a very negative image. As a result it was boycotted by many people. The political events there have now changed its image radically.

The image of a destination is also influenced by who else goes there and what they say about it. Leading personalities may speak well of a place. If well-known transnational companies set up operations in a country, this too exercises considerable influence. If major tour operators feature it as a part of their programmes, this too contributes to a positive image.

Generally it takes a long time to build up the image. To try and change it in a major way in the short term is difficult. Image-building promotion, using advertising, is expensive and not always effective. And it is obviously easier to strengthen an already positive image than to try and correct a negative one.

Image is best built, reinforced and strengthened as a continuing process. A destination should be present at all major international shows and exhibitions, and the media should be encouraged to talk and write about it. Writers, film makers, commentators, journalists, and opinion-makers of all kinds should be encouraged to take an interest in the place. Promotion and publicity should emphasize a destination's most striking features and associations. For example, Western Samoa has all the romantic pull of Polynesia while it was also the last refuge of Robert Louis Stevenson.

Because of its importance in tourism, image has been listed as a separate component in the marketing mix. Price, another component, is closely interrelated. It has to reflect and support the image not undermine it.

The following resumes some of the key points:

- The image may change from market to market.
- It is built up over time, as the result of a constant flow of messages and stimuli.
- It always needs to be strengthened and maintained.
- It is influenced by certain major associations and ideas.

- It should be kept at the forefront – people have to keep writing and talking about a place.
- Price should be in keeping with the image.

Once people visit a place they will form their own impressions. They will take an image away with them. What they say and the personal recommendations which they make exercise a major influence.

Price

Price is a part of the marketing mix. This gives it, quite rightly, a marketing focus. The price should be attractive and competitive, but in keeping with the image. It is the image which suggests a particular price/value relationship.

The end price of visiting somewhere is the total cost of the trip. It will cover the cost of travel, room and board, together with the optional purchases and extras at the destination. How much people pay, or commit themselves to pay before leaving, are the major determinants. People judge this payment in their own currency according to their normal system of values. The GTA can monitor and compare local visitor costs through a visitor price index.

The foreign exchange rate has a more direct impact at the destination. It establishes how much visitors get for their spending money. This determines their local purchasing power. If they can buy and do a lot of things, this is more likely to attract them back for a return visit.

Destinations tend to fall into price categories and this makes price a part of the image. Although prices will depend on the category of accommodation chosen, the overall price range offered will differ from destination to destination. Price levels can also convey the idea of relative exclusivity.

Any tour operator's catalogue will reveal the more expensive destinations as opposed to the cheaper ones. It is easy to see how each destination is positioning itself in relation to the others.

In price setting there are many cost considerations. In general, for example, the more distant a destination the higher the air transport cost as a proportion of total costs. Various cost considerations and influences are discussed in the next chapter.

Published prices are the most important in marketing. People ask – how much will it cost? Does this seem right? – does it support the idea of the place – its image? Is it worth it? Is it good value? Is it competitive? Price, above all, positions a destination in the market. Price may support the image but it can also undermine it.

The product life cycle

Over the years studies have shown that many products go through a life cycle. This work sprung from Levitt's original product life cycle concept (Levitt, 1965). The product is introduced, it grows, it matures, levels out and then declines. At the point of decline the product requires action to resuscitate it and further extend its life. This is shown in Figure 3.4. The curve will be of a different shape according to the various influences at work.

Many products rise and fall with current fashion. A product can lose its appeal.

Restaurants are notoriously vulnerable to changing trends and tastes. All design is subject to changing values – in art, clothes, architecture, interiors, and furniture.

One has the cyclical rhythms of nature itself, the seasons of life, the fading away and the constant renewal. This gives the cyclical effect a certain philosophical appeal. To endure, things may need a new face and a new form. The old is rejuvenated. It makes a full turn and returns to where it started.

As a consequence there are fashion revivals. The out-of-date returns to become the in-thing. Old hotels are renovated and exceed all their former glories. Forgotten authors are published again. Old makes of cars are declared classics and are rescued from the rubbish dumps.

It is often held that this same life cycle concept applies to tourist destinations.

The concept of a life cycle in tourism, however, relates to the

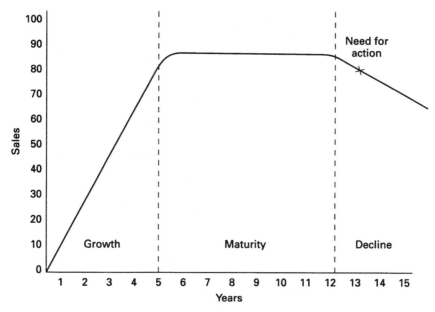

Figure 3.4   Typical illustration of the life cycle concept

broader concept of the changeability of the tourism product discussed in Chapter 1. Tourist destinations are usually in a constant process of change as they grow, develop and adjust to the market. Even when their carrying capacity is reached, they are still subject to a range of improvement, rehabilitation and redevelopment schemes. The tourism product, in this sense, is always an unfinished product. It is always responding and adjusting to planning and marketing imperatives and opportunities.

Product feasibility

Moving from the consideration of tourism as a whole to the consideration of a hotel or restaurant project, means changing from a macro to a micro viewpoint. Despite the change in scale many of the principles remain the same.

One looks at the relationship between the demand for facilities and

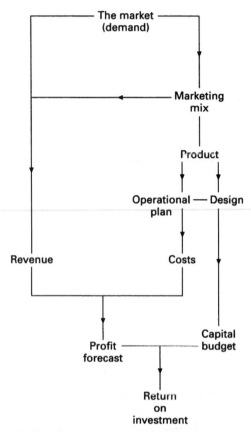

Figure 3.5   Project feasibility

services and the capital required to satisfy it; between the opportunity and the investment; between marketing plans and financial plans; between revenues and costs and between sales forecasts and operational budgets.

As seen in Figure 3.5 marketing, operational and financial criteria combine to determine the feasibility of tourism projects.

One conceives and operates projects based on the relationships between these three dimensions – market/product/costs. For a new project this will be expressed through the following steps:

● Market feasibility study
  – Product definition (location, facilities, services, image, price)

- Marketing forecasts and sales strategies
- Product development – Operational plan (What and How?)
  - Design brief – Plans drawings
  - Furniture/equipment schedules
  - Budgets.
- Investment appraisal – Capital budgets
  - Forecasts and projections
  - Operating profits
  - Cash flow
  - Debt/Service coverage
  - Returns

For the operation of an existing business, the same relationship is expressed through:

- Marketing Plan
  - Targets and forecasts
  - Marketing mix
  - Product and image
  - Promotional and distribution strategies
  - Sales and prices
- Operational plan
  - Organization and staffing
  - Operational budgets.
- Financial plan
  - Operating profits
  - Capital expenditures
  - Cash flow
  - Returns

The rate of return on the investment should be measured using the discounted cash flow method. This means discounting over the project's assessed life, the net future cash flows to equal the original capital cost. The discount rate used to produce this result is taken as the project's financial rate of return.

Feasibility studies on new projects, or the operational analysis of an existing enterprise, follow the same steps. Feasibility studies may not always provide the correct answers. There may be differences between the actual results achieved, and those forecast. Once a project is executed results may prove to be:

- a big happy surprise – far exceeding the projections
- encouraging – a little ahead of those expected
- as expected – approximate to the forecast
- disappointing – short of those expected
- the unhappy surprise – far short of the expected

If the actual results are either well over or well under the conclusions of the feasibility study, one or all of the following took place:

- apparently unforeseen circumstances and conditions developed
- the study overlooked some major factors or made serious errors in its assumptions
- a poor assessment of the risks was made

This may mean that the study was badly designed and executed. Or that it was executed merely to support conclusions and recommendations already formulated.

A study may be carried out too quickly and superficially. Consultants are sometimes willing to use industry-wide averages and cut and paste sections from similar studies elsewhere. Each project needs its own detailed study which should:

- make realistic assumptions about demand, the markets to be served and the needs to be met. Sales forecasts must be based on a complete analysis to include realistic estimates of visitor flows, occupancies, length of stay, seasonal differences and average price.
- include an operational plan with detailed staffing and cost estimates.
- detail an accurate and realistic capital budget.
- provide details of the proposed financing and loan conditions, debt/ service ratios, etc.

If a project is to be supported by the government, then the economic and social benefits should be established. Feasibility checklists, from government and private sector viewpoints, are included at the end of this chapter.

Transportation

A broader definition of the tourism product would include transportation.

People travel by air, road, rail or sea – and possibly by river or other waterway. The right access to a country or region is obviously essential. The number and location of airports, seaports and the development of road and other transportation networks are critical. Tourism uses many combinations of travel such as fly/cruise and fly/drive. People may also arrive and leave through different points.

Transportation opens up tourism opportunities and permits the linking of more places and experiences, often producing a longer length of stay.

Air transportation depends on airports and aeroplanes. Airports are an essential part of infrastructure. The superstructure comprises the airlines together with the full range of supporting services and facilities.

The term 'flag carrier' illustrates the importance which many governments give to nationally owned airlines. They are viewed as symbols of prestige, pride and national identity. They are also used in the conduct of foreign policy and are linked to the idea of national security and independence. Worldwide there are presently some 190 government-owned airlines.

Airlines operate under rules governing scheduled services set up in 1944 in Chicago. Although the Chicago Convention produced the freedoms of the air (covering the various rights to pick up and put down passengers, mail and cargo), governments decided to regulate airline operations country-to-country (bilaterally). This approach controls all the services by the two countries in question – one at each end of a particular route. Governments therefore may not only own airlines they can also control air operations.

Deregulation did take place in the United States in 1978 and led to very tough and competitive conditions, producing lower air fares. Efforts are now being made to deregulate in Europe.

Maritime transport and waterways. Ocean going liners now operate on few routes, many having been redeployed as cruise ships – a popular form of seagoing tourism. New and often smaller ships have been brought into service and new cruising waters developed, for example, in South East Asia and the Pacific.

Yachting, both bareboat and charter, has also grown.

New ferry services have been introduced, particularly with the addition of hydrofoils and hovercraft, for example, the hydrofoil types of vessel are now in service between Tanzania and Zanzibar, and Singapore and Batam island. Meanwhile in Europe the channel tunnel has provided competition for the corresponding ferry services.

Cruise ships may also make more stops at out-of-the way areas and islands. These places can obtain some benefit from this tourism through offering local tours, folkloric shows and the purchase of handicrafts.

Railways continue in many parts of the world as a popular form of transport. With product development, upgraded service, and imaginative promotion, various tourism train rides have been marketed successfully. For example special trains in India, Malaysia/Thailand and Europe have all been successful. This success is likely to be copied in other countries and regions.

Roads

Tourism needs an adequate road network, providing sufficient access to destinations and attractions. Urban planning in developed countries has followed the USA in catering to the private car as a major form of transport. It is not surprising therefore that the car is used extensively for tourism.

The car gives people control over when to leave and where to stop, how fast to go, what route to choose and how long to take. It gives a sense of freedom and independence, there is space for luggage, and journey costs may be lower than other forms of transport. People can also use the car, once at their destination. The popularity of the personal car, plus the use of long distance buses and overland tours organized by travel companies, make the development of the road network critical.

Road development, particularly new motorway construction, conflicts increasingly with environmental conservation objectives. There is evidence that new roads only ease congestion and speed up transit for a short time. Their development merely encourages greater use of the car and more journeys are made. No advantage is achieved, but the environmental costs are high.

This conflict between motor transport and the environment is a continuing development issue.

Development concepts

Staging points/areas

It has always been important to identify staging points in market feasibility studies for new hotels. These are the likely points or areas where people will choose to stage their journeys – stopping for one night or more. With tourism growth the concept of staging has developed. People will choose a staging point as an important part of the overall travel experience.

For example, European travellers to Australia, or Australians to Europe, may stop en route in Bali, Singapore or Bangkok for up to five nights or more. Or travelling the other way round they may stop in Los Angeles or Mexico City, or Hawaii or Fiji.

Staging criteria are important in any multi destination holiday. Tours stop where there are places to see and visit and things to do.

The cluster concept

Obviously a destination with high tourism potential is certain to bring together, within a cohesive geo-spatial framework, an ample range and variety of complementary tourism assets. The precise range of facilities, services and attractions within easy access of one another, will depend on the place. There is a core product and a peripheral or optional product.

The core product includes the right kinds of accommodation, restaurant and recreational facilities together with tourist attractions. The peripheral product builds onto this, adding the possibilities of other tourist attractions in the form of various scenic, historic, leisure, amusement, entertainment, shopping, recreational sites and installations. An ideal destination represents a cluster of all these components.

Resort complexes

Tourism enclaves consist of well-planned integrated resort complexes. They keep the tourists in one area, concentrate the infrastructural requirements, and enable a large number of hotels and accommodation units to be constructed quickly in a controlled and coordinated manner.

They can also balance this development with the right mix of supporting and complementary facilities and services. This type of resort complex requires the availability of sufficient areas of land. Land must be acquired at reasonable prices, since these are relatively low density developments.

From a marketing standpoint such resorts often represent a superior product, offering a well spaced, properly ordered and attractively landscaped environment.

Governments may set up a development corporation to take the lead role in planning and managing this type of project. Government may already own the land, or will acquire it, at desirable sites for development. The corporation takes over the land, develops a master plan, borrows the money to create the necessary infrastructure, and stimulates local and foreign investors to undertake the secondary development.

Integrated resorts of this kind are attractive and marketable. Being contained in one area, they avoid the potential disruption caused by more dispersed forms of tourism.

Examples of resort complexes of this kind are Cancun in Mexico, Playa Dorada, Puerto Plata in the Dominican Republic, Nusa Dua in Bali, and the Langkawi development in Malaysia.

People seek people

Man is a social animal. People want to mix, meet each other, look at each other, and find opportunities for social interchange. During a holiday experience people want, at certain times, peace and quiet and the conditions for rest and relaxation. They want the tranquillity of pleasant and attractive surroundings where they are left alone undisturbed.

At other times they seek other people, the hustle and bustle, and the colour and vitality of busy streets. They want the opportunity to look at and meet other people, to socialize and to form friendships and relationships.

It is essential to provide, in tourism planning, the gathering points to meet this need. Many coastal resorts in the Mediterranean originated as fishing villages. The centre of the old village with perhaps buildings, a square, restaurants and bars and an esplanade clustered around a harbour, now form the heart of the resort. Everybody gravitates here each evening at sunset. People walk, talk, have a drink and enjoy the crowd and the ambience.

Linear coastal developments often lack this type of focal point. One has a strip of hotels often continuing over a considerable distance, maybe ten to fifteen kilometres or more. Centres of activity may spring up along the strip, but sometimes this does not happen. This means that there is no cohesion in the overall product and people tend to become restricted to the confines of one hotel.

People seek people. New resorts need gathering points to fulfill this important purpose. This is a concept originally developed by Juan Fuster Lareu (Fuster Lareu, 1992).

Tourism – a street enterprise

One of the most important of all tourism enterprises is the street itself. When the street is taken altogether, with everything it comprises, it can be seen clearly as one of the key components of the total tourism product. The street, with its shops, window displays, its signs and hoardings, its stalls and street vendors, its sounds and smells, its colour, mood and atmosphere, plays an important part in the tourist experience. This is another concept developed by Juan Fuster Lareu (Fuster Lareu, 1992).

As noted above, in many coastal areas one finds villages and communities, previously based on fishing, which have adapted to tourism. And at certain times of the day people do take to the main streets, plazas and squares.

In many cities efforts have been made to pedestrianize the core tourism areas. It is here that people want to stroll and shop, stopping at the local bars and restaurants. The downtown area and its streets should create the necessary welcoming appearance and atmosphere.

Facilities and services

A wide variety of facilities and services contribute to the overall product: hotels and accommodation facilities, camping, restaurants and catering services, resorts, theme parks, casinos, information services, local tours and excursions, cultural attractions, shopping, entertainment, sports and recreational facilities.

In tourism, accommodation and food and drink are part of the core product – normally any visitor has to make use of the various facilities available. The use of other components is optional and depends on a visitor's needs and preferences.

To maximize the earnings from tourism, therefore, the visitor has to be persuaded to see and do and buy as much as possible. This requires up-to-date and readily accessible information on everything available, together with well-organized merchandising and promotion.

Project feasibility checklist

The following checklists make mention of environmental impact statements (EIS). An EIS is prepared so as to weigh the environmental costs and benefits of a particular development. The criteria associated with an EIS will be discussed more fully in Chapter 7.

From the government viewpoint

Policy and strategy
Clear development strategies. Reflection of the stated tourism policies. Definition of the market. Number of tourists the project will attract. Kinds of tourists. Seasonality of demand.

Development needs
New infrastructure needed – waste and sewage disposal, water, power, roads and access. Provision and financing of these needs. Integration of the project with local transportation development.

Environmental impact
Environmental impact of the project. Preparation of an environmental impact statement (as noted, to be discussed and detailed in Chapter 7). Adherence to all physical planning regulations. Review of architectural, design and engineering concepts. Contribution of the project to overall environmental quality.

Economic impact
Measurement of the project's economic impact. Method used and results obtained. Benefits to the local community. Contribution to the economy. Employment created.

Social impact
Consultation with the local community. Form of consultations. Explanations of the project. Feedback and reactions. Degree of local support.

Ownership and management
Ownership of the project – local/foreign/mixed. Management of the project. Type of enterprise – transnational, nationwide, other. Previous experience and track record. Use of local labour. Direct jobs created. Established marketing links. Sales projections. Financial feasibility.

From the private sector viewpoint

Market definition
Analysis of demand. Levels of demand. Identification of the market – marketing objectives. Market characteristics. Tourist flows. Seasonality and the distribution of demand. Preferences and needs.

Product definition
Overall description of the product concept. Local authority support. Planning permission. Reactions of local community. Criteria in the development of each aspect:

- Location – Ease of access. Catchment area. Characteristics of site and surroundings. Relationship to other services, facilities and attractions. Infrastructural needs and environmental criteria.
- Facilities – Range of facilities. Capacity. Design concepts – style and layout of buildings. Operational needs. Staffing and organization.
- Service – Definition of levels of service. Coverage and hours of opening. Staffing and organization.

Marketing mix
Definition of the product (as above). Promotional strategies. The image and appeal of the project. Market positioning and pricing strategy. Distribution/sales network.

Project justification
Revenue assumptions. Visitors/customers. Average expenditures. Operating costs by sales outlet. Projected operating results. Capital budget – construction, furniture, fittings, equipment, other costs. Financing costs. Return on investment.

References

Fuster Lareu, Juan (1992) *Turismo de Masas y Calidad de Servicios*, 2nd edn, Grafica Planisi.

Levitt, T. (1965) 'Exploit the Product Life Cycle', *Harvard Business Review*, November/December.

4 The travel trade

This chapter covers the structure and composition of the travel trade, explaining businesses such as tour operator, wholesaler and retailer. It describes the ways in which the travel trade works, covering the various interrelationships. It goes on to outline some travel trade characteristics such as price integrity, the tendency to secrecy and the risks and responsibilities of the tour operator. The relationships between destinations and tour operators are discussed, covering the choice of operators and various conflicting viewpoints. The chapter then summarizes the impact of information technology. It goes on to explain the importance given to consumer protection, and then describes national tourism offices abroad. The chapter concludes with a brief checklist to assist in coordinating with tour operators and the travel trade.

Organizers and retailers

In the 1980s the European Commission recognized a need to regulate the travel trade. In 1990 it adopted a directive on 'Package Travel, Package Holidays and Package Tours'. Member states were required to introduce legislation, implementing the directive, by the end of 1992. Accordingly the British regulations came into force in December 1992. Their provisions are discussed later in this chapter.

In the EU directive, the terms tour operator and travel agent are not used since they tend to have a different meaning from country to country. Instead, the terms organizer and retailer are used.

Organizer means the person who, otherwise than occasionally, organizes packages and sells or offers them for sale, whether directly or through a retailer.

Retailer means the person who sells or offers for sale the package put together by the organizer.

It is obviously sensible to frame regulations using precise and unambiguous terms. However, in the travel trade itself the terms tour operator and travel agent continue in common use.

In the travel trade, roles and relationships are flexible constantly adapting to changes in the market and new realities and opportunities. On one side there is a greater concentration of power in the hands of fewer large tour operators. On another side, as tourism diversifies, there are a greater number of agencies dealing with the more specialized types of tourism.

Vertical integration is also increasingly common with the same companies controlling tour operators, retail agencies, airlines and hotels.

What does the travel trade consist of?

The travel trade consists of those enterprises which produce (package) travel, and/or sell travel and/or arrange travel, or arrange meetings, conventions and exhibitions including the related travel.

The key verbs which describe the travel trade are: producing or packaging; organizing or arranging; selling; and booking and ticketing.

Tour operators, involved principally with leisure tourism, produce packages. They may sell these directly to consumers, or they sell them through wholesalers and retailers.

The travel trade can be broken down and described as follows:

Tour operators

Inclusive tour operators (mainstream markets) – outbound.
Inclusive tour operators (special interest markets) – outbound.
Inclusive tour operators – principally inbound.
Inclusive tour operators – principally domestic but some inbound.

Wholesalers

Enterprises which engage in on-selling an existing package or product to travel retailers.

Retailers

Retail enterprises selling existing packages, travel tickets and other services (e.g. hotels, rental cars), to the public.

Travel management services

Enterprises specializing in arranging travel for the business sector.

MICE Organizers

Enterprises which specialize in arranging conventions, meetings, incentive travel, conventions, conferences and exhibitions – hence the term MICE.

Transportation Companies (railways, bus companies, shipping companies and airlines).

Transportation companies may act, either directly or through subsidiary companies, as inclusive tour operators.

Clubs, societies, and associations

This category covers any other organization which acts in the same capacity as a tour operator. For example there are a number of sporting, religious and other special interest groups involved in tourism in a continuing and organized way. Acting for their members, they organize and sell various packages.

Wholesalers and retailers make money principally from commissions based on what they sell. This comprises the main proportion of their revenue.

Travel management services serving the business sector are also mainly rewarded through commissions on sales. However, depending on the range of services offered some customers may pay them fees.

MICE organizers may also be remunerated through a combination of commissions and fees.

Transportation companies obviously make money by selling tickets, either directly or through third parties. Many also control subsidiary companies acting as tour operators.

Clubs, societies, associations and other organizations which act as tour operators may be either profit or non-profit making. Any profits from travel are mostly used to support the organization's other activities.

Tourism and travel have grown more diversified, and the mix of enterprises selling travel has changed accordingly. Mainstream markets are controlled by fewer large tour operators, while a growing number of smaller ones concentrate on special interest and alternative tourism.

The growth of information technology and internet services may lead to new ways of selling leisure and travel services.

The following notes describe the characteristics of each of these principal types of enterprise.

Tour operators

Tour operators can often come to play the dominant role in most elements of a destination's marketing mix. This is particularly true in the case of comparatively small tourism sectors with limited marketing expertise and budgets. Tour operators may greatly influence prices, the image of the destination, the promotion and the sales network.

They may also influence the product by suggesting ways to improve.

Inclusive tour operators make money not only from their packages, but also by selling complementary services on commission, e.g. travel insurance, local excursions and tours.

Figure 4.1 shows the way in which tour operators work.

Wholesalers

Wholesalers respond to a demand for the onselling of packages to retailers. For example, a wholesaler in the States may on-sell a 'tour of the Shakespeare country' on behalf of a UK inbound operator. Or this

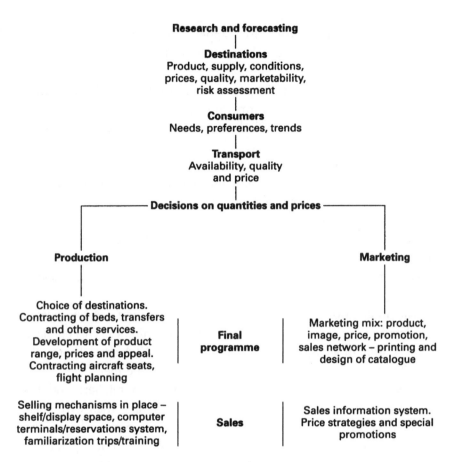

Figure 4.1 How tour operators work

same wholesaler may also sell the 'overland Jakarta\Bali tour' for an Indonesian inbound operator.

Retailers

The success of a travel retail business depends on three key considerations:

Location and physical facilities
The location and ease of access. Visibility, signing and shop window.

Interior design and layout. Eye appeal and merchandising impact. Brochure and catalogue availability and display.

Information systems, and the processing of tickets and bookings
On-line reservations and information systems. Rapid access to, and confirmation of, best prices. Technology-assisted speed of service.

Personal service
Human element. Knowledge and understanding of destinations and tour operators. Courtesy and attentiveness. Travel counselling and selling skills.

Retailers may sell a variety of travel and tourism services including bus, rail, shipping and theatre tickets. For most agents, however, the major part of revenues come from airline and inclusive tour bookings and tickets.

The International Air Transportation Association (IATA) licenses retailers to issue tickets on behalf of its member airlines. This entails an investigation of all aspects of the business, and IATA check thoroughly that its various conditions and requirements can be met.

Figure 4.2 illustrates the relationship between retailers and tour operators. Tour operators have increasingly acquired their own chains of retail agencies. Although these may sell a range of packages, they naturally favour and push the packages of the tour operator in question.

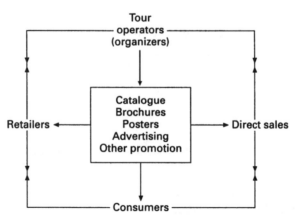

Figure 4.2   Tour operators and retailers

Many of the traditional independently operated retail agents may, just as many high street butchers and greengrocers, find themselves obsolete. This is a continuing trend.

A destination should know how many packages of various types have been sold by a tour operator over a certain period of time. Often the destination may have no effective way of finding this out for itself. It therefore depends on the tour operator for the information.

Tour operators, however, like to keep information to themselves. They realize that this may give them a future negotiating advantage.

Tour operators may also be reluctant to share information on their network of retailers, or to say which retailers sell most packages and where. A destination should know this. It should know how its product is being sold and how well it is selling.

Travel management services

Specialized travel services for business travellers often include the development, for many companies, of an in-house travel administration system. Such a system covers the formulation of travel policies and travel planning procedures, and the arrangements for all trips including health requirements, hotel and car rental bookings, the control of expense reports, reimbursements, and the reconciliation of related accounts.

These travel services have responded to a clear need. Many companies suffer from loose rules governing travel, often permitting staff to make their own arrangements (usually through their personal secretaries), with confusion over accountability and the correct budget. Well-organized corporate travel services have made the administration of travel more efficient and less costly.

MICE organizers

Companies specializing in the MICE market can create a package to meet the particular needs of each customer. They bring all the diverse facilities and services together, and they do this in competition with other destinations.

This means that they package hotel accommodation, meals, the use and organization of the convention centre, the convention registration and administration, an entertainment and recreational programme, a formal programme of dinners and receptions, possibly a civic reception given by the city or local government, sightseeing, and a programme for spouses or those not attending the convention sessions.

International competitive bidding is often employed. Different destinations bid for conventions and exhibitions including all the related needs specified

Incentive groups are holidays organized by a company, usually for its highest performing distributors or sales people, for example, Ford Motor Company or Nikon cameras for their top agencies.

Transportation companies

Many transportation companies have formed tour operating subsidiaries. This enables them to take control of more of their marketing and to be less dependent on outside interests. They may still do business with other tour operators, either alone or sometimes sharing space with their own tour operator.

Price integrity

Because of aggressive pricing policies, the passengers on a single scheduled airline flight may have paid a wide range of prices for the same flight in the same class. There may be as many as ten different price levels, and the lowest price in club class may be less than the highest price in economy class.

Similarly, the guests in a hotel may have paid different prices for the same accommodation.

The objective of pricing policies is to obtain the maximum revenue possible while selling all available space. This usually means using a varied marketing mix. The product is the same but pricing, promotion and sales approaches may differ. And they may differ according to the time of year, the market segment, the particular country and so on.

Hotels and airlines have published tariffs which list the highest prices. But the market willing to pay the highest prices may only use up a proportion of available space. The rest is filled up by discounted business.

The sales strategies will be influenced by the volume purchased and the continuity of the demand. Somebody buying half an aeroplane for a whole year will get a better price than the operator who wants only 10 per cent of the plane for three months. However, the first operator may decide to buy 60 instead of 50 per cent of the plane, and then onsell the additional 10 per cent to the second operator at a better price than directly obtainable from the airline. In doing this, he or she acts as wholesaler.

If a hotel, for example, exploits the concept of marginal costing and elasticity of demand, it prices to achieve the highest possible occupancy, to leave nothing unsold. However, in doing this it will drive down its average room rate, and the average room rate achieved has a direct effect on quality and image levels as well as profitability.

For this reason hotels, airlines and other providers of space are concerned to preserve the idea of price integrity.

Also if the price is too low the product is cheapened. It may no longer appear to give value for money. Discounted prices can damage the image, as noted in Chapter 3, especially of up-market products and services.

Customers resent paying more than the next person for the same thing. However, people appear willing to accept that previously contracted group prices may be lower. They also seem willing to accept the low package holiday prices paid at the last minute.

However, they tend to resent different prices charged for the same services at the same time, under what seem to be the same conditions and circumstances.

People lose confidence when price integrity is betrayed. It devalues the service in their minds, damages its image, and causes annoyance. Users expect a certain consistency in pricing levels.

Sometimes, it is wiser to maintain the product's price so as to protect the higher paying end of the market. When the marketing mix is too variable and tries to meet all tastes and all prices, the overall image and price may eventually find the lowest level.

Secrecy

All competitive business tends to be secretive. However, the travel trade's variable pricing tends to make it rather more secretive than many other types of business.

The wide variety of contractual interrelationships which grow up in tourism, between tour operators, airlines, hotels, local operators, car rental companies and so on, contribute to this secretive environment.

Prices may be constantly modified as new deals are negotiated or renegotiated. The travel trade around the world may make thousands of price changes every day.

The covertness of the travel trade makes it difficult to find out how it is operating, who is doing what, where most influence is being exerted, and what likely outcomes may result. This is all a part of insider knowledge. It comes from a wide network of relationships and sources of information, which may take years to build up.

This can also place GTAs at a disadvantage. They may lack the staffing and organizational continuity to acquire such knowledge. Similarly, an inexperienced private sector may also lack similar inside knowledge and understanding.

Risks and responsibilities

If tour operators contract seats from an airline, they may take on an obligation to pay for the seats whether they are sold or not. The precise terms of the contract will determine how much they pay and when, what cancellation rights they have, what penalties for non-performance will apply, and what guarantees will be necessary.

Generally charter flights enable tour operators to achieve lower seat costs, mainly because they can achieve higher load factors and lower overheads than with scheduled services.

An inclusive tour operator may buy 50 seats on an aeroplane as a component of an inclusive tour programme. He buys them for $200.00

a seat and there is no cancellation clause, i.e. no possibility of returning the seats to the airline unsold. Whether the operator uses the seats or not, they have to be paid for.

The operator, therefore, may price the package based on a 70 per cent seat utilization. This still enables a marketable price and a profit while minimizing the risk. It also means that anything sold over the 70 per cent will produce a higher return, and the remaining seats can be sold, up to the last minute, at heavily discounted prices.

Tour operators may use a variety of last minute deals to generate additional revenue from the remaining seats. As already noted, they can exploit both the concept of marginal costing and the price elasticity of demand. At the same time, they may be careful to maintain the idea of price integrity and value for money for their mainstream market – the people who have already bought holidays.

Contracts with hotels follow the same principles. The more risk a tour operator assumes, backed by appropriate guarantees, the lower the hotel price. In turn, the hotel must make sure that the contracted rooms are kept available.

A tour operator may decide to act in partnership with a local inbound operator. The local operator will then provide all the services at the destination, including both the hotel space and the ground transportation. This spreads the risk and the returns will be lower.

The tour operator's principal sales tool is the catalogue. This may include only the programmes for a specific region or country, or it may feature similar style holidays in different parts of the world. The product range responds to the operator's markets and normally tries to include packages at various prices for differing tastes. If operators are promoting a particular package of some kind, then they may produce a separate brochure for it.

During a certain time European operators tended to use surcharges, supposedly applied because of unforeseen cost increases in package components or wild swings in exchange rates, to produce the profit margin. This practice was open to abuse and the consumer protection measures, discussed later in this chapter, established controls.

Despite this change a substantial proportion of tour operating profits still come from the various extras: regional supplements, room supplements, cancellation charges, investment of deposits and balances, travel insurance and local tours and excursions.

The need to contract services and set prices far in advance, usually 18 to 24 months, introduces risk in the event of unforeseen fluctuations in costs. Operators have to use the devices of skilled money management to counteract such risks. Payments are often made by consumers well in advance of holidays. Operators can usually enjoy healthy cash flows, and are able to use large cash balances advantageously.

Choosing foreign tour operators

It is generally not for a government (except under the old centrally planned and controlled communist economies), to choose tour operators. It is sometimes mistakenly assumed, however, that governments can select tourism markets by exercising control over which tour operators can or cannot sell the destination.

This would tend to upset free market conditions. Selective controls would also impose impossible restrictions on the hotels and inbound operators. Normally they would like to be free to sell their product and the destination according to their own judgement. However, should people be free to sell a country's tourism product through whatever channel and at whatever price they choose?

The people producing Mercedes automobiles or Rolex wrist watches would not let just anybody sell them. They would develop quite stringent criteria and appoint dealers accordingly.

In many ways a tourist destination is like any other product. Whoever sells it should not undermine the marketing mix. Some control has to be exercised over the quality of all aspects of the product, including the quality of the companies which take on the responsibility for selling it. Also the quality of the ways in which they choose to sell it.

Tourism is not like marketing commodities such as oil, coffee, tea, copper, tin, tobacco or even vanilla pods. These are raw products yet to be processed and marketed as a finished product under a recognizable brand name.

The package of cigarettes, the jar of instant coffee, the petrol for the car, may not even identify a country of origin. But a tourist destination is already a product before it is packaged and marketed in a foreign market place. The way in which it is sold can undermine how it is viewed, and seriously damage its sales.

A GTA, working in close collaboration with the hotel and travel trade, normally tries to establish some working guidelines to ensure that the destination's marketing mix is maintained within agreed limits.

Conflicting viewpoints

International tour operators act as the conduit between each tourist origin country and its markets, and each destination and its products. They exercise considerable control over the market, while the destination exercises some control over its tourism product.

Destinations (through the GTA) may often view the operators with a certain amount of suspicion and mistrust. They often tend to think that operators have no particular loyalty to the destination, portray the wrong image, retain a disproportionate share of the benefits, and flout local tax and fiscal regulations.

Tour operators, for their part, often doubt the GTA's understanding of tourism and its technical expertise in marketing.

The relationship between GTAs and tour operators needs to be free of prejudice on both sides. It requires the free exchange of information, and a healthy understanding of relative roles and rewards.

Information technology and the travel trade

The development of information technology has had a profound effect on the travel trade. It has:

- put up-to-the-minute information on travel and tourism on the TV screen at home, or through other home-accessed information systems.

- given criteria about the enquirer's needs and preferences, it may enable a quick comparison of a wide range of alternatives.
- allowed access to a complete description of the destination together with all relevant details.
- also enabled the instant confirmation of availability and booking.
- also provided automated ticketing.

Information technology has changed the skills needed by travel trade personnel. Planning routes and itineraries, verifying schedules, looking up tariffs and writing out tickets were among the important skills of front line staff. These tasks are now becoming computer driven.

Staff can concentrate on the quality of customer service and sales and travel counselling.

Consumer protection

The history of the inclusive tour abounds with stories about holiday experiences which fell far short of the promises made. Half-finished hotels, uneatable food, filthy bed linen, five kilometre treks to the beach, and polluted swimming conditions. Everybody has a travel horror story.

The evidence suggests that since the introduction of package holidays back in the last century, most consumers have been more than satisfied. But sometimes because of poor quality control and entrepreneurial error and business failure, serious problems have occurred.

In tourism many people buy a product which they have never seen firsthand. They buy it on trust based on a sales blurb, some photographs and a salesperson's reassurances. Even when it turns out as expected, perhaps the operator goes bankrupt and leaves them stranded at the destination. Obviously the nature of tour operation requires that consumers are protected.

The 1990 EU directive on 'Package Travel, Package Holidays and Package Tours' was mentioned at the beginning of this chapter (it was incorporated into British legislation in December, 1992). It sets out the regulation of inclusive tours and serves as a good example of this type of legislation.

The directive stipulates that brochures and advertising must not have any misleading information. They must contain clear, complete and correct information about:

- the destination and periods of stay involved
- the transport used
- the class of accommodation and its characteristics (listing the category of accommodation according to any official system of classification)
- the meals provided
- the itinerary
- the passport and visa requirements
- any requirement as to the minimum number of participants and if and when there is a cut-off date
- arrangements in case of delays
- guarantees for advanced payments made and for repatriation in the event of insolvency

The directive also describes the precise requirements about each of the above. In what circumstances and how they apply, what must be made part of the contract, and when information must be provided.

The contract must contain not only the points listed above, but also:

- the dates, times and points of departure and return
- any visits or excursions, or other features, included in the price
- the names and addresses of the organizer and, where applicable, the retailer
- any taxes or additional charges not included in the package price
- the price may be revised before departure but only under certain conditions. Any revisions will relate to transport costs including fuel costs, increases in taxes, dues or fees for services such as landing and departure taxes, and the foreign exchange rates governing package costs. No increase at all is permitted after 30 days before departure, and an increase of up to two percent must be absorbed by the operator
- the payment schedule and method of payment

- any special needs requested by the consumer, and agreed when the booking was made
- the period within which any consumer complaint for non-performance must be made

The directive gives people the right, under certain circumstances, to transfer their bookings to another person. It also deals with alterations to the conditions, and any resulting cancellation by the consumer. It covers other situations when a significant proportion of the services are not provided. And it goes on to deal with all aspects of liability on the part of the organizer.

The regulations also require organizers to provide evidence that any needed refund of advanced payments and repatriation of holiday makers are assured. Such arrangements may be made through bonding (as in the UK), insurance, or funds in trust. In the UK, for the purposes of the regulations, the Civil Aviation (Air Travel Organizers Licensing) regulations are judged to meet this requirement satisfactorily.

In any proceedings connected with an organizer's non-compliance, defendants may show that they took all reasonable steps. Consumers may have to show that it was unreasonable to rely on the information provided to them.

In the UK other legislation, such as the Fair Trading Act 1973, the Restrictive Practices Act 1961, and the Trade Descriptions Act 1968, provides for various complementary consumer protection.

The European directive is one example of the regulation of travel and related consumer protection. Other countries have adopted similar regulations covering broadly the same issues. Bonding, requiring that tour operators create the means to repatriate or refund clients in the event of business failure, is a measure increasingly adopted on a worldwide scale.

National tourism offices abroad

National Tourism Offices may be set up by a GTA in one or more of the countries representing its major markets. Any such offices should be well located, attractively designed and efficiently operated. They should project in every way the destination's desired image.

Offices have an important role in distributing printed material and providing information. They also play a key part in monitoring the market and collecting all relevant and up-to-date data about it.

An office does not have an independent role, it is an extension of the GTA and represents the tourism sector as a whole. It should reflect the tourism policies of the country in question and help to cement working relationships and solve problems. It should liaise closely with the local travel trade, particularly the tour operators selling the destination, and provide the necessary marketing support.

Checklist – working with the travel trade

The following brief checklist covers the main points for a GTA when dealing with the travel trade – especially with foreign tour operators handling inbound traffic. The trade and professional associations provide the essential channel for close consultation and collaboration.

The issues included in this checklist are discussion points. They can help to raise and consider various actions and questions strategy and possibly regulation.

Regulatory framework

A framework which ensures that:

- the consumer is adequately protected against travel trade mal-practice and/or financial failures.
- the travel trade is assisted through regulation to achieve certain minimum operational standards and, through its trade associations, to police itself more effectively.

Strategy checklist

(This checklist shows how a GTA might monitor questions of destination marketing through tour operators. As result a GTA may coordinate, working with the sector, the development of a number of guidelines).

Is the marketing mix of the tour operators, selling incoming inclusive tours, compatible with the marketing mix of the destination? In particular:

- what is the difference (distinctiveness) and positioning of the destination, in relation to the other destinations offered in the operator's catalogue?
- what image of the destination does the operator project in the catalogue and other printed material? Does this reflect the desired appeal?
- what is the positioning of the price/value relationship in comparison to the other destinations offered? Does it appear to make sense?
- what is the promotional impact of the tour operator's material? Is it suitable in terms of layout, copy, graphics, quality etc?
- how much material and how many catalogues are distributed? How and where? What is the coverage in terms of retailers and geographical areas? What promotional programmes support retail sales?

Are operators selling one or more destinations within the region? Do they favour one destination more than others? Do they sell any multi-destination packages within the region? Do they offer two and three day 'add-ons' within the region? How does all this affect the destination?

How many other tour operators from the country of origin are selling this particular region? Which destinations do they favour the most? What are the relative shares of the market? Because of this which destinations represent the main competitors?

What are the comparative advantages or disadvantages of each tour operator? A better or worse product, product range and image, price/value relationship, promotional material and appeal, and sales and marketing coverage?

Are there any tour operators active in the region which do not sell the destination? Why?

Are all the tour operators satisfactory in the way they do business? Terms of contracts, payment schedules, guarantees, advance payments, honouring cancellation clauses and commitments, local representation?

Do tour operators appear committed to the destination? Do they provide helpful feedback? Do they do market research, demand forecasting, trends analysis etc? Are they willing to share information?

Are programmes sufficiently focused or are they messy — with too many hotels, and too many variations in the packages offered?

What transportation is used and what are the contractual relationships made? With which airlines — how many incoming seats are controlled by each operator? What are the options for obtaining additional seats? Are reliable carriers being used? Are national carriers used or not? If not why not?

What more can you do as a destination to encourage the tour operators to sell more?

Are any national tourist offices located in the major markets performing their role effectively, e.g. providing up-to-date market information, monitoring market performance and the promotional activities of competing destinations, and providing marketing support?

5 Government tourism administration

This chapter looks at the issues related to public sector administration and tourism. It discusses the purposes of public administration and examines the concepts of absorptive capacity and cultural compatibility. It goes on to explore issues about strengthening the capacity of the public sector and problems of malpractice on the part of government officials. The role and scope of government tourism administrations (GTAs), and the various forms of organization found, are discussed as are questions of decentralization and private sector organizations. The importance and influence of government/business relationships are also discussed. The chapter then goes on to consider the legal framework for tourism and concludes by describing various international organizations.

The purpose of public administration

The purpose of public administration is to establish the framework by which a country can develop and foster the good of all its citizens, while protecting the rights of the individual. Human rights and the good of all are generally defined by a country's constitution. The constitution is then interpreted to reflect the policies of the political party in power.

Public administration is then aimed at the implementation of government policies and plans, and the operation of its routine affairs. In practice this consists of administering the laws, collecting revenues, operating social services, allocating funds, and generally running the country.

Great emphasis in public administration is placed on the rule of law.

For example, legal conditions are established in which a business can hope to meet its own objectives as well as the broader objectives of society. Business would not be able to function effectively without such a framework.

All aspects of business are subject to some form of regulation — adherence to building regulations, tax laws, labour codes, laws of contract, financial regulations, environmental codes, commercial law, and business licensing requirements, etc. Business must be conducted within the rules.

The success of a legal system depends largely on the public's willingness to play by the rules. People must first be aware of the law, then they must believe in it and follow it. Law enforcement agencies can deal with a small number of transgressors. They cannot cope if the majority of people transgress.

Aspects of public administration

Politics, economics and public administration are closely related. Public administration is influenced by the wisdom of the day, by cultural norms and historical influences, by economic priorities and by political beliefs and expediencies. And where there is a permanent civil service — a body of career professionals — it is also influenced by a set of institutionalized beliefs and values.

It is these various influences which make countries different in their responses to similar needs and circumstances. Differences occur in the following ways:

- The cultural conditions for certain things to be done.
- The professional capacity to do them — trained personnel, technology and know-how.
- The political, economic and social justification to do them — the impulse to do them.
- The sense of public service and professional integrity to do them.

Depending on the circumstances, therefore, some things may never get done successfully. This leads to the consideration of two interrelating concepts – absorptive capacity and cultural compatibility.

These two concepts can be described as follows:

- The capacity to absorb and harness new technology, or to cope with the pace of new development – in knowledge, skills and resources.
- The compatibility of particular systems or approaches within the cultural framework of the country. Because something has worked in one country, can it work in another? Are there cultural reasons why it can't? Do new ways of doing things clash with limitations of a cultural nature?

The public sector tends to suffer more than the private sector from these limitations.

The private sector may be quick to try and catch up or adapt. It imports any resources lacking and sets about learning the necessary techniques and skills. It adapts to change. This change rebounds on the culture which, in turn, also starts to change. This is part of the development process. The public sector, by contrast, is more set in its ways and less ready or able to contemplate change.

Public sector officials tend to be more change resistant, less adventurous, and more fixed in their cultural traits than their private sector counterparts.

Key issues in strengthening the capacity of a country's public administration

Depending on the part of the world, public administration deficiencies tend to be of the following types:

- Low pay is common in countries with budget problems and where the private sector offers insufficient alternative employment opportunities.
- Patronage is also common. Government jobs may be exchanged for political support or favours. There may be examples of nepotism, and posts given to people for reasons other than their competence.

- Overstaffing. Because of low pay, low productivity and patronage, too many people are employed.
- Lack of political independence of the public service leads to an extension of patronage. In some countries all employees in the public administration are political appointees. When governments change, the public servants change. There is no continuity and the level of technical competence is affected.
- Inappropriate skills. Employees may be trained in general administration but often have little technical knowledge or skills in the area of specialization, e.g. tourism. Administrators are often required to make technical decisions, and should possess the necessary expertise and specialized experience.
- Poorly defined jobs. People may not know what they are supposed to be doing. This leads to confusion and duplication, since the roles and responsibilities of staff are not clear.
- Lack of clear objectives. Personnel become lost in routine repetitive work that appears to have little real purpose. They are unaware of any clear objectives. A job becomes an exercise in filling up time.
- Poor intragovernmental communication and coordination. This is characterized by a duplication of effort, by activities which overlap and conflict and by fragmented decision making.

Sound management practices can offer a cure for these various problem areas.

Malpractice by government officials

The UK's 1993 Audit Commission investigation revealed, in local government, 54 cases of fraud involving the award of contracts and granting of planning permission (HMSO, 1994).

In many countries government officials may be offered money for a variety of reasons, for example:

- as an appreciation for pushing the products or services of a particular company
- by featuring them in Government sponsored promotion

- by recommending them to potential investors
- or by ensuring that these are the goods and services purchased by the government itself
- for choosing not to enforce a particular piece of legislation, code of practice, etc
- for expediting the issue of a particular licence — regardless of whether or not the correct criteria have been met
- for issuing a planning permission or a similar authorization, in contravention of the established conditions, for some kind of proposed development
- through the payment of commission from a supplier or contractor
- for arranging the approval of special grants or subsidies although the proper conditions have not been met
- through defrauding the government by falsifying claims for the reimbursement or payment of services never undertaken, or salaries for personnel who do not exist.

Attractive and competitive pay and conditions, and well established career paths help to eliminate such malpractices. Public administration should be as transparent as possible, and held accountable for all of its actions.

The role and scope of a government tourism administration

A government will set up its form of tourism administration according to local practice and preference. Each GTA attempts to deal with tourism in its own manner. While there may be no single or best type of organization, there is a range of responsibilities which a GTA should cover. GTAs may take different organizational forms while tackling the same tasks.

A GTA exists to plan and manage the sector, working in close collaboration with all other interests. It does not have, in the management sense, an executive responsibility. While it may coordinate the planning for tourism it is, for the most part, the private sector which executes the plans. The GTA's management role is therefore an indirect or indicative one.

A number of variables affect the precise nature and functions of a GTA:

- the priority accorded to tourism by the government
- the size and scale of the country's tourism sector, and its level of development
- the degree of centralized planning and administration, and the role of government in relation to the private sector
- the roles undertaken by other organizations and agencies – both public and private sector
- the relationship with other government ministries and agencies, and the degree of coordination which exists.

A GTA may include some or all of the following departments under its management: administration; legal counsel; information systems and research; marketing; product planning and development; regulation and control; tourist information services; human resources development; public awareness programmes; and international relations. A typical GTA organization chart is illustrated at Figure 5.1.

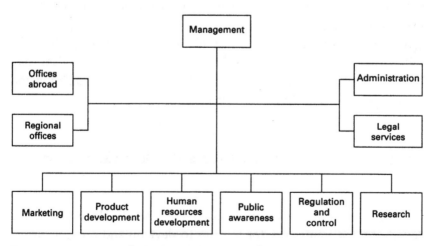

Figure 5.1   Typical GTA organization chart

GTAs do not handle directly all public sector tourism matters. On many questions the GTA will only have a consultative role – and this is often overlooked. For example, economic and fiscal policies are the responsibility of the ministries in charge of finance and economic planning. Land use and physical planning are usually under the ministries responsible for the environment and public works.

Tourism is multi-sectoral and crosses many different areas of responsibility. This complexity makes coordination between various government agencies difficult.

Because of the degree of interdependence, a number of countries have chosen to establish interministerial tourism committees, to try and ensure the necessary coordination.

Special committees, however, seldom seem an effective remedy. Although the task is difficult, the channels of communication should already exist for good interministerial working relationships. This is part of the effective functioning of any government.

From the cabinet and higher policy making level down, there are usually sufficient bodies already in existence to enable interministerial contacts, consultation and coordination. What is less likely to exist is a shared recognition of the priorities, and a common understanding of agreed policies and strategies.

This is sometimes due to the absence of any strong central directive on tourism, causing it to become fragmented across the various branches of government. Each ministry develops its own ideas about the priorities and the needs.

Where tourism is of great economic importance, it helps to make tourism a senior ministry with the appropriate status. Tourism may then stand a better chance of ensuring the necessary coordination and prioritization of its activities and needs.

Forms of government tourism administration

It is evident from the above that government should establish the conditions and framework for tourism to develop and prosper.

It is a government's direct responsibility to frame the policy for the sector. Some of the implementation of the policy, however, may be delegated to an independent form of organization, representing the sector as a whole. A government may set up such a body when it wishes to:

- ensure the full participation of the industry in decision making
- tap the best technical expertise available
- free decision making from the possible slowness and unresponsiveness of government bureaucracy
- shift the decision making responsibility from itself to the sector as a whole
- create more transparency in decision making.

Government takes the overall management role and selects the appropriate form of organization for its GTA. It may choose to separate policy making from policy implementation, while also splitting up other functions.

A GTA, therefore, covers all branches and levels of government and may not comprise one organization alone. This concept replaces the more traditional idea of a National Tourism Organization (NTO). Historically an NTO tended to represent a narrower concept, concentrating mostly on domestic and international marketing, tourism statistics and some regulatory functions.

In practice a GTA may range from a ministry in central government to tourism development corporations or boards with independent powers, to provincial government and municipal tourism offices. What is set up is an overall organizational framework, capable of operating in an integrated fashion while satisfying all the various needs.

A government chooses the form for its GTA which it considers best suited to fulfil the required role:

- A full ministry dedicated to tourism. This is wholly government staffed and managed but with various kinds of advisory and consultative committees.
- Part of a ministry. The ministry has a mixed portfolio and tourism may be linked with such areas as civil aviation, culture, information and the media.
- A quasi autonomous non-governmental organization (QUANGO)

set up through the government, but with a high degree of autonomy. Often taking the form of a statutory board; a board established through legislation to fulfill stated aims.

A QUANGO is generally a government-sponsored agency or authority with independent powers. It is a term commonly used in the United Kingdom.

- A ministry or part ministry, with certain activities also entrusted to a QUANGO. A ministry may assume responsibility for policy, research and statistics, planning, regulation and control, public awareness and international relations, while a QUANGO takes the responsibility for investment promotion and marketing.

However, the various functions may be split up in other ways.

- Such a QUANGO as above may take the form of a joint promotion or development board. This is a board often registered as a company with its equity distributed between the government and the tourism private sector. It takes on the responsibility for marketing, spending funds which may be jointly contributed by the public and private sectors. Such a board, may or may not assume responsibility for some jointly sponsored development projects.
- A QUANGO which takes the form of a non-statutory board. It is set up by a ministry but has no formal powers. Its authority is derived from the government department or ministry to which it is subordinate.
- A tourism development corporation. Again this may be a wholly owned or partly owned government-sponsored corporation, similar to the joint promotion or development board mentioned above.

Governments may decide to initiate the development of major tourism projects themselves. They may own land, or intend to acquire it, for this purpose. A development corporation is formed to take the lead role in planning and managing these projects.

As described in Chapter 3, on resort complexes, the corporation takes over the land, develops a master plan, uses loan finance to create the necessary infrastructure, and attracts investors to undertake the secondary development.

A development corporation should usually confine itself to the specific projects, and not encroach on the functions of the GTA. This can lead to a duplication of activities, a fragmentation of efforts, and a dilution of professional expertise. The relative roles of the GTA and a tourism development corporation can become confused, with a number of overlapping activities.

Whatever way responsibilities are divided and whatever the final form of organization chosen, the GTA still assumes a catalytic role in the management of the sector. It should try to find the best way of playing this role while involving the private sector to the maximum degree possible. The exact answer will differ from country to country depending on government, culture and circumstances.

The above forms of organization are all more or less instruments of government. They all tend to be set up through government initiatives and are dependent wholly or partly on public funding. While a QUANGO may have independent powers, it is still indirectly dependent on government.

The membership of a QUANGO's board of management takes advantage, in principle, of former civil servants, prominent business people and other leading specialists.

Full time government tourism officials should be supported by the close involvement of a wide range of industry leaders and specialists. The best form of organization satisfies this requirement while achieving close coordination within the sector.

Generally the GTA in any form should not run commercial tourist facilities directly. This would normally represent unnecessary government involvement and is best left to the private sector.

As to the running of tourist information offices, this is best organized at the level of the area or municipal authorities or also by the private sector. This gives the responsibility to those parties most affected by the quality of a local information service.

Decentralization

The GTA normally involves a number of different levels: national, regional, area and municipal. The needs across the whole country should be addressed and coordinated effectively.

Decentralization in many countries has given regional and local government authorities autonomy over many development decisions.

Many of the needs and problems are only fully understood in the regions, the outlying areas and the cities themselves. They can only be investigated in collaboration with the local administration. While tourism development policy is agreed at the national level, the central GTA should provide regional and other levels of government with the necessary guidelines and advice.

Economic and social planning, in all its dimensions, is intersectoral and operates at all levels of government. The proposals on strategy and the relevant tourism development programmes need to be discussed with the regional and local authorities and their staff. Their inputs and agreement are essential.

It is important to involve the key personnel of the regional tourism and other local government offices as closely as possible. These are the personnel who will initiate and follow up on all subsequent actions and resulting projects.

At the national level the role is to consolidate views from around the country, and develop them into a logical overall framework. In this way the policies and strategies are built through a bottom-up approach, but are then fed back down. This combines top-down and bottom-up approaches, with key people at both levels making an appropriate contribution.

Central government coordinates, with wide consultation and discussion, the development of the policies and strategy frameworks to follow. Then, acting with any help and advice from the centrally based specialists, the regional and local authorities develop their objectives. They do this in close collaboration with all local interests; the community, other agencies and institutions, and the private sector.

Private sector organizations

Principal among the tourism private sector organizations are the trade and professional associations. For example, the hotel and restaurant associations, the travel agent's association, the tour operator's association, together with other organizations representing such interests as tourist attractions, convention centres and hotel and tourism training centres. On the professional side there may be associations or guilds representing particular specialists such as tourist guides, hotel managers and chefs.

The membership of these organizations may be fully representative of the particular sub-sector or group of people in question.

One of the major roles of trade associations is to lobby on behalf of their members. The various organizations join associations to be able to speak with a single voice. For this reason it is important for the GTA to consult with them on a continuing basis. Consultative or advisory committees or councils provide a forum for the expression of viewpoints. In some countries, a combined tourism association is a way of bringing the various professional and trade associations together. Such an association can then speak for the tourism private sector as a whole.

Whatever the case the sense of partnership between public and private sectors is essential. It should be fostered at every opportunity.

Government/business relationships

Government can coordinate long-term policies and strategies; this is a part of macro economic management. Governments tend to take a broad view. Business, however big the interests represented, tends to take a narrower view.

However, many different sets of interests will try to exercise influence over the decisions which governments make. Special interest groups and lobbyists of all kinds will try to persuade government to support their own particular aims. Governments may sometimes respond to the loudest voices and strongest influences.

Democratic government permits a continuing debate between all the competing and conflicting sections of society. Public administration is a balancing act, full of trade-offs, ambiguity and compromise. But while one may try to do better for everybody, some people come off best.

In pluralistic societies, there is a system of countervailing power at work. Each viewpoint on tourism may have opposers. Amidst this the government takes action (e.g. cuts or increases taxes, introduces incentives, intensifies particular marketing or training efforts, etc). It maintains contacts and discussions with various interests, and passes laws to regulate business activities. It keeps the institutional framework updated and responsive to national needs.

All governments intervene in business. Without intervention business could not exist. It is in the degree of intervention that governments differ. Some governments may demonstrate an attachment to free market principles. Others intervene constantly to regulate or influence the performance of markets.

As already noted, one school of thought holds that government interference in free trade, manipulating prices and regulating supply, is always regrettable. Others see it as the proper exercise of government leadership, accepting responsibility to maintain social harmony and to protect the interests of the state.

Governments normally explain their intentions and actions. They talk to business interests and try to convince them about the rightness of intervention. On the other hand, business talks to government to seek intervention favourable to its own interests.

Common in tourism, for example, is when existing hotels want to prevent additions in the number of hotel rooms. This is justified, it is claimed, because of an apparent threat of over capacity. But it is often just a protectionist manoeuvre.

In the case of government intervention, both sides have to take notice of one another. This tends to make the relationship more structured. The GTA meets formally with the trade associations and representative institutions.

The relationship tends to become institutionalized through the creation of councils and committees, through which formal contacts and discussions take place. This formal framework, however, produces a whole range of informal contacts as well. These informal contacts may bring together senior government ministers and business leaders through dinner parties, lunches, receptions, special events and other social activities.

Governments may tend to recognize only particular organizations as representative of the sectoral interests. These may include both employers' associations and trade unions. In some situations governments choose to interrelate with only a handful of major corporations. Some political parties may lean more towards business than others. Others may be more aligned with the trade unions.

The tripartite relationship of government, employers and unions is a concept promoted over the years by the International Labour Organization (ILO). Business has often feared the unions because of the traditional antagonisms between labour and capital. The employer/labour relationship often seems poised on the edge of conflict. The tripartite concept brings people together to resolve their problems harmoniously.

It is also in countries where the business/government relationship is most institutionalized that one tends to find the unions joining in as well. The same principle of tripartism is at work. This is a sensible approach not only in questions affecting employment and training, but in all matters affecting sectoral performance.

Business (just about everywhere) often sees itself as more hindered by government than helped. Business normally seeks various kinds of preferential treatment:

- lower rates of taxation
- grants, exemptions, subsidies and incentives of various kinds
- protection from competition
- assistance with exports (including invisible exports) e.g. export credit schemes
- funds for research, training and marketing.

In areas such as training, the environment, safety standards and so on, a regulatory approach is often needed. A voluntary approach is always preferable if it works. It is usually worth giving it a chance.

Countries have to choose to lean one way or another.

- In interventionist countries, business will wait for the government lead. There is less inclination for business to take initiatives.
- In non-interventionist countries, businesses may take action themselves through their trade and professional associations. They collaborate together, regulating and policing themselves, participating in joint marketing and training programmes, and protecting and promoting their own interests.

It is for each country to determine its policy, and decide which of these approaches it prefers.

A legal framework

The legal framework set up to regulate tourism may not differ greatly from the regulation of other types of businesses. There may be some particular legislation related to tourism, aimed principally at consumer protection, for example the 'Package Travel, Package Holidays and Package Tours' regulations already discussed in Chapter 3.

As indicated previously, a GTA should not intervene in setting and enforcing standards if they are not essential. Acceptable performance standards can often be left to the power of market forces. This makes it unnecessary, for example, to classify hotels and other tourism enterprises or license tourist guides. Additionally, the trade associations themselves may ensure that certain standards are provided by their members.

Government regulation may be justified when competition is limited and consumers need protection against gross inadequacies.

It is often practical to establish an umbrella tourism act which will set out the principal tourism development policies, and define the role and powers of the government tourism administration.

As a part of this, the GTA may be empowered to make regulations controlling various types of tourism activities. Such an umbrella act may permit the GTA to make minor adjustments to these regulations from time to time, without having to pass through the full legislative process again, for example, the registration and regulation of travel agencies and tour operators, hotels and other tourist accommodation, and possibly tourist restaurants and other facilities.

The act may also make cross reference to other relevant regulations, administered by other ministries and government agencies. The GTA can then monitor the sector's compliance in accordance with these. For example, in the case of new or expanded buildings:

● a licence to build (meets planning and building regulations)

- a certificate that the enterprise meets the fire regulations (if separate from building regulations)
- a certificate that public health regulations have been satisfactorily met
- an approved environmental impact statement.

It may also be possible for this same act to make reference to:

- the designation of tourism development zones
- the control and regulation of such zones.

The act may also set out the country's tourism policies.

Chapter 10 further discusses various aspects of regulating the tourism sector, including the licensing, registration and classification of tourism facilities.

The way in which a government divides up the responsibility for various legislation, between its branches and departments, differs from country to country. The level of efficiency in enforcement may also differ. In developed countries long years of experience may have entrenched these responsibilities. In areas such as business registration, planning permissions, building regulations, labour laws and fire codes, for example, the GTA may have no involvement.

In developing countries, however, a GTA may be expected to help ensure the compliance of the tourism sector with all legislative requirements. In this, it assumes some overall responsibility for the sector.

At whatever stage of a country's development, however, a GTA should be consulted in the framing of legislation which in any way affects the development of tourism.

International organizations

As the countries of the world grow closer together, there is more international collaboration. Countries agree common standards, international codes and practices, and statistical definitions. They also seek to make more inter-country comparisons and to share knowledge and experience. They try to learn from each other through the transfer of technology.

Technical cooperation takes place not only between developed and developing countries, but among the developing countries themselves. This international activity is undertaken mainly through intergovernmental organizations. The collaboration is multilateral – between all the member countries.

Bilateral initiatives, of course, comprise the arrangements for cooperation between just two countries.

Examples of major intergovernmental organizations are the United Nations Educational, Scientific and Cultural Organization (UNESCO), the United Nations Environmental Programme (UNEP), the International Bank for Reconstruction and Development (IBRD – the World Bank) and the International Finance Corporation (IFC), and the International Labour Organization (ILO). All of these organizations have activities directly or indirectly related to tourism.

The specialized intergovernmental body for tourism is the World Tourism Organization (WTO) in Madrid.

There are also regional intergovernmental organizations such as the European Travel Commission (ETC), the Caribbean Travel Organization (CTO) and the Tourism Council of the South Pacific (TCSP).

Internationalization has resulted in many different organizations representing private sector interests. These various organizations represent a wide range of tourism related activities. For example, the International Air Transportation Association (IATA) for the airlines, the International Hotel Association (IHA) for the hotels, and the Universal Federation of Travel Agents' Associations (UFTAA) for the travel agents.

The World Travel and Tourism Council (WTTC) covers the sector as a whole, with the participation of many of the leading private sector companies.

Internationally there are also organizations for a variety of tourism related professions. For example, conference interpreters, congress organizers, tour managers, and travel journalists and writers. There is also, for example, a World Association for Professional Training in Tourism.

There are also a wide range of regional private sector organizations.

For example, Europe has regional associations for hotel managers, hotel school directors, hotel and tourism schools, airlines, and tourist guides. It also has, among many other organizations, the European Federation for Farm and Village Tourism. In other regions there is the ASEAN Tourism Association (for the seven ASEAN countries – Brunei, Indonesia, Malaysia, the Philippines, Singapore, Thailand and Vietnam), the Latin American Confederation of Tourism Organizations, and the Pacific Asia Travel Association (PATA).

The world has also tended to become regionalized into economic and political blocks. These start perhaps as trading blocks, expand their common activities into other areas, and become more integrated as time goes by. The European Union is a good example of this process. As this happens the business/government relationships become internationalized. For example, business now concentrates many lobbyists on the European Commission in Brussels.

References

Her Majesty's Stationery Office (1994) *Protecting the Public Purse: Combating Fraud and Corruption in Local Government.* London, HMSO.

Part Two
Tourism's Impacts and Other
Management Criteria

6 Tourism and the economy

The chapter lists the components of economic policy and shows how tourism relates to each of them. It goes on to examine the concept of development planning and the constraints to economic growth. It then explores the part played by foreign investment, and examines the case for incentives. The process of economic development is discussed, and the chapter then goes on to cover techniques for measuring the economic impact of tourism. Tourism multipliers and input-output analysis are discussed, and ways of improving tourism's economic performance are identified. The chapter concludes by examining ways of reducing economic leakages.

Taking a comprehensive view

Many economists approach tourism by measuring its impacts – using particular analytical and economic accounting techniques. This is an entirely descriptive approach. The word impact refers essentially to what has happened, not what should have happened.

Tourism should first be seen in the context of overall economic policy and planning. It has to be slotted into a macro-economic view. In attempting to manage an economy many different factors have to be kept in balance.

The study of economics generally divides between:

- the criteria used in developing economic policy, to arrive at objectives and forecasts
- the techniques used to influence economic performance, to achieve these objectives and forecasts
- the techniques used to measure past economic performance.

Economic policy and planning

Economic policy and planning will revolve mainly around certain fundamental objectives. The potential contribution of tourism is noted under each of these.

- Balancing the make-up of the economy – sectors and targets
  Tourism dominates the economy in some countries, for example, the Bahamas. In others it represents an important way of diversifying the economy – often away from commodities, for example, Australia and Indonesia.
    Whatever the case, it is important to target tourism's role, and to commit resources accordingly.
- Maintaining macro-economic stability
  Tourism is assisted by price stability, low inflation and equitable foreign exchange rates. Stability is an essential condition for a successful tourism sector.
- Allocating resources – often scarce resources
  Tourism's importance must be recognized, for it to be given the resources it needs.
- Achieving economic growth
  Tourism's contribution is often significant. Its growth rate may exceed that of other sectors.
- Ensuring the sustainability of economic activities in environmental terms
  Tourism has to achieve sustainability if it is to succeed in the long run.
- Achieving the equitable distribution of economic activities by region of the country
  Tourism is an important way of achieving regional development. For many regions it represents the best economic option.
- Balancing the geographical distribution of the population
  Connected with regional development, tourism can create jobs where they are needed.
- Achieving an equitable distribution of economic benefits per capita of the population

Many types of tourism, with high multiplier effects, can result in a widespread of economic benefits.

- Minimizing the level of unemployment
  Tourism is a major source of employment.
- Maintaining a low and acceptable rate of inflation
  Tourism is sometimes developed quickly in formerly under-developed regions. Substantial inflows of revenue may occur, ahead of the capacity to fully supply the demand for goods and services. This can create an inflationary effect, and put tourism out of balance with the more traditional sectors of the economy.
- Maintaining the stability of the currency
  Inbound tourism as a substantial source of foreign exchange earnings, helps to maintain the stability of the currency.
- Achieving an acceptable balance of trade
  Again, inbound tourism is an invisible export and contributes to an acceptable balance of trade.
- Achieving a balance between consumption, saving and investment
  Like any other sector tourism can contribute significantly to this objective.
- Funding a budget to enable the public sector to fulfil its role
  Tourism is a good source of government revenues. In addition to normal tax revenues, it may also generate revenue through, for example, bed taxes and airport departure taxes.

Government will set economic policy as it relates to these various areas. However, in some countries the central bank may be an independent branch of government and will undertake responsibility for monetary policy.

Linked to the areas of economic policy and planning, are further objectives of public expenditure and social policy. The economic policies support the social policies and vice versa.

- Generating sufficient government revenues to meet public expenditure
- Providing an adequate educational and vocational training system
- Providing an adequate public health system
- Providing an adequate legal framework – from the judicial system to law enforcement

- Providing an adequate network of other essential social services; fire, post office, ambulance etc
- Maintaining an agreed range and level of other social services
- Providing an adequate system of national defence
- Maintaining overseas diplomatic representation
- Ensuring adequate maintenance and expansion of the country's physical infrastructure and public utilities – roads, harbours, airports, railways and transportation systems, telecommunications
- Ensuring an adequate supply of produce, goods and services for the consumption of all sections of the population.

All governments, whatever their particular political and ideological beliefs, understand that they must satisfy the above needs. However, it is unlikely that they will agree on how to go about it.

The success of any economic system depends on providing people with an acceptable standard of life.

The origin of national development plans

The term 'development plan' is used mainly in the context of macro-economic management. The emphasis of such planning tends to be on public expenditures, where and how they are to be prioritized and allocated, and how government revenues are to be raised to meet them.

The economy is analysed sector by sector, and then viewed as a whole. Government decides how to best influence economic performance.

This process takes place in every country in the world, although it may not always take the form of a comprehensive development plan. Sometimes it is associated with national budgeting, the allocation of public expenditures and the corresponding forecasts of overall economic performance.

As long as governments have governed, they have engaged in some form of economic planning to work out how much money they need to spend and how much they need to raise. As a part of this, each government department has to prepare its proposals. Each has to ask for its share of public funds.

Departments compete for funds. The result depends on the influence of each minister of government, on how well the case is argued, and how good the lobbying is. People fight for the biggest share possible.

Development plans owe their origin, therefore, to the budgeting process. The need to set up an ostensibly rational basis for setting and funding budgets and establishing a system of priorities. Governments allocate funds to best reflect their policies.

Plans gradually become refined to guide the development of the particular sectors, setting out performance targets and ways to achieve them. Since one year does not allow a long enough period, most plans are developed for four or five years. Such plans contribute to the programme on which governments are elected for their particular term of office.

Tourism will usually comprise one part of the plan. All planning should be viewed as a continuous process. Plans should be constantly reviewed, updated and adjusted, according to newly-assessed needs and priorities.

When an ongoing tourism planning process is in place it is easy to make a summary for inclusion in the government's development plan.

Preparing national development plans

A plan normally starts with a review of recent economic performance together with future prospects. It will go on to summarize its main contents, and explain why the chosen government policies are the most appropriate.

It will describe in more detail the substance of the plan. It will list the public expenditure planned under each particular category, e.g. transport, energy, water supply, health, education, and natural resources management and the environment.

It will then deal with the expected role and future development of the private sector. It will generally do this sector by sector: agriculture, forestry, fishing, trade, mining, manufacturing, tourism and other service sectors.

The rate of economic development depends more on private sector performance than public sector expenditures. Governments like to help promote (markets and investment) a sector which it views as having potential. It will look at current supply and demand, the marketing opportunities, and the development needs. It may also examine promotional needs for specific markets.

Governments cannot look at one sector alone in an isolated way. Sectors are interdependent, and have to be related to the economy as a whole.

To safeguard against misguided assessments, there should be close consultation with the private sector. Industry leaders can help to judge current conditions and prospects, and to predict likely performance.

The main elements to be judged, in formulating an economic development plan, are as follows:

- Identification of development opportunities. Results of surveys, technological and scientific research studies, market studies, and surveys of natural resources.
- Development of appropriate levels of infrastructure, e.g. airports, seaports, inland waterways, roads, railways, water and energy supplies.
- Development of the appropriate legislative framework for economic activities – foreign investment, land tenure, contracts law, commercial law, banking law, etc.
- Development of training facilities and programmes aimed at defined skill standards for the necessary occupations, as well as the continuing and related levels of general education.
- Promotion of particular types of investment, seeking proposals from foreign and domestic investors and giving assistance in the formulation of projects.
- Achievement of the best resource-use through land use planning, zoning and planning regulations, and the application of any incentive schemes and tax breaks.
- Achievement of improved savings levels, public and private.
- Development of improved business and financial services, e.g.

banking and credit facilities, insurance, commodity markets and security exchanges.

Constraints to growth

The principal constraints to growth are generally:

- skilled manpower
- the necessary natural resources
- finance
- the capacity of the capital goods sector

The need for skilled manpower is obvious. Even though many tourism and hotel jobs have a relatively low skills base, there is still a need for many highly skilled workers and supervisors. Unless skills training is well developed, its absence represents a major bottleneck.

Secondly, the necessary natural resources are obviously a prerequisite for certain types of development. For example, if new land for development is being used up, this represents a major limitation. Some countries may have a shortage of tourism sites for development, for example, in a developed European country. By contrast, others may have an abundance. Indonesia has 17 000 islands many of which have tourism potential and are yet to be developed.

Money itself may represent a constraint. An approximate capital output ratio can be 3:1; this is to say that to achieve a 5 per cent growth rate in GDP requires an annual net investment equal to 15 per cent of GDP. This exceeds the savings ratios of most countries. In consequence, development has to fuelled by foreign investment and this is not always easy to attract.

Finally, the capacity of the capital goods market is no less important but is often underestimated. Capital costs in hotel facilities are broken down between construction (about two thirds of the total), and furniture, fittings and equipment (about one-third).

A main constraint in construction may also be lack of skilled workers. It requires at least a year to train general construction workers and longer for more specialized jobs. If the construction sector is already working at full capacity, then this, too, will represent a major constraint.

Building materials, if locally produced, may also be short. Items of furniture, fittings and equipment, if locally produced, may also pose a supply problem. This may create a need to import items adding to costs and using foreign exchange.

Foreign investment

If the intention is to attract foreign investment, then the law should obviously be designed to facilitate this objective. Both the law and the procedure in handling development proposals should be helpful. They should not be so ambiguous and slow as to deter potential investors.

The two essential criteria are clarity and speed. The law should be clear, with applications processed in no more than 4 to 6 weeks. Investors should not be pushed from one government agency to another, seeking a variety of licences and approvals. An investment board or similar agency should act as a one-stop shop, capable of giving the one comprehensive approval to cover all aspects of the investment.

Investors want a stable investment situation without surprises; transparent and equally applicable to all.

It is essential to screen foreign investors thoroughly. One has to ensure that they are serious persons or companies with good financial credentials and a sound business track record.

There may be a need for brokers or promoters to pursue the right kind of foreign investor. If so, they should be chosen by the government on the basis of their established reputation and past proven results.

Among the key provisions which should be included in a foreign investment law, are the following:

● The training of local personnel should be one of the requirements. It is important to ensure the comprehensive transfer of technology. Investors should give details of their proposals.

- Approval should be extended to projects which support the Government's socio-economic objectives and priorities. Among the criteria may be job creation, regional development, export earnings, income generation, import substitution, environmental sustainability and the upgrading of skills.
- Investments may be restricted to particular sectors only, reserving certain kinds of enterprise for local investors.
- Undertakings may be given by the Government not to expropriate or nationalize the enterprise or any of its assets, or take any measures having the same or similar effects. And not to impose price controls on the investor's products or services.
- Permission to purchase foreign currencies and to remit them abroad to meet all obligations associated with the investment; imports of supplies, repayment of principal and interest on international borrowings, reasonable royalties and management fees, dividend remittances, and the repatriation of invested capital.
- Incentives may be extended to projects which:
  - develop high technology industries
  - create a significant number of jobs
  - increase exports
  - foster regional and/or rural development
  - protect and/or conserve the environment
  - locate in priority development zones
- Incentives are usually of the following types:
  - exemptions from, or reductions in, various kinds of taxes, customs duties and other government levies
  - the grant of land or money as a contribution towards a certain type of development, provided that the development meets the agreed conditions and requirements specified
  - the provision, at no cost, of the infrastructure required to support a development
  - the provision of loan finance at concessionary rates of interest and an extended period for repayment
  - the provision, at no cost, of government guarantees, to provide additional security for the necessary loan finance.

An incentive is really a form of government subsidy. But many commentators consider it a pity that incentives are offered at all. They consider it preferable for investment projects to stand or fall on their merits without any form of government intervention, or interference with market forces.

Generally, however, incentives are offered for the following reasons:

- When competition for investment is fierce. One must offer competitive conditions – at least comparable and perhaps superior.
- When incentives lessen risk and increase the probability of a good rate of return on the investment. They therefore induce people to invest where and when they might not otherwise invest.
- When the cost to the government of the incentives in question is far outweighed by the economic benefits generated.

There are three basic principles for governments to follow:

- Do not give away more than necessary.
- Be sure that benefits will exceed the costs.
- Apply incentives fairly and equitably – do not negotiate them in an inconsistent and uneven manner – the 'horse trading' approach.

In many free market economies there are frequent examples of selective government intervention; subsidized credit, ceilings on borrowing rates, public investment in selected sectors, protected import substitution, and assistance to export marketing. In tourism, for example, it may even go as far as the payment of financial incentives to foreign tour operators who produce a certain volume of inbound tourists. Or sometimes, providing substantial capital grants towards the costs of developing hotels in certain areas.

The free market does not always work in attracting investment in the best interests of the economy. Incentives are sometimes essential to get the kinds of investment needed to achieve certain economic and social objectives.

However, if government money is to be given away (in the form of grants or foregone revenue) to encourage private sector investment, it has to be very well justified. It should only be done as a very last resort, and wherever possible it should be avoided.

The development process

Underdeveloped countries are rural by nature. Most people live in rural areas and depend on agriculture for their livelihood.

An efficient agricultural sector is a key to progress. It produces increasing yields per hectare and high productivity per worker. This stimulates development. It creates more prosperous communities and a growing domestic market for manufactured goods. And it creates surplus labour from the farms which is absorbed into new industrial enterprises in the towns.

By 1850 Britain was the only country in the world where the number of agricultural workers had fallen below 50 per cent of the labour force.

A corresponding improvement in access to health and educational services, raises the capacity of people to work effectively. Agriculture becomes mechanized and highly productive, and industry expands. This provides the basis for more infrastructural development.

At the same time, domestic and export markets develop. Prosperity boosts government revenues and this allows for universal health services and education. This is followed by the development of a full range of social services. As people earn more they may save more. Capital markets grow and stimulate more industrial expansion. A country breaks out of underdevelopment.

All this may sound an ingenuous view of the realities of development in the contemporary world. However, many economies have to be restructured. There are many problems: for example, limiting population growth, safeguarding the environment, conserving resources, controlling urban expansion, reforming and deregulating bureaucracies, mobilizing investment, improving education and health, and transforming traditional values.

Tourism is a flexible economic force that responds well to a variety of situations. It can trigger large new resort complexes in hitherto undeveloped regions, or it can equally well create new economic options through small tourism enterprises in undeveloped rural communities. Tourism offers many possibilities.

Tourism multipliers and what they measure

Clearly tourism should have a favourable economic effect. The tourism multiplier is one way of measuring it. This multiplier analyses the leakages of tourism revenue out of the economy, and the knock-on effects created within the economy.

Just as a note of music may linger on and gradually die away, so a tourist dollar may echo on through the economy.

Within the economy, the front line of people and suppliers providing goods and services benefit from a direct impact. A second line less involved with tourism, benefits from an indirect impact. And finally as expenditure filters on down, there is an induced impact.

This multiplier effect can be measured in different ways, for example, on income (rent, profit, interest, salaries) – the tourist income multiplier; on employment – the number of jobs created by tourism revenues; or on the government revenues generated.

To calculate the multiplier effect, data about operational performance and expenditures are analysed together with the characteristics and knock-on effects of transactions. The multipliers are then expressed as ratios, for example, the income multiplier will lie in most cases between 0.4 and 2.0. The number of direct jobs created may be expressed per thousand dollars of revenue, and government revenue as a ratio of total revenue.

For example, Archer and Fletcher show Turkey with a tourist income multiplier at 1.96, Jamaica at 1.23, the Bahamas at 0.79 and Fiji at 0.72. In Jamaica the government revenue multiplier was 0.306 – for every US$1000 of tourist expenditure the government received $306. The employment multiplier was 0.000128 – an increase of US$7682 in tourist expenditure would create one new job (Archer and Fletcher, 1990).

Large well diversified economies will be more self-sufficient in meeting tourism's needs, and the income multipliers are the highest (at from 1.5 to 2.0). In smaller economies, less diversified and with a narrower base, they will be the lowest (around 0.5). Such small economies will require the importation of many items, resulting in a higher leakage of expenditure abroad.

Comparability of multipliers between countries

For this reason alone, care should be taken in comparing the multipliers between different countries. There are also other reasons why comparisons can be misleading. First, the methodologies employed may differ; the way business activity is sampled, the extent that the indirect and induced benefits are included, and the range and accuracy of the revenue and cost data which are collected may all combine to produce varying results. Also economists sometimes guard the details of their methodology, and it may be impossible to establish the reliability and comparability of results.

Large and small hotels

Yet another reason lies in the composition of the hotel sector. Small locally owned hotels usually attract a lower spending market, but have a higher income multiplier. These small operations are generally better integrated into the local economy. Large luxury hotels, by contrast, may attract a higher spending market but import more supplies and generate a lower income multiplier.

Large hotels, because of the above, will for the most part achieve more revenue per visitor than small hotels, and visitors from the upper market segments may also indulge in far more discretionary spending in the destination. As a consequence the net benefits to a destination may be higher, even though the income multiplier is lower.

A higher multiplier, however, does tend to indicate a wider distribution of benefits among the society. Small locally owned hotels generate a smaller pot of money, but spread it around more.

Large hotels and resort complexes may generate more government revenue as well as more employment.

These are all very broad generalizations. It might be possible to find situations in which some small hotels have very high room rates and revenue, while maintaining close linkages with the local economy. Or where large hotels have low revenues as well as high patterns of leakage.

The need to disaggregate the sector

For this reason, it can be both misleading and of little practical use to calculate only an aggregate multiplier for the sector as a whole. A sector needs to be disaggregated and structured according to its different characteristics, types and size of hotel, and markets. Multipliers can then be calculated according to each sub-sector.

This enables policy makers to analyse more effectively the relative strengths and weaknesses of each, and to see where the opportunities for improvement exist. It will also help to indicate the best types of tourism for the future expansion of the sector.

The main characteristics

It is important to understand first the types of tourism which it is possible to attract, supply and serve, and second the relative benefits of each. Yet in economic analysis the measurement techniques sometimes come to overshadow the reasons for their application and the use of their results. Multipliers are sometimes calculated, but not understood or related to future improvement and development strategies.

One must not lose sight of the purpose of the technique. The income multiplier is designed to assess how much expenditure stays in an economy, and how it works its way through to provide wide economic benefit. It is easy to see where leakages occur to diminish this effect. And then, very important, to concentrate (where possible or desirable) on eliminating or reducing these leakages.

Tourism professionals should grow accustomed to identifying and thinking about tourism revenues and expenditures, and what leaks out or stays in an economy. They will be able to develop a feel for the economic effects; the cognitive skill of seeing and knowing. Looking at a particular tourism sector, they should be able to formulate a close assessment of its performance. Informed judgement of this kind is not a substitute for more rigorous study, but it helps to keep the economic impact of tourism in constant focus.

The input – output approach

Related to multipliers in the sense of exploring how expenditures repercuss through the economy, is the input-output approach. The multiplier effects on incomes, employment and government revenues were mentioned previously. A multiplier can also be developed to assess the impact on both sales and output. However, the technique most currently used to measure these latter types of effects is input-output analysis.

Wassily Leontief, a member of the economics faculty at Harvard until his retirement in 1975, advanced the development of input-output analysis and was awarded the Nobel Prize for his work.

This type of analysis has some similarity to the tourism multiplier, but is more sophisticated. It measures the overall impact of revenues in a more detailed and comprehensive way. It takes into account the intersectoral structure of an economy. Any economy is locked together – a system of interdependent relationships. One sector supplies another – the sales from one become an input to another. A model can be developed to simulate how the economy works, reflecting the relationships between inputs and outputs. This is obviously of great assistance in economic forecasting and planning.

Based on detailed study of economic behaviour, a series of input-output coefficients are developed based on different types of transaction. These will enable the model to work in the same way as the economy works. Once the input-output tables have been constructed, the effect of various levels of economic activity can be tracked through the model. This can help to provide answers to the policy makers' questions, for example, what if so many international visitors were received a year, each spending so much money?

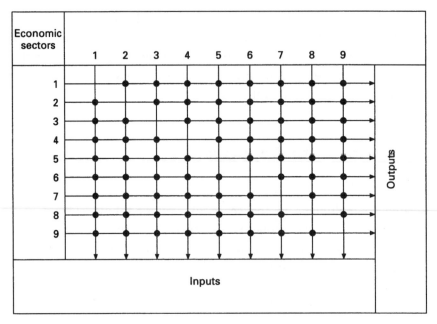

The points of interactions between sectors are shown across
the matrix producing the series of inputs and outputs

Figure 6.1   Schematic view of an input–output table

Figure 6.1 gives a schematic idea of an input-output table.

A great number of calculations are needed in such analysis, and this
technique has been greatly assisted by the development of computer
technology. Input-output analysis, as tourism multipliers, is another
useful way of monitoring the development and performance of the
sector. Tables can be developed specifically to monitor the tourism
sector, and included within the scope of a computerized information
system designed for this purpose.

Critics of input-output analysis point to the difficulty in defining in a
constant way the relationships between sectors. Underlying assumptions, they say, are often too shaky to allow accurate results. However,
accuracy can be improved as the technique is refined, permitting closer
adjustments to be made. The technique is now used not only at the
national and regional levels, but also at the global level.

As noted in Chapter 1, tourism is not an economic sector in itself but
an economic activity which flows into a number of sectors. It does not

fit, therefore, into the classifications used for national economic accounting. One has to tinker with various categories, making a range of further assumptions and adjustments, in order to apply the technique to tourism.

As time goes by, new approaches will be developed to address the place of tourism in economic accounting, and to refine the economic models used to monitor the sector's performance.

Leakages

The payments outside the country to support international tourism are usually called leakages. As noted, the economic benefits of tourism arise from only those earnings which remain within the economy.

It is also more accurate to talk of the import components of tourism in general, since domestic tourism will be affected as well as international tourism.

The items which are imported to support tourism fall into the following categories:

- construction equipment used to build new hotels and tourism installations
- construction materials similarly used
- furniture, fixture and equipment used for these new hotels and tourism installations
- operating supplies such as food and beverage, paper supplies, spare parts and engineering supplies, etc.

Some of these represent capital expenditures and some revenue expenditures, either costs towards the creation of the tourism asset (capital costs), or costs incurred in operating the tourism asset (revenue costs).

Apart from items of this nature, capital, services and manpower may also be imported. Capital, both equity and loan finance, may be brought in from outside depending on the legislation governing foreign investment. This will mean the subsequent payment to external sources of dividends and interest.

Services from outside the country may include design and planning work which come to represent a component in the capital costs. They may also include management fees, if the hotel or installation is to be managed by a foreign company or multinational, and they may also include marketing fees, if monies are to be paid out through advertising agencies, hotel representatives (and overseas representation and sales in general including public relations companies), and fees to purchasing companies, maintenance companies, training companies, etc.

They may also include foreign personnel, whose particular technical knowledge, skills and experience are needed for the success of the enterprise. Apart from recruitment costs, a proportion of the wages and salaries paid to these personnel is likely to be remitted outside the country.

Leakages of this kind are usually viewed in an entirely negative light since they are a loss to the economy. They do foster international trade, however, and in this sense are positive.

Trade is based on concepts of equity and reciprocity, and the balance of trade is a fundamental discussion issue in the development of relations between different countries. Japan, for example, has chosen to use outbound tourism to help reduce its excessive trade surplus.

Reducing leakages

The term 'leakage' implies something that can be repaired; one finds a leak and fixes it. All of the above leakages, however, cannot be fixed although many can be reduced. For example:

- Capital costs can be reduced by using local construction methods, emphasizing the use of local materials.
- By reducing construction costs, the capital investment required may all be available locally.
- Many items of furniture, fittings and operating equipment can be produced locally.
- Many imported foodstuffs and other supplies can be substituted by locally available items.
- Design and other consultant expertise may be available locally.

● Foreign personnel can be substituted by local personnel.

However, there are dangers in rushing into these various measures. One can lessen the quality of the tourism product, and it may no longer satisfy the intended markets. As a result the sector can finish up producing reduced net economic benefits. In the development of tourism strategy these various considerations need to be carefully weighed.

One of the induced effects of tourism is to change a population's pattern of consumption. Tourism gives exposure to imported food-stuffs and other goods, and local people may develop new preferences. This stimulates an increase in the importation of such items. This effect is often highlighted by critics of tourism. However, it is best viewed as a normal result of development and people's increasing prosperity. The internationalization of consumption tastes is a way of expanding world trade.

References

Archer, Brian and Fletcher, John (1990) Tourism: Its Economic Importance in *Horwath Book of Tourism*, (ed. Quest, Miles). The Macmillan Press.

7 Tourism and the environment

This chapter deals with the interrelationships between tourism and the environment. It discusses the awareness of environmental issues, and the need for preventative and remedial action. It describes the competition for space and resources, and the ways of ensuring that conservation measures are adopted. It lists tourism's potential contributions towards these objectives. It goes on to identify and outline aspects of project appraisal, cost/benefit analysis and the concept of an environmentally adjusted domestic product. The chapter also describes the issues related to zoning, planning and land use, and the concept of yield in the physical planning of tourism facilities. It outlines some other issues in facilities planning, and introduces the idea of paying environmental and cultural royalties. The chapter concludes by listing environmental management standards, and a checklist for the preparation of an environmental impact statement for tourism projects.

Development and the environment

The fulfilment of human needs causes environmental change of some sort. To adapt the natural environment to human existence is part of being human. Every time people cultivate crops, divert rivers, construct buildings, engineer new roads, or undertake any development, it rebounds in some way on the environment. The arguments are about whether such actions are detrimental or not; whether the environment is harmed, and whether development is sustainable.

Development cannot mean growth alone. Growth may make some people richer but it doesn't necessarily add to everybody's state of well being. It was noted in Chapter 6 that economic development should have broad and interdependent effects which lead to the improvement of life. Are people better off not just in financial terms, but in access to health, to educational opportunities, to housing, leisure options, recreational facilities and so on?

In the past, progress was measured principally by GNP *per capita*; a measurement which does not reflect either the distribution of benefits or the quality of life. In an effort to move forward and take a more appropriate view, the United Nations Development Programme (UNDP) introduced its human development index. This index takes into consideration not only the *per capita* GNP, but also people's life expectancy and rate of literacy. This gives a more complete view of people's well being.

Sustainable means something which can continue. Development should enhance and conserve the world for future generations. There is a danger of using up non-renewable resources while starting off degenerative processes and leaving the world a progressively poorer place. This is not sustainable.

Trade offs

Every time people act, it usually means that something is gained and something is lost. Environmental issues are largely a question of trade offs; for example, development takes place but resources are used. Access is improved but views are lost or trees are cut down. New factories are created but the air is polluted.

Some trade offs when examined may make sense. Other trade offs may be unacceptable. Urgent short-term economic advantage should not be used to justify lasting environmental damage.

In tourism, destroying the resource that attracts tourists, e.g. a coral reef, for immediate economic gain, makes little sense.

There are many pressing global environmental issues, for example, global warming (greenhouse effect), the ozone layer and the use of chlorofluorocarbons, pesticide use, desertification, and the problems of urbanization, air, water, and noise pollution, waste disposal, habitat destruction, soil depletion, endangered species, acid rain, and rain-forests, oceans, wetlands, coral reefs, rivers and estuaries. All of these pose many urgent needs.

Costs

Environmental targets often mean either higher costs or short-term losses in revenue. In response, companies draw attention to their responsibility to shareholders. They reason that action is not urgent, and that the threat to the environment is exaggerated. They play for time. Environmental costs have to be paid. If measures are delayed the costs increase.

As illustrated in Figure 7.1, costs are of three types:

- The costs which are preventative – expenditures are made to prevent specific, foreseeable and negative outcomes. They are costs which should be included as part of a given investment.
- The costs which are remedial – expenditures which have to be paid out by someone eventually, to remedy the damage caused by ignoring them in the first place. Those who damage the environment should be penalized and made to pay compensation.

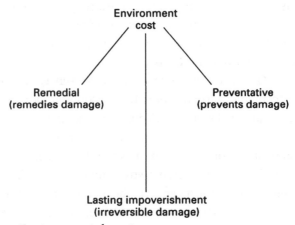

Figure 7.1   Environmental costs

- The costs of causing lasting impoverishment – these are costs which are difficult to quantify, but which represent a lasting impoverishment in the quality and variety of life. They are often incalculable.

A responsible attitude recognizes realistically all of these costs.

Two decades of turmoil in Cambodia have resulted in the planting of some eight to ten million landmines. It is estimated that the cost of planting a mine is US$15.00, but that the cost of safely removing it is US$1000.00. It is an example of outrageously inflicted damage at little cost. The cost of repairing the damage is very high, not only financially but also in lost limbs and lives.

Using tourism to justify conservation

If the use of natural resources is denied to people because of conservation, it is likely to mean a loss of income-earning opportunities.

If conservation causes a loss of income, the local population should be somehow compensated. Tourism may be able to provide this compensation in a variety of ways. It may create jobs as well as opportunities for the provision of various produce and services.

In one area of Zanzibar there is presently only one small hotel. The closest village, some two kilometres away, started to sell sea shells to the tourists. The hotel, to protect the natural environment, urged their guests not to buy the shells. It therefore deprived the villagers of a source of additional income. In compensation, however, all the hotel's staff are employed from the village. The hotel also tries to buy as many supplies as possible from there, and it has counselled the villagers on how to grow various vegetables which it needs for its menus.

In the Himalayan Kingdom of Bhutan one can note the case of Phobjika valley. It is one of the well-known wintering places for the rare black-necked crane. But it is also home to a community which could develop the region by cultivating potatoes – a high yielding cash crop. If the cranes are valued more highly than potatoes, then the people of Phobjika need to be compensated.

The game parks of East Africa provide another example. Considerable land is set aside for the parks. However, people may compete with the animals for this land. Poachers may kill the animals. It is only by allocating a proportion of the game park benefits to the local people that their support can be obtained. Such local support is essential for conservation.

These various initiatives illustrate certain principles. One should:

- Recognize that if people's livelihoods suffer, however important the environmental issues, their support and collaboration are unlikely to be given.
- Provide alternative sources of employment, income and/or compensation, using the opportunities offered by tourism.

Environmental measures do not tend to work without the support of the local population. Tourism can help obtain that support.

Tourism's contribution

Tourism can focus attention on important environmental issues, and can trigger projects which both conserve and enhance the environment, for example:

- It creates an audience for historical and archaeological attractions, and may generate funds for their conservation and upkeep.
- Similarly, tourism develops a flow of traffic to beauty spots which while putting pressure on them, also generates funds for their protection and management.
- Because of the importance of sunshine as one of tourism's principal themes and motivations, it highlights the seriousness of ozone depletion.
- It draws attention to the issue of biodiversity and the numerous endangered species – particularly the more spectacular ones such as elephants, rhinoceros and tigers.
- Because so much tourism revolves around the sea and the marine environment, it draws attention to problems of pollution, destruction of reefs and damage to coral, the plight of dolphins, whales and other marine mammals, and the dangers of overfishing.

- Similarly, it highlights the need to conserve and protect forested areas and wetlands, and stimulates funding for the creation of national parks and reserves.
- Tourism installations often create an example of energy-saving through the use of solar energy, wind-generated power, and natural ventilation.
- Tourism can often use landscaping and improved architecture to reduce the needs for expensive cooling, heating and lighting systems.
- Tourism has often been the predominant influence in the redevelopment and beautification of factory sites, mining areas, and riverside locations, all of which have been abandoned after years of former industrial use.
- Similarly, tourism has enabled the conservation of period transportation systems, old steam railways and sailing ships.

Approaches to cost/benefit analysis

Cost/benefit analysis justifies the use of resources. It attempts to calculate a rate of return for society as a whole. The costs of some resources, such as land or labour, may not be based on market values. If there is no demand for an alternative use, resources can be valued and below normal market prices.

In a situation of high unemployment and underemployment, labour may be costed at below market rates. Similarly, government owned land, undeveloped and without any obvious alternative use, may also be costed at a figure seemingly below market value. This approach is known as shadow pricing.

Similarly, there may be costs due to environmental losses or damage, which may not appear as commercial costs. However, they may be so high that they should prevent any project from going ahead.

In calculating a project's rate of return, market prices do not always reflect the true value to society of using resources. This technique makes objective value judgements about the true costs to society, to arrive at the true benefits.

Political decision making often relies on value judgements. The values assigned to costs and benefits may depend on the opinions of decision makers at a given moment. These values may change over time as circumstances and priorities change.

In Bhutan, the quantity of water channelled through the country's numerous rivers is known as white power. But to harness all of this power through more and more hyydroelectric projects is thought to have too high an environmental cost. The environmental costs are judged to outweigh any benefits from the export of the additional electricity generated.

An environmental impact statement (EIS) is prepared so as to weigh the costs and benefits. A checklist for an EIS is included at the end of this chapter.

Environmentally-adjusted domestic product

Until now environmental costs are not usually reflected in national economic accounting. The use of natural capital is omitted from the customary methods of measuring economic performance. Although many environmental assets are not subject to market transactions, they are being used up and should be costed.

A monetary value is therefore included for all natural capital used and environmental damage suffered. This allows for the calculation of an EDP – the Environmentally-adjusted Domestic Product – known as the Green GDP. As noted by Glenn-Marie Lange and Faye Duchin, 'sustainable development is said to be achieved if EDP is not decreasing with the passage of time.' (Lange and Duchin, 1993).

As tourism uses natural resources, so it can conserve and enhance them. It depends on the concept and type of tourism, and on the effectiveness of tourism planning.

Zoning, planning and land use

Zoning and planning regulations are fundamental in all development. Tourism should not be allowed to grow in an explosion of random development. Land use planning is essential. It provides a framework for what can be built where, how big, how high, and in what form and style.

Intersectoral coordination is essential for effective land use planning. Different sectors compete with each other for space. Interests need to be reconciled to arrive at the best use of different areas.

Part of zoning for tourism can consist not only in designating certain areas and sites for development, but also in indicating their minimum and maximum yield in rooms or beds.

A minimum yield is an important concept. It may be wasteful, for example, to take five hectares of prime beachfront land, and build no more than 20 rooms on it (four rooms – eight beds per hectare). Yet where land is initially cheap this sometimes happens.

In agriculture one measures appropriate development in terms of sustainable yields; cattle or fruit trees per hectare, tonnes of wheat, tons of potatoes etc. In tourism one should think similarly.

If key sites are used to maximize the number of beds up to a certain limit, then this means a better yield for the land area used. It means that less land is needed, more green spaces remain and more land is left free from development.

On a number of small Caribbean islands (where land is a very limited resource) this principle is not necessarily followed. All beachfront land is often developed. While much of it is very low density and no building is above the treetops, it does not always represent the most efficient use of land. In many places one could have achieved the same height restrictions and as many tourist rooms, while leaving more green and empty spaces for the enjoyment of all.

While yields in rooms should not be too low, it is often too many rooms per hectare which is found to be the case. Depending on the resort location and type of development, ratios from 20 to 60 rooms per hectare might be considered, the difference, say, between cottage or bungalow type projects and two or three storey blocks. Yet developers may succeed in putting 500 rooms or more onto a five hectare resort site, and far more on a city centre site.

Land prices are related to permitted height. As height restrictions become relaxed, land prices tend to increase and the buildings go higher. Twenty and thirty storey hotels or more are common in some urban environments.

In some areas of the United States, high rise buildings are often favoured while maintaining a low ratio of rooms to the land used. This places a modern multi-storeyed building in a spacious landscaped setting – for many a very agreeable planning solution. It may also allow for greater operational efficiency; the services are concentrated more closely together, resulting in the economic use of labour.

Restrictions on the use of land conflict with the idea of an individual's right to own and develop land as he or she chooses. Most societies, while recognizing this right, do not allow it to be exercised in an unrestricted manner. There are clear limits as to:

- the right to develop land or not
- what the land can be used for
- what can be demolished or not
- upper and lower limits on how big or small the development can be.
- the design; the form, positioning, architectural style and height of building
- the setback (distance) from roads, other buildings, the shoreline or riverside as the case may be
- regulations governing the buildings themselves
- requirements as to drainage and waste disposal
- requirements about parking
- access and landscaping requirements (including tree conservation and planting), ensuring the right treatment of surrounding areas.

Planning need not be over-restrictive. It will not prevent the individual touches which make a development distinctive. Paint, banners, awnings and canopies, whitewash, sunshades, statues, flowers, shrubs and trees, help to make places feel distinctive, welcoming and loved. In tropical countries the appropriate use of landscaping, with shrubs and flowers, can transform a basic concrete block building into a visual delight.

The system of controls over land should be as transparent as possible. The approval process should be open and participative. There should be open discussions of the issues, time allowed for publicizing decisions, public hearings and the right of appeal and review. The environment and what happens to it involves the society as a whole; everybody can have a say. These issues are further discussed in Chapter 15 on public awareness.

Some guidelines in facilities planning

Those responsible for the planning of tourism facilities need above all to conform to all related regulations and codes. Beyond this there are some other useful guidelines. Projects should:

- Respect the spirit of the place. Buildings should be congruent with their surroundings. Development should be sympathetic to the local culture and environment.
- Restore old buildings but respect their original use. They should be adapted if necessary, while respecting their integrity.
- Allow high rise building only when it is in keeping with the overall development concept, and when it conforms with local density standards.
- Leave green spaces and animal habitats intact and undisturbed.
- Conserve trees wherever possible, plant flowers, and revegetate any disturbed areas.
- Conceal plant and machinery as well as car parking.
- Leave views unblocked by buildings. If possible, views should be opened up from every balcony, terrace and window.

Visual pollution is often a controversial concept. Some things can be agreed as universally ugly. Others are only ugly as a matter of personal opinion.

Carrying capacity

In Chapter 1 carrying capacity was summarized as the point when more visitors would damage the environment or lower people's enjoyment below an acceptable level.

Every destination has a limitation as to the total number of people that can visit. It is this limitation which defines the destination's carrying capacity. It can be further broken down into five elements; two are quantifiable and three qualitative.

- *Damage*. The number of visitors without causing measurable damage to the environment.
- *Delay*. The number of visitors without causing intolerable delays in the use and enjoyment of attractions, with people having to queue or wait in traffic.
- *Overcrowding*. The number of visitors without giving a feeling of overcrowding, so that people are not jostled and squeezed.
- *Image*. The number of visitors in and around a destination without changing its image, and the necessary atmosphere and ambience which form a part of the enjoyment.
- *Reaction*. The number of visitors before there is a strong reaction, on the part of the local population, to the excessive pressures created. A feeling of cultural invasion is provoked when religion, language, heritage and traditions seem threatened.

The current carrying capacity of a place can often be increased through careful planning and management. By improving existing facilities and the organization of tourists, greater numbers can be received in still acceptable ways.

The payment of environmental and cultural royalties

Many natural attractions and cultural attractions can be visited free of charge, or they may only have a nominal entry charge. It may be considered a fundamental human right to allow everyone to enjoy these attractions. It may be a sound principle to give people equal opportunities to visit and enjoy not only their own national heritage but also world heritage. It is the concept of generational equity – of passing on a heritage as rich or richer than the one received – that underlies much of the philosophy of sustainable development.

However, as noted, the demand to visit a place may exceed the limit set by its carrying capacity. As time goes by, incomes rise, available leisure time expands and tourism increases, so the pressures on places and their carrying capacity grow correspondingly.

One way of limiting demand and decreasing this pressure, is to raise admission charges. This excludes all but the people who can afford to pay. This is a policy, however, which appears elitist, favours the well off, and discriminates against the poorer sections of society. Basing the enjoyment of heritage on buying power seems an unfair policy to adopt.

Heritage is simply viewed as something to be shared by all. A country may also extend this idea of sharing to foreigners. Nominal entrance fees to attractions may be paid as at home, while the general environment of the country is free. Visitors do not expect to pay for it.

However, should this principle also apply when people from rich countries enjoy the heritage of poorer countries? In such cases, many believe that the constraint of price control need not exist. If you want to go to Bhutan, for example, you have to pay for it. The Government levies a substantial royalty for the privilege of visiting and enjoying the country.

Bhutan can be regarded as futuristic in its application of this concept.

- It views carrying capacity in the widest possible sense – looking at the assimilation of tourism not only in terms of environmental impacts, but also in terms socio-cultural criteria and the potential disruption to the local way of life.
- It chooses, though a poor country, not to develop resources to the detriment of the environment. It levies a royalty for the store of pleasure which it is conserving.

Land tenure

Systems of land tenure are at the heart of any culture. The individual right to own and develop land has represented a fundamental value in many societies. At the same time the acquisition of land by the State, to carry out works which will serve for the common good, has become an important feature of policy and planning. While ostensibly fair compensation is paid in such cases, people seldom like to suffer the loss of their land.

In a similar way the restriction of the ways in which land may be used, as already noted, also affects its value. Land is the basic resource for all human activity. As such its ownership and use are not only the basis of economic development, but also lie deep in the human psyche. People's relationship to land – the territorial attachment – is an integral part of their make-up. Deep down, people often believe that doing whatever they want with their land is morally right.

However, people are told what they can or cannot do with the land. There is the right to appeal, the right to argue one's case, but the overriding rule of law is based on the needs and interests of the community as a whole. Land can only be used by individuals in such ways as to serve the common good.

In many parts of the world, land ownership is often collective by nature. Land belongs to the tribe or the community, to be used and enjoyed by all. Individual use is the subject of group approval.

The regulation of land ownership requires a very effective system of registration, allowing for the efficient transference of ownership in the event of sale, gift or inheritance.

Land tenure, the use of land, and zoning and planning regulations are among the most charged of all development issues. Any ambiguity or confusion may represent a major barrier to development. It is essential that the legal system is rapid and efficient, and that any doubts can be quickly removed. It is equally essential that published policies and permitted land use are made widely known.

Environmental management standards in Europe

It is useful to review the range of environmental management standards now adopted by the European Union.

The eco-management and auditing scheme regulation

This was introduced in July 1993, and compliance is to be voluntary for the first four years. An environmental agency monitors participating enterprises. The enterprise carries out an environmental auditing procedure. An environmental standard is reported which is then reviewed by an accredited external environmental auditor.

Air emissions

This governs emissions from plants, for transport fleets, and includes substances damaging to the ozone layer.

Amenities, trees and wildlife

There are numerous national regulations designed to control the conservation and upkeep of amenities, trees and wildlife. Enterprises need to be sensitive to their responsibilities in accordance with local requirements.

Noise

This refers to established standards for permitted noise for various types of plant and equipment including, for example, motorized mowers.

Nuisances

This includes a variety of nuisances affecting the environment. For example, drainage systems, caravans, temporary buildings or sheds, or even vehicles.

Physical planning

The principal provisions of physical planning will cover, according to local conditions; density, height, setback, etc. The assessment of environmental impact has become a prerequisite to obtain planning permission.

Radiation

This embraces all the regulations governing permitted levels of radiation.

Urban renewal

These regulations differ in application according to the area. They cover protected buildings, the need for renovation to achieve health and safety standards, and the designation of areas and sites for urban renewal schemes.

Waste

This deals with waste management and includes the disposal of toxic waste. It also covers dumping at sea, transportation of toxic waste and other special provisions.

Water resources

This covers water pollution, discharges, and water quality standards. Inland waters and the sea are both included.

Water supplies and sewage treatment

This covers questions of contamination, and safeguarding the water supply system.

Safeguards as to the proper use of products, the disposal of waste materials, energy conservation, and health and safety regulations (already well developed in European countries) are also covered. EU regulation is also expected to encompass packaging, so as to encourage recycling and lessen quantities of waste destined for landfills.

Rothery (1993) lists a fuller summary of EU provisions.

Voluntary codes

Education and the development of the public consciousness are essential in maintaining environmental quality. This requires that most people observe requirements, complying voluntarily without the need for enforcement.

It is easy to choose between 'have to' versus 'want to'. When people want to do something, it is much more effective motivation than when they have to. When people have to, it requires constant supervision and enforcement to ensure that they do. And this is often ineffective.

Codes should be agreed after full and detailed discussion of the standards which are in the best interests of all. People will then choose to keep to them. Indeed they will tend to police the sector themselves, and ensure that the codes are observed and standards maintained.

Sensitivity should also be developed towards building conservation provisions which protect historical buildings and heritage sites, and countryside conservation measures which designate national parks, protected areas, and nature reserves.

Checklist for developers

For the development of designated tourism areas:

- Ensure the participation of the local community in planning approvals.
- Develop areas in strict accordance with the legislation governing all aspects of physical planning.
- Do not demolish any protected buildings or, if possible, any buildings of historical or architectural interest.
- Enhance the distinctiveness and authenticity of the development.
- Make sure that long-term considerations take precedence over the short term.
- Use environmental conservation as a feature of the development.
- Make the development a reflection of local values.

- Minimize all economic leakage; try to develop linkages with local enterprises and use local resources.
- Prioritize job creation for the local labour force.
- Charge the costs of environmental measures, and the corresponding precautions that need to be taken, to the development itself.
- Retain flexibility to review and modify plans in the light of experience.
- Check that the zoning policies and physical plans are achieving the best use and interrelationship of land areas.
- Make sure that the provision of infrastructure is adequate and unobtrusive.
- Check for the introduction of imbalances in the local economy.

Checklist for the preparation of an environmental impact statement (EIS) for tourism projects

The approach to an EIS is illustrated at Figure 7.2. An EIS can take as its starting point the feasibility study described in Chapter 3; much of this study can be used to form a part of the EIS. The EIS focuses more on the physical planning and environmental aspects of the project.

Executive summary

A brief description of the project, its justification and a summary of the main findings and conclusions.

Terms of reference

The precise terms of reference in relation to the requirements of the planning authority for which the statement is being prepared. This should cite the particular regulations which the statement is intended to satisfy.

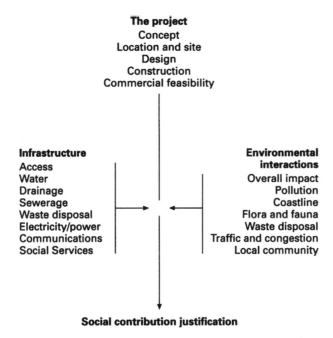

Figure 7.2 Environmental impact statement

Project Description

A description of the project which should include the following:

The project concept

Its nature, form, size, category, capacity, and range of activities. Its principal markets and pricing policies.

Location and site

Precise details of the location of the project and its site. Surrounding areas and uses. History of the site. Effect on adjacent and neighbouring land and property. Plan of the site area showing options for future development and expansion.

Design/Architectural solution

Key aspects. Functional interrelationships of areas and buildings. Site limitations. Application of planning regulations and building limitations. Style and image of the proposed scheme. 1 : 1000 scale drawings plus cross sections and elevations.

Construction
Construction methods and timetable. Organization of work, materials and equipment during the construction phase. Site preparation, transportation of materials to the site, blasting, excavation and earth-moving. Disposal of construction spoil. Control measures during construction – dust, noise, drainage and runoffs, water pollution, waste disposal.

Planning controls
Conformity with current regulations affecting the project.

Commercial feasibility

Statement of marketing feasibility
Principal market segments to be served and their characteristics. Market assessments and forecasts by each sales outlet.

Statement of financial feasibility
Summary of financial projections, with underlying assumptions and key operating ratios.

Infrastructural requirements

Transport access
Implications and needs. Car parking provisions.

Water supply
Demand as the development proceeds. Special needs, e.g. swimming pools, fire fighting, etc.

Drainage
Drainage needs. Any problematic aspects. Proposed stormwater drainage.

Sewage treatment
Treatment and disposal. Proposed installations.

Waste disposal
Proposed provisions for waste disposal.

Electricity
Demand as the development proceeds. Eventual annual energy needs. Provision for emergency supply. Alternate energy sources.

Communications
Proposed installations and needs. Demand when project is fully operational.

Social services
Specific requirements and provisions for the labour force. Housing, health, education and other social services.

Environmental impacts

Change
Change to the whole character of the area. What this represents. Assessment of impact acceptability. Visual impact. Effects on landscape and views.

Pollution
Dangers and safeguards against all types of pollution; water — including the sea, rivers, lakes etc, air, noise. Visual pollution.

Coastline
If the project is on the coast, compatibility with overall coastal management objectives.

Flora and fauna
Any danger of damage to vegetation and wildlife.

Waste disposal
Acceptable provisions for all waste disposal.

Traffic and congestion
Any danger of causing a deterioration in local traffic conditions.

Local community
Possible disruptions to the local way of life. Effects on neighbouring building and population.

Social contribution and justification

Contributions to the local community. Improved amenities and services. Boost to the economy. Generation of jobs. Linkages with other economic sectors. Evaluation of costs and benefits. Overall assessment, and justification of the project in terms of its social contribution. Chapter 9 further describes socio-cultural impacts.

Results of consultation with the local community

Consultations conducted with the local community. Where, and in what form? General reactions. Principal objections. Overall assessment of both majority and minority opinions.

Conclusions and recommendations

Approval recommended or not, with a list of the conditions and any modifications to be required. Details of the corresponding measures to be taken against any dangers of negative environmental impacts. Related reporting, evaluation and monitoring requirements.

References

Lange, Glenn-Marie and Duchin, Faye (1993) *Integrated Environmental-Economic Accounting, Natural Resource Accounts, and Natural Resources Management in Africa*, Institute for Economic Analysis, New York University.

Rothery, Brian (1993) *What Maastricht Means for Business*, Gower.

8 Sociocultural effects

This chapter explains the sociocultural effects of tourism. It covers the impact on a destination, its way of life and its arts, and the possibility of local resentment and resistance to change. It explains what is meant by culture and explores the idea of a common culture. It describes typical antitourism sentiments, and cultural concepts relevant to the development of tourism such as orientalism, xenophobia, ethnocentrism, primitivism and cultural atonement. It goes on to examine the impact of travel on the traveller, the influence of religion and the process of development and change. It also explores the connection between migration and tourism, and examines particular views about service. It continues by discussing price irritations and concludes by looking at the problem of AIDS.

Introductory note

There are three aspects to the sociocultural effects of tourism:

- On the destination – how well a destination is able to assimilate given numbers of visitors.
- On the way of life – the impact that visitors have on people's values and the local way of life.
- On the arts – the influence of the visitors on the arts; music, dance, painting, sculpture, theatre, architecture, handicrafts, etc.

These three types of impacts have the following positive effects:

- The numbers of visitors boost the local economy (as discussed in Chapter 6). They create wealth, generate jobs, produce improvements in the local infrastructure, trigger a range of new facilities and services, and stimulate other types of investment.
- Secondly, tourism creates more contact with the outside world,

fosters a process of internationalization, stimulates two-way flows of information, promotes cultural exchange, leads to the import of more goods and services, and generally acts to develop the whole field of trade and communications.

- Finally, it creates an audience and patronage for the local arts – particularly for music, dance, theatre and handicrafts. It also has a significant indirect impact on all other artistic expressions – including literature, painting and architecture.

Impacts can also act in a negative way:

- First, there can be some local resentment to sharing amenities with a large number of visitors. As already noted, tourism competes for space.
- Secondly, there may be some resistance to the changes in values and the way of life, brought about not specifically by tourism but by development in general.
- And finally there can be some resentment of the impact of the new market forces on both the traditional and contemporary arts.

Figure 8.1 shows the interrelationship between development, the changes it brings and both the improvements and resentment which can result.

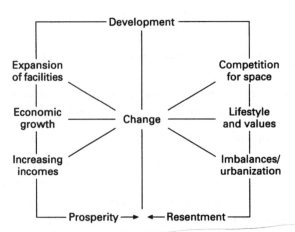

Figure 8.1   Development and cultural change

What is culture?

The cultural dimension is important in any consideration of society and human behaviour. It is also important in the international context because of the marked cultural differences between one country and another.

Culture can be described as the sum of ideas, beliefs, values, knowledge and behaviour which forms the shared basis for all social action. This description is hardly broad enough. Culture underlies all of life's actions and characteristics – for individuals or for groups, and to a large extent it dictates how a country functions and performs. Culture, according to Enzensberger, may be simply defined as 'everything that humans do and do not do' (Enzensberger, 1994).

A country's culture takes on a distinctive stamp; its way of life, the way people dress and look, all of its institutions, its street scenes, its markets and buses, and its rhythms and patterns, the whole character and appearance of its cities and its countryside; everything about it – its fundamental character – its ethos.

It is difficult to see a country's culture in its totality, because there are so many factors and variables involved. Culture is always in a state of flux. No group of people keeps on living in exactly the same way. The culture of a country changes in some way about every five minutes.

The myths of a common culture

The concept of a common culture, within a given country, is often much debated. There are certain national characteristics which people may share, but there are also significant cultural differences. The ways in which market segments are classified (discussed in Chapter 2) illustrated the criteria by which cultural differences can be assessed. Cultural differences usually accord with distinct market preferences. The way in which a market is segmented is the same way in which the culture differs.

Therefore, how much do people of the same nationality have in common? People certainly share a sense of national identity. There are common ideas about who they are, what they believe, what they stand for. There are historical reminders in the collective psyche of adversities overcome, battles won, enemies conquered and great works achieved.

Politicians play on the idea of national identity. They justify their policies on the need for the country to make its way in the world. For it to be competitive, to keep up with the others, to retain its advantages, to take its rightful place and so on. What people definitely have in common is nationalism. And nationalism has little to do with a unifying ideology, or any other set of values. The Russians will now be as nationalistic under capitalism as under communism.

The idea of a common culture among people of the same nationality can be misleading. People may have less in common than is thought. But there is certainly a sense of national identity, a common language, and a tribal ethos.

The anti-tourism schools of thought

During the 1960s the anti-tourism schools of thought gathered momentum. They were fuelled by the popular radicalism of the time. Tourism was a new form of imperialism, it eroded the culture, damaged the environment, cheated people out of land, trivialized art and handicrafts, left few economic benefits, often brought social ills such as drugs and prostitution, and spread elitism, snobbery, consumerism and false get-rich-quick values. In a wave of righteousness community leaders, among them many teachers and youth organizers, criticized tourism. They preached the anti-tourism slogans vigorously and rapidly recruited many supporters.

School children were given biased texts and encouraged to criticize tourism. Negative views became fashionable – the accepted wisdom of the time. The universities joined the bandwagon although specialized studies and courses in tourism hardly existed at this time. The social sciences departments were in the vanguard. This was particularly true

ces may even be revelational and they tend to give passion-
ort to their new beliefs. They will give their total loyalty to
ure in question, and attempt to convince other people of its

of course, an objective reality that many cultures have been
ued and little appreciated by the outside world. This is being
d. Other cultures are now more widely studied and better
od. This is a positive trend offering many opportunities to

hobia

bia denotes an unreasonable hatred or fear of strangers and
s or that which is strange or foreign. Where there is an
to develop tourism it may be more likely to find xenophobic
es among a proportion of the population, rather than
bia itself.

tourism is upmarket there is usually less evidence of these
es. Host populations do not tend to resist the visitors who
s of money. Economic benefits, if clearly seen, tend to defeat
reaction.

entrism

n describes a belief in the inherent superiority of one's
nic group or culture. There is a corresponding tendency to
er cultures from the point of view of one's own. Every-
ethnocentric to some extent. The majority of tourists will
ally compare the countries visited against their back-home

amework within which people live is usually narrow. As
vel further afield and add a variety of cultural experiences, so
horizons expand. They will start to view other countries
ectively, and are likely to become less ethnocentric.
does, in most cases, widen people's understanding.

in the universities from some developing regions, for example in the Caribbean from where anti-tourism ideas spread to universities in other parts of the world.

What tended to arrest the anti-tourism lobby was, in part, tourism's rapid growth. However, the introduction of tourism at the university level, as a serious and important area for academic research and study, was a major breakthrough.

Today tourism has become viewed, because of its social and economic importance and continuing growth, in a far more objective way.

Tourism in some countries, when it has been poorly planned and controlled, has produced bad effects. All development can pose problems. Tourism like immigration can also change the ethos of a place, not necessarily for the worse and sometimes for the better. Yet people mourn change; this is normal; people dream of what places used to be like – a nostalgic recollection of another time.

Relevant cultural concepts

In considering the sociocultural impacts of tourism, the following concepts are relevant. All cultures differ but each of these concepts will be found to a greater or lesser extent. They influence one culture's view of another and, for this reason, are important in the study of travel and tourism.

Norms and rules

The way in which people and societies choose to regulate their behaviour, and the rules which they follow need to be noted. A particular legal framework is agreed by each society and establishes certain limits. People are also restricted through social norms – the etiquette and the codes of conduct which govern the ways in which people behave.

Emotionology

This is the study of how people, during a given period and in certain circumstances, observe specific emotional norms. In some societies, to show certain feelings may be judged acceptable, even expected. The display of these emotions is approved by society. The display of others is not.

The way in which emotions are hidden or expressed is likely to change from country to country. It may also change over time.

In many societies, for example, anger is permitted if channelled towards a justifiable cause and a constructive end. In other societies to show anger in any circumstances is unacceptable.

A review of the culturally approved emotions of a given time, and in different societies, can open up new understanding.

Orientalism

Orientalism both creates and perpetuates false ideas about the culture and behaviour of others, particularly as they relate to western views of the East. The mysteries of the East are due mainly to the West's incomprehension of eastern cultures. Descriptions may often touch on banality. But it is these myths which are not only frequently repeated but may also influence contacts and relations.

Primitivism

In the nineteenth century it was common to proclaim primitive societies as idyllic. There existed a belief that any simple communal society reflected the earliest human settlements and the original concept of human happiness. These societies were seen as sharing and caring, while the western societies of the time were seen as selfish, grabbing, and callous. The western world was judged as lost, while these primitive societies seemed to conserve the true essence of the human spirit. In a similar way the term primitive in art meant to flatten and simplify, to emphasize straightforward values without any multi-dimensional embellishment.

Primitive society meant a natural state full of goodness and

simplicity. This idea still has considerable a is not far removed from Rousseau's ei between the noble savage and the disloca(

Some past cultural anthropologists, exar beliefs, have also tended to view certain co(primitive way.

Present schools of anthropology reco sweeping the world. They now attempt a looking at the various influences on developi example, universalization, the media, consun education, health, family structure, travel, n criteria.

Tourism is often viewed as disrupting sometimes argued that they should be iso ences. This, in a sense, equates people wit through the creation of conservation areas. It of development and participation in the mo(

Leanings towards primitivism contribute to atonement.

Cultural atonement

This is common among Westerners. It may als in Japan. Cultural atonement may be motivate past excesses, coupled with the desire to reje(culture. It is flavoured with primitivism, and virtues of alternative cultures. It produces inversion of bias.

The bias and preferences of the people affe(side of these other cultures, cultures which ar(developing world, belonging to the less privi exploited and the formerly colonized countries. forward as purer, deeper, more humanistic and

It is a viewpoint almost romantically on the : the oppressed. It says that those who have bee(may actually have the most value in the presen

The followers of this creed want to holiday i(

experie(
ate sup
the cu
value.

It is
underv
correc(
unders
tourist

Xeno(

Xenop
foreig
attem(
tende
xenop

Wl
tende
spen(
any s

Eth(

This
own
view
body
auto(
setti(

T
peo(
will
mor(

T

The impact of travel on the traveller

Even if people have little cultural sensitivity or curiosity, the act of travel brings them into contact with different environments. And even if they meet only a few locals other than tourism employees, they still capture a series of experiences and impressions. They learn, at the very least, something about the look of the place, about the food and drink, about the way people appear to behave.

A small proportion of travellers are motivated by the idea of discovery. They are intent on learning about different cultures. They may be encouraged to study about a country's culture – its history, art and language – both before leaving and after returning home.

All travellers are affected in some way. They become more international in their tastes, their experience and their understanding.

Travel contributes to the process of internationalization; to the cross cultural interchange which tends to make people's lifestyles increasingly similar.

The influence of religion

Religious beliefs are among the most emotional and deeply felt. In many cultures they come to form the most predominant influence in people's response to life.

Where there is a strong institutional religion, it may play a major role in the country's life; there is little division between the state and religion. The constitution recognizes an official religion so that the link is clearly prescribed. In such cases there may even be a Ministry of Religious Affairs.

Religion has always been one of the major contributors towards a sense of national identity. To be English was to be God fearing and Church of England. To be Malay is to be Muslim. To be Balinese is to be Hindu and so on. To be English and Muslim or Hindu has now emerged as a new subculture, of increasing significance as the overall national identity develops and changes. As Britain has become more multicultural and multiracial than before, what it is to be British assumes different meanings.

In certain cases, for example in some Islamic countries, the state and the religion are made virtually indivisible. The legal system (Shariah) and the whole system of government reflect the values and the codes of Islam.

In tourism, however, it is plain to see that when the visitors are of one religion and the visited are of another, there are grounds for confrontation.

Separate religions need to show great tolerance and sensitivity to one another. An interchange of ideas between religions, together with other cross cultural activities, can form a positive part of tourism.

Development and change

All development brings change. Federico Retamar, the Cuban poet, says that 'only the dead are not men in transition'.

In developing countries, as previously in developed countries, large numbers of people leave their rural setting to seek industrial jobs in ever expanding cities. At first many encounter poor conditions of work, or no work at all. Many find only urban poverty, and the fear and loneliness which often accompany it. Gradually, however, most people prevail and improve their lot.

This happened all over Europe, only differing a little in the manner and pace in which it came about. It introduced a growing working class, a new middle class, and an urban culture. Expectations and aspirations grew, more rights were granted, and trade union movements gathered momentum.

Development brought entirely new values and ways of life. Between 1800 and 1900 Europe changed completely. Since then technological advance, two world wars, and continuing social and economic development have continued to change life.

Economies diversify. The unchanging nature of life is gradually lost. Modern sectors move ahead and traditional sectors restructure themselves; housing, education and health improve; the birth rate falls; women advance; youth flourishes; people live longer; culture loses its former stasis; society is in a state of rapid change.

Looking around at the newly industrializing countries of the world, the same patterns of development recur. Places like Malaysia, Thailand and Indonesia are living through years of momentous change. Countries welcome such change; people live better, achieving more, consuming more. But as society prospers, so it must remain stable. As traditional ways of life become lost, many related values disappear.

Lee Kuan Yew, Singapore's Senior Minister, has commented that, 'Prosperity brings a certain materialist set of values. It brings about changes in behaviour. If you know this and you set out consciously to prevent certain core values from being eroded, you stand a better chance of preserving basic standards. Change is unavoidable, but that need not dissolve your way of life' (*Time*, 18th April, 1994).

In most countries tourism is only one part of development. However, in major resort areas tourism itself may become the principal cause of rapid change. Here it is predominantly tourism, not indus-trialization, that brings jobs and boosts incomes.

People who regret change will regret development. Corrubias in his commentary on Bali, published in 1937, described the island as 'a living culture that is doomed to disappear under the merciless onslaught of modern commercialism and standardization'. Nearly sixty years later Bali continues to change and develop. Its economy has grown and it is now a major tourist destination. Its culture is still vibrant.

In the developed world cultural change has been a slow process. In the developing world there is often an accelerated period of catch-up which brings relatively quick change.

A country can certainly foster its own cultural development. It can stimulate artists to create, and it can help to provide the conditions under which its arts can flourish. But it cannot stop the tide of international cultural influence that now washes over the world at large.

This is fed by commerce, advertising, fashion, entertainment and the media. It is heralded by the signs and symbols of our times, which bring in their wake an abundance of ideas about values and lifestyles. Coca Cola denotes more than a soft drink, Christian Dior more than a fashion house, Levis more than a pair of blue jeans, and McDonalds more than a hamburger. 'Dallas', and other major soap operas, seem to be everywhere. Films are released on a worldwide basis. Everybody listens to the same pop music. Much of modern culture has become universal.

Tourism in a new destination

Tourism directly affects the lives of people living in the tourist areas. The following are some of the effects which the development of tourism will bring to a new destination.

- It brings new jobs. This can displace people from existing jobs — because tourism jobs may be better paid, cleaner and more agreeable. This is true in former rural communities. Tourism is usually better paid than agricultural work or fishing.

    This will put pressure on the agricultural sector to develop, and rural communities will change profoundly.
- Many women may be given opportunities to work for the very first time in their lives. This will give them new skills, new confidence, and new economic power. They will start to control their own lives, their discretionary spending, careers, sexuality and fertility, etc.
- There may not be enough people in the area to fill the jobs. Development will require a steady inward flow of migrant workers. They may be from a different area of the country, they may even be foreigners. They may have different cultural traits, even a different religion. They will start to integrate with the locals, get married, buy houses, have children.
- Tourism will raise peoples' incomes. They will have money to buy and do things as never before.
- Development will add to the government's capacity to improve health and educational systems. Better educated and healthier people view life differently. Within a few years the younger generation will be very different from the preceding one. Education and improving standards of living tend to influence spiritual and religious perceptions. There will be a widening gap between the old and the young.

- Housing will improve and a variety of new housing projects will develop.
- Vocational training programmes will teach a wide range of new skills.
- Mechanization and automation will replace manual labour; machine-made will replace hand-made; information technology will replace manual systems.
- Since menial tasks are mechanized, many of the quaint sights conducive to tourism will disappear, for example the boy on the buffalo – a common sight in parts of Asia. This same boy will now go to school.
- As noted, tourists are customers willing to pay for craft items, works of art, and live performances. The traditional cultural pursuits will undergo a process of commercialization.

Migration and tourists

Tribalism unifies groups of peoples to resist invasion and intrusion. Tribes are united by a common identity and purpose. A person identifies with the tribe and not with humanity at large. Nations are built on tribal foundations, and they turn inwards to protect themselves from outsiders (Enzensberger, 1994). It takes time for any migrants to be accepted.

As long as any minorities remain distinctive and unassimilated, they may clash with the tribal ethos. People may join forces to resist newcomers.

At various stages of development, a country may lack sufficient workers of various types. When and where there is such a need for labour, countries seek workers from outside. Migrant workers are recruited and admitted often in significant numbers. However, when there is no further need for these workers they are expected to leave. A welcome is extended on the basis that visitors are there for a given time only. They are not expected to outstay their welcome.

When migrant workers do stay and settle it tends to create, as evidenced in many countries, social unrest. They clash with the tribal ethos. Hospitality is based on the idea that people visit and then leave. Tourists do not stay. They visit a country for a short period and then leave, or so it seems. But this is not how it seems to the local population when tourism is sustained at fairly constant levels throughout the year. The tourists are there all the time, they represent a constant presence.

If there are 20 000 beds in a destination operating at an average of 50 per cent occupancy, this means that an average of 10 000 visitors have joined the resident population. They have become a permanent part of local life. How well they are accepted will depend on how culturally dissimilar they are, where they are and what they are doing at any given point in time.

If they are so culturally dissimilar as to be obtrusive and if they all assemble at the same time in space shared with the local population (e.g. downtown), then their presence is bound to cause irritation. If, on the other hand, they are not culturally dissimilar and remain principally in the space assigned to them (e.g. the resort areas), then their presence may come to be well accepted.

There are obviously strong reasons to try and control the distribution and movement of tourists. To try and keep tourists within designated areas and circuits may be relatively easy with mainstream resort tourism; it is much harder with urban tourism. Tourists visiting Paris, London or Rome want to experience the centres of these cities.

Even in cities, however, much can be done to control the tourists' distribution and movement. Particular areas can be zoned for hotel development, sightseeing can be given particular routes and schedules, and parking and gathering points can be suitably planned.

As already discussed in earlier chapters, some of the key action steps in controlling tourism development are:

- To be clear about the types of tourism to develop or what types not to develop. About the markets to attract, and those not to attract.
- To establish clear planning criteria for the distribution and movement of tourists; where they will be housed and where and how they will spend their time.
- To monitor issues of carrying capacity, ensuring that attractions and installations are improved wherever possible, and that maximum numbers are not exceeded.

in the universities from some developing regions, for example in the Caribbean from where anti-tourism ideas spread to universities in other parts of the world.

What tended to arrest the anti-tourism lobby was, in part, tourism's rapid growth. However, the introduction of tourism at the university level, as a serious and important area for academic research and study, was a major breakthrough.

Today tourism has become viewed, because of its social and economic importance and continuing growth, in a far more objective way.

Tourism in some countries, when it has been poorly planned and controlled, has produced bad effects. All development can pose problems. Tourism like immigration can also change the ethos of a place, not necessarily for the worse and sometimes for the better. Yet people mourn change; this is normal; people dream of what places used to be like — a nostalgic recollection of another time.

Relevant cultural concepts

In considering the sociocultural impacts of tourism, the following concepts are relevant. All cultures differ but each of these concepts will be found to a greater or lesser extent. They influence one culture's view of another and, for this reason, are important in the study of travel and tourism.

Norms and rules

The way in which people and societies choose to regulate their behaviour, and the rules which they follow need to be noted. A particular legal framework is agreed by each society and establishes certain limits. People are also restricted through social norms — the etiquette and the codes of conduct which govern the ways in which people behave.

Emotionology

This is the study of how people, during a given period and in certain circumstances, observe specific emotional norms. In some societies, to show certain feelings may be judged acceptable, even expected. The display of these emotions is approved by society. The display of others is not.

The way in which emotions are hidden or expressed is likely to change from country to country. It may also change over time.

In many societies, for example, anger is permitted if channelled towards a justifiable cause and a constructive end. In other societies to show anger in any circumstances is unacceptable.

A review of the culturally approved emotions of a given time, and in different societies, can open up new understanding.

Orientalism

Orientalism both creates and perpetuates false ideas about the culture and behaviour of others, particularly as they relate to western views of the East. The mysteries of the East are due mainly to the West's incomprehension of eastern cultures. Descriptions may often touch on banality. But it is these myths which are not only frequently repeated but may also influence contacts and relations.

Primitivism

In the nineteenth century it was common to proclaim primitive societies as idyllic. There existed a belief that any simple communal society reflected the earliest human settlements and the original concept of human happiness. These societies were seen as sharing and caring, while the western societies of the time were seen as selfish, grabbing, and callous. The western world was judged as lost, while these primitive societies seemed to conserve the true essence of the human spirit. In a similar way the term primitive in art meant to flatten and simplify, to emphasize straightforward values without any multi-dimensional embellishment.

Primitive society meant a natural state full of goodness and simplicity. This idea still has considerable appeal; the myth lives on. It is not far removed from Rousseau's eighteenth century contrast between the noble savage and the dislocated societies of Europe.

Some past cultural anthropologists, examining different values and beliefs, have also tended to view certain communities in a romantically primitive way.

Present schools of anthropology recognize the rapid changes sweeping the world. They now attempt a multidisciplinary approach, looking at the various influences on development and social change; for example, universalization, the media, consumerism, politics, economics, education, health, family structure, travel, migration and other social criteria.

Tourism is often viewed as disrupting primitive societies. It is sometimes argued that they should be isolated from external influences. This, in a sense, equates people with wild animals protected through the creation of conservation areas. It denies people the benefits of development and participation in the modern world.

Leanings towards primitivism contribute towards feelings of cultural atonement.

Cultural atonement

This is common among Westerners. It may also exist to a lesser extent in Japan. Cultural atonement may be motivated by guilt for a nation's past excesses, coupled with the desire to reject and revise one's own culture. It is flavoured with primitivism, and a desire to extol the virtues of alternative cultures. It produces what amounts to an inversion of bias.

The bias and preferences of the people affected are always on the side of these other cultures, cultures which are mainly rooted in the developing world, belonging to the less privileged, the poorer, the exploited and the formerly colonized countries. These cultures are put forward as purer, deeper, more humanistic and so on.

It is a viewpoint almost romantically on the side of the victims and the oppressed. It says that those who have been devalued in the past may actually have the most value in the present.

The followers of this creed want to holiday in these cultures. Their experiences may even be revelational and they tend to give passionate support to their new beliefs. They will give their total loyalty to the culture in question, and attempt to convince other people of its value.

It is, of course, an objective reality that many cultures have been undervalued and little appreciated by the outside world. This is being corrected. Other cultures are now more widely studied and better understood. This is a positive trend offering many opportunities to tourism.

Xenophobia

Xenophobia denotes an unreasonable hatred or fear of strangers and foreigners or that which is strange or foreign. Where there is an attempt to develop tourism it may be more likely to find xenophobic tendencies among a proportion of the population, rather than xenophobia itself.

Where tourism is upmarket there is usually less evidence of these tendencies. Host populations do not tend to resist the visitors who spend lots of money. Economic benefits, if clearly seen, tend to defeat any such reaction.

Ethnocentrism

This term describes a belief in the inherent superiority of one's own ethnic group or culture. There is a corresponding tendency to view other cultures from the point of view of one's own. Everybody is ethnocentric to some extent. The majority of tourists will automatically compare the countries visited against their back-home setting.

The framework within which people live is usually narrow. As people travel further afield and add a variety of cultural experiences, so will their horizons expand. They will start to view other countries more objectively, and are likely to become less ethnocentric.

Travel does, in most cases, widen people's understanding.

● To monitor carefully any economic imbalances created by tourism. Assist the sections of the community which suffer – introducing modernization, providing loans and advice, increasing mechanization and productivity.

The pejorative view of service

In many cultures service is viewed in a pejorative way; this is true at the national as well as the personal level. The nation itself may view tourism as a low priority option. Politicians may prefer to make or produce things rather than serving visitors. 'We are not a nation of waiters,' they say.

Tourism may be seen as placing oneself at the disposal of others; to be at the beck and call of foreigners, and it may be judged as demeaning.

At one time Cuba appeared to neglect its opportunities in international tourism. Tourism hardly seemed to fit with Fidel Castro's image of the future; in more recent times he has changed this view. Tourism has been recognized for its economic importance, and its value as a foreign exchange earner. Now in a moment of extreme economic limitations, tourism is able to make a significant contribution.

In a similar way, young people have often seemed reluctant to choose tourism careers. It was undignified to be seen serving other people. Tourism has now tended to overcome this attitude. However, it has to maintain its image as a modern, international sector capable of offering attractive and competitive career opportunities.

Price irritations

Price irritations often exist when visitors may be rich in terms of their discretionary spending power, while many local prices may be only a fraction of those at home. In response to this spending power, prices are inflated to exploit the tourist. This is motivated by opportunism and greed; tourists are scalped.

Certainly some tourists are generous and outgoing and pay high prices without hesitation. Others resent the constant attempts at overcharging. Lack of tourist information on prices creates a potentially harmful situation. Price guidelines should always be provided.

Equally, two-tier pricing systems where the locals pay one price and the visitors another represent a serious source of irritation and are open to abuse. Market mechanisms can be left to operate, but visitors should be informed about the normal range of local prices.

AIDS

The spread of disease through travel and tourism is a continuing problem, but has been largely responsive to vaccination and control. However, the transmission of AIDS on a worldwide basis remains one of the major sociocultural concerns of tourism.

In tourism AIDS is spread principally through sexual contacts. These can be either heterosexual or homosexual and can involve prostitutes, other tourists and ordinary members of the host population.

It is likely that prostitution is the most common initial vehicle for the spread of the disease. The following points are central to the study and control of this situation:

- Tourism does not tend to create prostitution – but when prostitution already exists it tends to create a certain type of tourism. A supply of prostitutes will exist, in the first place, through a domestic demand. A foreign demand then builds on this domestic demand.
- The demand, therefore, is best regulated through restriction of the supply. It is impossible to eliminate prostitution. However, economic growth, development and improved living standards tend to reduce the supply and availability of prostitutes. This tends to reduce demand.

The example of Thailand serves as a case study. A domestic demand existed. A drift from the rural areas to the town tended to produce a supply of new young prostitutes. Demand increased through the use of Bangkok for rest and recreation by the American army in Vietnam. The organized and well packaged prostitution available in Bangkok then created its own tourism demand.

The advent of AIDS has produced a demand for younger and younger prostitutes. There is often a belief that younger girls are less likely to be infected.

The manner of packaging of prostitution tends to stimulate demand. If prostitution is available in night club settings it becomes more marketable. This is where restriction and control of the supply become important issues. Prostitution should be confined to a special category of establishment, conceived for the purpose.

The problem requires a complete approach to its control involving registration, education, and rehabilitation. The key action steps should include:

- To intensify public awareness programmes on AIDS. Discourage the patronage of prostitutes, while encouraging the use of condoms.
- To train social/health workers to help prostitutes avoid contracting AIDS, and to seek opportunities to rehabilitate girls and boys to follow more normal working lives.
- To target police for special training on prostitution, sex-related crime, and precautions against AIDS.
- To register prostitutes, check them regularly for infection, and control establishments through regulation.

References

Corrubias, Miguel (1937) *Island of Bali*, Oxford University Press.
Enzensberger, Hans Magnus (1994) *The Great Migration in The Civil War*, Granta Books.
Time, 'Frank Words for America', Interview with Singapore Senior Minister Lee Kuan Yew, 18th April, 1994.

9 Development issues

The chapter has selected a number of issues central to many tourism planning and management decisions. It discusses the tourism product and marketing outcomes, and the place of small hotels. It then considers old and new destinations, established tourism zones and new zones, investment aspects and the need for balance and harmony in tourism development. The chapter goes on to examine the role of the flagship product, and the idea that everyone should have a chance. It then discusses tourism's need for things to do, the integration of cultural attractions with tourism, and tourist information services. The chapter concludes by examining some aspects of tourism and crime.

The tourism product and marketing outcomes

Destinations are often told to go up-market and concentrate on higher spending tourists. They are told to attract richer people, induce them to stay longer and try and get them to spend more money.

However, it is the nature of a destination's tourism product which determines the type of tourists. In this sense, as already noted, tourism is supply led. The people who visit are attracted by what is on offer. It is pointless to propose a marketing strategy which has little relevance to the actual tourism product. If, for example, the supply consists mainly of modest guest houses, the visitors attracted are generally those people happy with this type of accommodation.

The way to achieve marketing objectives is to control the quality of the product, for example, tourism planning can specify that only projects of a certain standard may be developed in particular areas and locations.

Figure 9.1 illustrates changes in the market through modification of the supply.

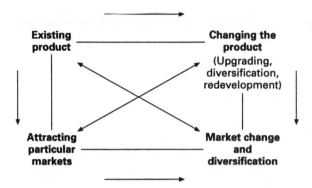

Figure 9.1   The supply grid

The planning, licensing and the control of minimum standards are the key. A GTA can control the quality of rooms, and even the quantity of rooms. It can improve the quality of existing hotels and accommodation facilities through:

- Raising, from time to time, the minimum standards required for licensing and registration (if a classification system exists minimum standards can be raised by category). One or two years' notice of this may be given, to allow operators sufficient time to make the improvements.
- Introducing a system of investment incentives and funding; tax breaks, low interest loans or financial grants to permit facilities to be easily upgraded. Operators are given sources of funds to make the improvements.

Minimum standards may in some cases be set on the high side, covering items such as roofing materials and exterior and interior finishes. The standards required may result in higher capital costs. This indirectly levers up prices inclining the product towards higher spending markets.

Bold GTA intervention can change the product markedly, but this should be well justified from a marketing standpoint. Any changes to the product and price have significant marketing implications; for example, a destination may decide to upgrade the marketing mix in the small locally owned hotels. As a result the product improves, prices rise, the image develops and promotion and distribution are adjusted accordingly. However, there may be insufficient market demand to make this new marketing mix feasible. Lower spending visitors are now excluded, but there are not enough higher market segment visitors to replace them.

It may have been better to keep the marketing mix, improve the product and continue with the lower spending market. Low spending visitors staying in small, locally owned hotels, may still generate profits and make a significant economic contribution.

However, destinations sometimes introduce various strategies to discourage low spending international visitors. For example, high hotel taxes and high entry fees to museums and tourism attractions are introduced.

This can handicap the small locally owned hotels which depend on the lower spenders. A policy of favouring high revenue earning tourism and trying to exclude all other types of visitor seldom makes sense. It can ignore significant marketing opportunities, and deny local entrepreneurs the chance to operate successful small businesses. The tourism product is just as segmented as the market. To narrow the product appeal narrows the market.

A diversified product is able to satisfy a wide variety of markets. It also widens entrepreneurial opportunities. However, all segments of the tourism product should still achieve planned standards of quality appropriate to the particular marketing mix.

Only small destinations, for example some of the small island countries, may tailor their tourism product to the needs of a few higher spending market segments, but the size of their tourism sector may be small, with easy access to major markets and a limited tradition of local entrepreneurship.

A destination tries to harmonize its range of products with its markets. It may favour a particular mix and balance between these various markets, and encourage the development of one type of product more than another. Whatever it does selectively should fit with the marketing realities, while meeting the needs of the local community. And this includes the creation of business opportunities for local companies and individuals.

Small hotels and tourism enterprises

As described above, a product of local small hotels is often built up based on the lower spending market. Up-market small hotels are more usually found in developed rather than developing countries.

As noted, small locally owned and managed hotels may help to diversify tourism. Certainly, small hotels usually play a significant role in domestic tourism, where there is a large demand for cheaper accommodation, and in most countries, they may represent by far the largest proportion of the accommodation supply.

For a strong small hotel subsector to be developed, one should:

- Accept a component of small hotels and tourism enterprises as a strength.
- Build on this strength, and improve quality and efficiency through technical assistance and advisory services.
- Develop training programmes to assist in improving standards.
- Develop lines of credit to assist in the improvement and further development of facilities.

Old and new destinations

In old destinations there may be few new hotel extensions or hotels. Most of the hotel stock has already existed for some years. This differs from new destinations where supply is still growing rapidly.

In these older destinations, therefore, the size, category and mix of facilities are for the most part already fixed. As noted in the previous section, it is the nature of this product which preselects the type of visitors. What gets marketed is what there is. Blackpool, Mykonos or Benidorm attract certain markets simply because of what they have and what they are. What they could or might have been is mostly an idle question.

The major difference between destinations relates largely to the age of facilities and the corresponding needs for renovation and redevelop-

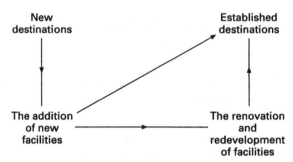

Figure 9.2   Changing emphasis between new and old destinations

ment. This is influenced by the proportion of new facilities to older ones. For example, most European resorts in the north are now more fully developed than equivalent resort centres in the south.

Figure 9.2 illustrates the different development emphasis in new and old destinations.

In old destinations, a major task is the renovation of facilities and the maintenance of acceptable standards. In this it is necessary to keep the architectural integrity of old properties. The preservation of certain buildings as well as cultural attractions, is an important consideration. Steps are needed to ensure that designated buildings and sites are protected.

At worst the demolition of buildings and the redevelopment of sites may threaten the scale and character of the place. There should be a clear idea of the overall environment and atmosphere essential to conserve. Physical planning controls should ensure that this happens. Additionally, one can identify particular renovation and redevelopment projects which can enhance the destination.

An old destination can come to be viewed by the market as a classic. It takes on all of its historical and romantic associations and assumes a distinctive and timeless image. On a small scale this has happened to some of the Cotswold villages in England's Shakespeare country, like Broadway, or to Nelson's Dockyard in Antigua. On a larger scale, it is true of places like Venice, Toledo or Biarritz.

An old destination is made and needs only resuscitation − even some occasional rejuvenation. A new destination is in the making and there should be a clear vision of the expected final product. Planning controls should ensure that new facilities are in keeping with this objective. As the destination expands and develops, it should be seen to take on the desired characteristics. The end result should be as envisaged.

In Chapter 3, it was noted that the tourism product is nearly always an unfinished product. It is in a state of change, aging but adjusting to new needs and markets, partly declining in quality, partly undergoing improvement and renovation, or redevelopment and expansion.

Old zones or new zones

An existing zone may be far from fully developed. However, it may be well established, attractively conceived, and have sound infrastructure and substantial remaining carrying capacity. Further development in such a zone is likely to improve it. It may make the product more complete by adding complementary facilities and services and enhancing the environmental quality. It may also achieve some economies of scale and add marketing punch. Expanding and improving the product within such a zone may also make the most of existing infrastructure and other assets.

Also resources are more readily invested in a product which has already proven successful. It may also be a zone which has been carefully controlled under a well conceived design concept, one that has prevented incongruous or unsuitable projects from marring the rest of the development.

Further expansion within this one zone may improve prospects and continue to create jobs and boost local incomes, attracting both new workers and businesses.

A zone like this may experience continued growth of the right kind, attracting more investment and expansion. One or two zones of this kind may come to dominate a country's tourism sector. However, there are sometimes dangers in allowing such concentrations of tourism to develop. It is argued that:

● This creates resentment elsewhere, and leads to unequal population distribution.

- Wherever possible, jobs should be spread around and taken to where people live;
- Economic development should be spread more widely so as to keep a balance between the different parts of the country;
- Tourism should be developed without delay, wherever the right conditions are found.

This raises the question of whether to concentrate tourism or diffuse it. Political pressure is often on the side of diffusion. This has sometimes led politicians to push tourism in areas where an insufficient demand existed.

Even given that markets do exist, are the timing and location right to initiate tourism development immediately? Should it be now or later? Should the development be in this zone or that zone?

The Bahamas has pondered the continuing development of Nassau, as against the development of some of its other islands. Rarotonga in the Cook Islands has pondered the same issue. Indonesia has been anxious to develop alternative islands to Bali.

In developing other locations one may not necessarily create the same product. Also a different product may generate new markets. Different types of special interest tourism, for example, can attract new market segments.

A new zone attracting the same mainstream market with roughly the same type of product is a different matter. This may merely create a competing destination within the same country. This may dilute both demand and available investment.

Any local authority wishing to develop tourism is free to do so. It should, however, plan accordingly. It should participate in the regional planning exercises, and follow the guidelines established. It should carefully observe land use and planning regulations, and ensure that buildings and businesses meet minimum requirements. The GTA may also encourage it to start cautiously, and not launch immediately into the development of a major resort. For example, it can start with small hotels serving the domestic market plus some special interest segments.

It is a question of timing. At a certain point a country may wish to see the development of alternative resorts in other zones. These can learn from past experience, and improve on previous developments.

They can also be distinctive from existing resorts. Demand may also be growing sufficiently to warrant substantial product expansion and diversification.

Once a new resort is started, it is often advisable to have a substantial first phase, counting new rooms not in the twenties but in the hundreds or even thousands. This will permit a resort to enter the market, in the early years, with a composite, well planned and major product. This is when proper zoning pays off, ensuring environmental quality and controlling development to clearly specified standards.

A new resort development may be initiated through either the public or private sector. Whatever the case, plans should be shown to be feasible, with private sector interests convinced and quick to take up opportunities. If proposals are not taken up by the private sector, this creates a vacuum. It also creates pressures to change or modify the plans and standards proposed. This is why the early involvement of a number of private sector developers is important, and why plans should be realistically based on sound marketing and financial criteria.

Zones with tourism potential should be designated early on. It is then just a question of when, at what pace and how completely to develop them. Alternatively, some zones may be placed on indefinite reserve; particularly where there are no immediate pressures from either the local people or the politicians to start development.

In the case of a particularly undeveloped country with the potentialities to develop tourism, it may be better to concentrate tourism within well controlled resort complexes. This makes tourism easier to manage, given the country's current stage of development.

Investment aspects

Tourism may be capital intensive in the case of up-market resorts and first class hotels. Other types of facilities may require far less capital. For example, bungalow type hotels with clusters of one storey buildings built from local materials in a typical style, using natural ventilation. There are many such developments, for example, in parts of East Africa. Modest land costs have allowed low density development, and tropical surroundings and attractive landscaping have created a relaxed and natural atmosphere.

It is therefore impossible to make generalizations about capital intensiveness. Different types of tourist facility can be created at widely varying levels of cost.

Tourism generally requires considerable new infrastructure. The ratio of infrastructural costs to subsequent investments in secondary development varies. A ratio of 30:70 is often found, and may rise as high as 40:60. This depends on the quality of the development and the marketing objectives. Undeveloped areas, particularly islands, require large investments in infrastructure. And infrastructural costs may be disproportionately high, when insufficient secondary development takes place.

Many governments have financed tourism infrastructure themselves, recovering their costs through private sector secondary development (through land sales, leases and joint ventures). Governments now tend to look to the private sector to undertake the complete development of areas, investing in both the infrastructure and the secondary development.

Balance and harmony

As noted, under normal conditions it may be advisable to diversify tourism. The eventual strategy is to expand and spread the range of facilities provided, to broaden the overall product, and to encourage the widespread participation of local people.

However, this depends on the characteristics of a destination and its stage of development. If feasible it is generally better to open tourism up, than to narrow and limit the numbers and types of development (a small destination – Bhutan for example – may be an exception to this). And it is better to disperse tourism, allowing a wide range of communities to benefit.

As noted this may be a question of timing, sound planning and the mobilization of adequate resources. A role of the GTA is to help promote development, allowing tourism to respond to the many opportunities. Tourism should have a broad and sensible balance. The various parts of the product should fit together, complementing each other in a variety of ways. The total product should be balanced according to the markets served, with the appropriate facilities, services and attractions and matching capacities and quality levels. The need to match various parts of the tourism product was discussed in Chapter 1.

Some Caribbean destinations, for example, have switched to a large number of all inclusive hotels. In these operations everything is included in the price; accommodation, food, drink, entertainment and recreation. Guests have little reason to venture out, and these operations lower the demand for local restaurants and bars.

The total product has to adjust to the new and specialized types of tourism which spring up.

The interdependence between various types of facilities and services may become frustrated by market and product changes. The necessary balance and harmony becomes disrupted. A GTA may be able to provide valuable advice about such change. A SWOT (strengths, weaknesses, opportunities and threats) analysis, discussed in Chapter 10, should help to identify changes of this kind.

The flagship product

The flagship product is that part of the tourism product which most influences, even sets, the overall tone and image of tourism. It is usually made up of the prestigious hotels and resorts; the price leaders and the pacesetters in quality and service. These are the hotels which tend to put a certain stamp on the destination.

The right flagship product may open up a destination to the most remunerative markets, while not excluding other markets and types of project. It often consists of operations of the brand name multinational hotel and resort companies: for example, Hyatt, Hilton, or Sheraton.

Their presence in a destination may have many benefits. It usually brings more innovation in design, more muscle to international marketing, and more know-how in training and operational systems.

The flagship product may also include world famous properties, managed either independently or by a chain, like Sandy Lane in Barbados or Raffles in Singapore. Apart from the flagship product a destination may have a range of facilities serving different market segments. Both Barbados and the Bahamas, for example, have a quite singular image but a fairly diversified product. It is the flagship product which tends to distinguish the destination.

Everyone has to have a chance

Tourism is seen as creating a chance for many local people to build, own and operate a small tourism business, for example, a hotel, guest house or restaurant. Regulation and controls are sometimes wrongly perceived as a way of preventing them from taking this chance.

Such a situation usually occurs when tourism and communities first discover each other. There may be an urgent need for the rapid addition of facilities, with tourism quickly offering new economic opportunities.

However, in the building of new facilities, minimum standards may be seen as inappropriate, expensive and difficult to follow. Land use and zoning regulations may also seem too restrictive. This is often made to seem like a conflict between dynamic development and unnecessary over-regulation. One should try to obtain people's understanding of the value of regulatory control. People should be encouraged to develop projects while keeping to the established limits.

Even at the level of micro enterprise conflicts can arise. People need a chance without threatening the quality of the product; for example, itinerant vendors on a beach selling perhaps handicraft items, post cards and trinkets. While tourism has offered them a new opportunity, their pushy selling techniques may molest tourists.

In such a case, the GTA should take action in consultation with these vendors. For example, it may start licensing, designate only particular areas for selling, allocate vendors to areas, develop codes of practice, and organize training. Through one or more of these courses of action, the GTA and local authority can organize the activity in a satisfactory way. The needs of both the vendors and the tourists can be better served.

Everybody can have a chance but only within an established regulatory framework, a framework reviewed and discussed with all the parties involved.

Things to do

The Bahamas have used the slogan, 'You never run out of things to do'. The number of things to see and do is one of the keys to successful tourism. Visitors should never feel bored. Even if they do not choose to do things, it is important that they are there to do.

In beach-based tourism, the sun, sea and sand represent the major component. It needs to be complemented, however, by a full range of other activities. For example, tours and excursions, cultural attractions and activities, sporting and recreational activities, and day-time and night-time entertainment. And even this may not be enough.

For mainstream tourism, resorts should also organize activity programmes. These may include competitions, games, fashion shows, folkloric shows, participative workshops, music recitals, language lessons, films, dance lessons, talks and discussion groups, and handicrafts demonstrations. These various activities are of course optional. Many people want to be left alone to rest and relax, but others do want to participate in some or other activity.

In urban tourism, the range of things to see and do influences the length of stay. This applies to all cities or towns. It will depend on how many museums and attractions there are to visit, how many shopping areas, how many interesting walks, how many theatres and nightclubs, restaurants and bars. How many days can be filled by this variety of attractions? It is easy to see that London can expect a longer length of stay and more return visitors than, for example, Birmingham.

The tourism product needs to be diversified and enriched as much as possible. Singapore lacks outstanding natural resources, and has little in the way of heritage attractions and cultural sites. Yet it has made the most of its shopping, restaurant and entertainment facilities adding attractions, tours and excursions. It has also, for example, developed one of the world's most up-to-date airports full of facilities and services. Singapore has built, out of apparently very little, a successful and growing tourism sector.

Product development, in any destination, must constantly try to add to the attractions and activities on offer.

Cultural attractions

Cultural attractions mean all those physical or formal expressions of the country's culture which can be visited, exhibited or performed. They are a part of the tourism product.

Cultural attractions are either hard or soft:

● Hard includes historical sites, museums, architecture in general, monuments, religious buildings (mosques, temples, cathedrals), and cultural centres, archeological sites, and centres of contemporary community life.
● Soft includes music, drama, poetry, literature, painting, sculpture, engraving, folklore and handicrafts.

The hard and soft should be imaginatively combined.

In many parts of the world museums have come under harsh criticism during the course of this century. Exhibits have often seemed buried within the walls, poorly displayed and explained. A major task has been to bring these institutions back to life, to link the past and present, to combine one cultural medium with another, and to develop a whole range of lectures, presentations, special exhibitions, live performances, demonstrations, instructional and learning activities, competitions and special events.

The range and diversity of such activities has led to the concept of the living museum, accentuating the relevance of national heritage to everyday life. This has resulted in putting museums back into the mainstream of life, and increasing their attendance and support. Cultural attractions should be interpreted in such a way as to make them living, vibrant and entertaining.

This process of interpretation in tourism is essential. It packages the visit to a place, adding to the quality of the experience. It can add to the way in which tourists are informed and the degree to which their interest is stimulated.

The skills and knowledge of a tourist guide alone are not enough. Interpretation can adopt a multi-media approach and may include video presentations, talks and lectures, regular guided tours, music and poetry recitals, reconstructions of the past, guided trails and walks, books and published information, posters and postcards, and other printed material, special displays and exhibitions, and signboards and explanatory notices. It is an overall approach.

Tourist information services

Good information services are essential in tourism. Tourists are in a place for a short period of time only, they have to learn rapidly about what there is to see, do and buy. They need to be informed about the destination and the range of services which it offers. Some of this information is closely linked to promotion. Informing somebody about a service will promote its use.

The purpose of an information service is to let tourists know:

- how to adapt to local conditions (mode of dress, health hazards, drinking water, power supply etc.)
- how to find one's way around (maps, routes, walking tours)
- how to behave (cultural norms and codes of behaviour)
- where to stay – this can comprise a reservations service operated by, or in collaboration with, the private sector
- what to see (places to visit, museums and other attractions)
- what to do (sports, recreation and entertainment facilities and centres)
- what to buy (shopping, handicrafts and souvenirs, food and drink

specialties, local textiles and fashion goods, duty free concessions etc.)
- how to travel (buses, trains, car hire, internal air services)
- what and where to eat (local specialties, menus, recommended restaurants)
- how to keep safe (any crime or security problems, precautions — what to avoid, where not to go, what not to do)
- where to worship (according to one's religion   places to worship and other associated services)

This information can be published in printed form through local business sponsorship. Tourist newspapers can also include most of the information listed above.

Guide books also provide a valuable source of tourist information and are purchased at a tourist's own expense.

Tourist information offices are essential — usually run by local government under the advice of the GTA. Offices need to be well located, in relation to tourist flows, and attractively designed. They should reflect the character and image of the destination. They should also be well organized in terms of administration, layout, counters, display racks and seating areas, and they should be staffed by multi-lingual well trained personnel, appropriately dressed.

Records should be maintained on all tourist contacts to analyse the information sought, noting any feedback on various aspects of the tourism product.

The content of public awareness programmes (see Chapter 15), aimed at tourists, is closely related to information needs.

Tourism and crime – security considerations

Good security has become a major component of tourism, and sound tourism management should try to deliver a safe environment.

Tourists are often targeted as victims of two types of crime:

- Common crime — tourists are at risk with regard to certain types of common crime, particularly assault, mugging and highway robbery.

It is fairly certain that tourists will be found carrying cash, travellers cheques, and credit cards. Tourists themselves are usually conspicuous. Hire cars and tourist cars are usually easy to identify.

- Politically motivated crime – tourists are made the targets of political movements – usually through kidnapping and sometimes assassination. By committing crimes against tourists, revolutionary groups hope to gain publicity for their cause.

Destinations often try to keep quiet about crime and visitors may be unaware of the dangers. They may also lack familiarity with the culture, surroundings and the language. Areas are often crowded and a tourist's attention is easily diverted.

Tourists may also leave belongings unguarded, sometimes just for a moment. They are also in a carefree mood and may have enjoyed a few alcoholic drinks. This makes them more relaxed and less vigilant. Added to this local police are often slow to follow up. They also tend to blame victims for not taking enough care and they can adopt, because of the frequency of petty crime, a callous attitude.

Tourists may also disregard security warnings about areas of a city or country which are potentially dangerous. Backpackers in particular, usually young and adventurous, are often careless. They may stray off track, court danger, and offer themselves as easy targets.

Tourists obviously need to be given information, guidance and protection. They also need to be helped when they are victims of crime. While the GTA can take care of many of the information needs, it should also work closely with the police force on all aspects of security.

Many countries have decided to set up a tourist police unit. For example such a unit was established by the Royal Malaysian Police in 1988. The objectives of this unit can be summarized as supporting tourism by providing tourists with security and assistance, and by preventing crime against tourists or crime committed by tourists.

The roles and functions of this police unit are:

- to have a thorough knowledge of tourist destinations and attractions
- to provide security and assistance
- to provide information and guidance
- to make areas safe for tourists and free from criminal activities

- to ensure that tourists are not victimized or cheated
- to ensure that tourists are informed about local norms, customs, laws and regulations
- to take fast action on criminal cases involving tourists, expediting investigations and prosecutions
- to prevent fraud or any unsavoury activity linked with tourism
- to help tourists involved in accidents, theft or the loss of important documents

This unit is staffed, organized and trained to fulfil these roles and functions.

10 Planning and management

This chapter emphasizes the role of planning as a part of management as opposed to the idea of a one-off master plan. It then describes ongoing planning. It goes on to discuss the need to monitor what is happening sector-wide and the nature of public sector planning and management. It then explains the functions of tourism management and a management by objectives approach (MBO). It describes private sector involvement, planning at different levels, the basic components of a plan and the allocation and use of resources. It then discusses aspects of regulation, tourism facilities classification systems and computer-assisted planning tools. The chapter concludes with an explanation of a SWOT analysis (strengths, weaknesses, opportunities and threats).

Planning as a part of management

Tourism planning is often treated separately from management. This is partly due to the influence of physical planners. For them the term planning has tended to apply historically to the design of buildings and urban areas. The design was completed and then construction took place. This is a project oriented approach.

Marketing, financial and operational inputs may well influence this design, but not in a continuing way. Design and planning are not seen in an overall management context. Tourism development master plans are often treated in a similar project oriented way. Planning is not seen as a part of a complex sectoral management process but merely as a forerunner to construction.

Of course, physical planning may also deal with spatial strategy, land use, zoning and physical interrelationships. At the local level it may define narrower planning criteria in the design of specific resort areas and installations. It tends to focus on design, however, and is not management oriented.

A GTA may also need a tourism master plan as a starting point to provide an overview of the sector and a clear idea of future development strategies. A GTA's main need, however, is to develop its own capacity to manage the sector. Planning is only a part of this.

The idea of a master plan

A tourism master plan as a one-off exercise, to be perhaps updated on a periodical basis, is an idea more commonly found in developing countries. In a developed country, a national tourism master plan may not exist as such. Planning as an ongoing function does, however, exist.

For example, one might find, in published form, a statement of future policies and strategies. One might also find tourism officials willing to discuss strategies and perspectives for the future. Tourism officials would know where they want to develop new hotels, and how they wish to improve standards. They may be contemplating new investments of various kinds, or the modification of certain laws and regulations, or changing the emphasis in their marketing strategies. They may be moving forwards in a variety of ways, planning as they go.

By contrast, master plans as projects have been promoted for developing countries by many of the aid agencies. Funds provided, however, often cover only the fielding of an outside team of consultants. This means that master plans tend to be prepared by these consultants, working under serious time constraints with the inadequate involvement of local personnel. This sometimes means that the work undertaken:

- tends to overlook important cultural, political and socio-economic constraints
- may not transfer sufficient knowledge and skills to local personnel
- may not identify all important background information

- may include courses of action which are beyond current institutional capacities
- may fail to obtain a local commitment to recommendations
- omits any agreed follow-up or action programme
- and becomes frozen in time.

A master plan undertaken by outside consultants is usually a task with a short duration – usually 12 to 18 months. Once it is completed, the budget is usually exhausted and the team disbanded. Once finished the plan tends to become quickly out-of-date. It is immediately subject to a whole series of changing conditions, priorities and circumstances.

The success of a master plan, therefore, is that it should mark the start of an adequately organized and resourced planning and management process. By the time the plan is completed, the organization must be in place to take over.

However, the transition of a one-off plan to a continuing planning and management process does not always take place. The need for this final transition is often overlooked. Organizational arrangements are not made, monitoring systems are not established, recurrent expenditures are not budgeted, and adequately trained personnel not left in place.

Emphasis should be given to the development of the management process itself rather than to a one-off plan.

Ongoing planning

Where master plans are produced in a manner external to the ongoing operations of a particular ministry, they will obviously run into problems at the implementation stage.

To be successful the plan is best implemented by the people who have participated in its preparation. The preparation and implementation of plans is a part of management. Plans need to be prepared with the wide involvement of all key technical and operational staff.

Four clear points emerge here.

- First, that a one-off plan is not sufficient in itself, and is of only short-term utility.

- Second, however, that the preparation of an initial master plan can be used to organize and set up the necessary ongoing process.
- Third, this can only be done if a team of competent local officials and technicians participate in the plan's preparation, with the complete involvement of a wide range of local public and private sector interests (assisted if necessary by outside consultants and experts).
- Finally, the planning process cannot be completely centralized but must involve the regional and local authorities. They should participate in the formulation of plans which they may eventually have to implement.

The GTA should manage tourism and coordinate sectoral planning. The task is often to create a planning function where none existed before; to work on planning, keep it updated and implement it. The GTA should not need somebody else to do this. But it may need specialized inputs and help in developing its own capabilities.

The whole concept of a planning process means that there is no end as such, only a beginning. It means that things, once studied and agreed, can start to be implemented. Action can be taken from the start. It also means that the committees and working groups, organized to consult on an initial plan, can be left in place to play an ongoing role.

Knowing about what's going on

Planning should never overlook the multitude of various private sector and other public sector initiatives which are already going on, and which characterize the tourism sectors's expected future development.

It may seem that a particular country or region has no tourism policy or development strategy. And it may be true that no strategy or plan has been agreed in documented form, or made the subject of close consultation with the private sector.

A strategy, however, may certainly exist. It will consist of the aggregate of ideas, projects and schemes already under consideration or in progress. Various individuals and organizations may be working on these, and a great deal may actually be happening.

It is usually assumed that governments, because they normally screen and license new business activity, know exactly what is going on. However, with a variety of government departments and agencies involved, and with increasing decentralization and deregulation, this is not always the case. No single government department may be monitoring the current situation comprehensively. Nobody has the complete picture.

However, bankers and investment houses, travel trade interests, hotel companies, airlines, training companies, educational institutions, and property developers may all have clear and well developed strategies for future development.

They may also exercise influence on each other, and they may lobby government in support of their plans. All of these influences push development forwards in certain directions.

Planning should not ignore the multitude of various private sector and other public sector initiatives which are already happening. These will contribute to the sector's future development. The GTA should maintain a comprehensive view.

The nature of public sector planning and management

All approaches to planning, e.g. economic development planning, land use planning, and infrastructure planning, are only appropriate as related to the management of the tourism sector as a whole.

There should only be one framework for the management of the country's tourism. If other separate initiatives are taken, there is a danger of fragmentation of effort and a breakdown in coordination.

Corporate plans, particularly those prepared by the major hotel and travel trade enteprises, should also be in keeping with national policies and strategies. The GTA should keep these questions under discussion with the key private sector interests.

There is a well-established way of looking at the functions of management as divided between planning, organizing, directing, coordinating, and monitoring. This approach was first put forward by Henri Fayol (1841–1925) (Krainer, 1995). Fayol was French and a management pioneer, remaining with the same company all his life and rising to the rank of managing director. He is recognized as a major thinker in the development of management theory.

Fayol's management functions are as follows:

Planning

Planning is about where one is going and what one is trying to achieve. The process outlined in Chapter 1 described the translation of policy into strategies, objectives, results and activities.

Organization

Organization relates to the mobilization and deployment of resources and technology. It provides the foundation for working towards the objectives and results. In this, the GTA should understand its role in relation to the private sector. It should organize itself into a sensible range of departments, defining their various roles and responsibilities.

Direction

Directing includes leadership, encouraging the various parties involved, maintaining a sense of purpose and achieving objectives and results.

GTAs tend to be weak in this area. They often tend to be passive, following behind the private sector, not identifying and reacting to needs, and not taking initiatives or action. The GTA should often take the lead on solving problems, on developing ideas for additional services and facilities, for prompting new projects, formulating new marketing ideas and promoting new training courses and programmes.

A prerequisite of leadership is purpose. Public administration tends to lose a sense of purpose. In many countries the administration tends to drift, and there may be no national consensus on development policies. As a consequence no sound basis exists for the allocation of resources or the distribution of benefits.

Coordination

This is the unifying activity that keeps everything moving together, maintaining harmony and building close working relationships.

No organization is in the same key position to coordinate the sector as the GTA. The public sector has a wide range of ministries and other agencies involved with tourism. As noted in Chapter 5, the private sector is represented by its various trade and professional associations, by major companies — travel, hotel, airlines, tourist attractions, entertainment complexes, trade unions and consumer groups. The GTA should coordinate with all of these interests, trying to arrive at a consensus on future action.

Monitoring

Monitoring represents the control function; the reporting and analysis of results. This may indicate where and how performance may vary from the plan, and how to take evasive or corrective action.

As already noted, the GTA should monitor the performance of the sector as a whole. It should maintain a comprehensive information system, including tourism statistics which meet with WTO standards.

When things go wrong or threaten to go wrong, the system has to give a quick response. Damage control systems provide for rapid action. For example if a tourist destination suffers from sudden, adverse publicity. Or if one of its major markets show signs of slumping.

A GTA's feedback system, through various kinds of published material — newsletters, bulletins and periodical reports, should keep people informed about the trends and the needs. It should be open, transparent and be able to answer for the tourism sector.

These five functions can be viewed as the cycle of management shown in Figure 10.1. On the basis of performance and analyisis, plans will be modified and adjusted. This makes tourism development planning an incremental process. On the basis of experience and analysis one keeps adding to, and refining, plans.

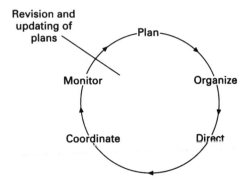

Figure 10.1   Cycle of management

Management by objectives (MBO)

The term MBO was first employed by Peter Drucker in the 1950s (Drucker, 1954). It was seen as one way of uniting organizational objectives with the aspirations of individual managers. Managers could reach higher satisfactions through the achievement of organizational objectives. This would produce a sense of common purpose.

MBO should be considered as an approach to management rather than a technique. As an approach it proposes that people and organizations focus on the objectives and results they want to achieve. Involving key people in setting these objectives and results encourages participation and commitment, and taps creativity. Objectives which link the GTA with the sector and which are widely supported by all interests, are likely to be achieved.

A plan has to be prepared showing the objectives, results and activities to be pursued. There are elements within the control of the GTA itself, and elements which depend on the performance of the sector as a whole.

Such a plan has to be divided between the appropriate GTA departments, making specific individuals and groups responsible. For sectoral objectives there should be a sense of joint reponsibility, with public and private sectors sharing a common purpose.

A GTA helps to create the conditions for plans to be implemented, and monitors the progress achieved. It shares responsibility with the sector as a whole for the achievement of objectives and results. Achievement does not depend on the GTA alone, but on private sector efforts as well as the prevailing local and world conditions.

Management by objectives:

- Involves key members of the organization in the setting of objectives.
- Concentrates on results rather than on activities and how busy or not people seem to be.
- Translates strategies into specific departmental objectives and results.
- Tends to improve the performance of the organization, simply by achieving better and more timely results.
- Enables a GTA not only to plan comprehensively for the sector, but also to implement plans. It achieves more effective management.
- Makes it easy to monitor the implementation of plans, and to see where results have or have not been achieved.

The achievement of results indicates that everything is proceeding as planned. Results not achieved indicate problem areas. It is on these deviations from the plan that management can concentrate its time and efforts.

Effectiveness among the various GTA departments can be improved in two ways:

- By ensuring that each department participates in formulating objectives, and is committed to their achievement.
- By improving interdepartmental relationships – making the organization as a whole more results oriented. And, where there are overlaps, by setting up interdepartmental working groups.

As the use of MBO spread, during and after the 1950s, it was seen to suffer from an obvious shortcoming. Some managers, recognizing that they would be evaluated against results, were inclined to set objectives too low.

As noted, many of the objectives such as growth in arrivals and earnings and the expansion of supply, are sectoral. Politicians, if they can, do tend to set these objectives and results too low. They want to exceed expectations; just like a manager who wants to keep his job, politicians want to win re-election.

Technical expertise has to try to overcome any political motivations. Objectives should be set realistically.

MBO is no longer a term frequently employed. However, its principles of setting objectives and being results oriented are of continuing value.

To sum up:

- GTA work plans should be developed and discussed, and objectives and results agreed, with the persons in charge.
- Sectoral objectives should be agreed by representatives of the sector's main branches.
- Interdepartmental and intersectoral tasks should be identified, over-laps agreed, and working groups (both internal and external/consultative) set up to tackle them.

Private sector involvement

Much of the GTA's management of the sector, as noted in Chapter 5, is indirect. A function of this management is to coordinate all public and private sector interests involved in the sector.

All the various private sector interests, working through their associations and organizations, should contribute their thinking on future needs and strategies.

The GTA is in the key position simply because it is the only body capable of playing the required coordination role. This, as already signalled, is the proper function of government – to act as the catalyst, to agree the directions to take, and to help create the necessary conditions.

As noted, the GTA needs to create a network of committees, councils, consultative groups, working groups and other appropriate mechanisms (at central and local levels) ensuring close collaboration between all parts of the sector. The nature of these coordinating mechanisms is organic; they should form, adjust and re-form according to needs. Many groups can be brought together to fulfil specific terms of reference, disbanding once the task and purpose have been achieved.

While the GTA accepts its responsibility to direct and coordinate the preparation and implementation of tourism development planning, it does so on behalf of the sector. It does not work alone – it works together with the sector. It is vital that the private sector participate to the very fullest.

The GTA gives the private sector the opportunity to speak up; the private sector should take this opportunity.

Planning at different levels

Nationally, tourism plans are needed at various levels:

- National – for the country as a whole.
- Regional – the government unit by which the country is divided up, for example, provinces, states, counties, or departments, and possibly designated development regions which group together a number of these units because of their common characteristics and markets.
- Areas – particular tourism and resort areas within regions, that because of their tourism importance require their own complex and detailed plans. The administrative unit may be a borough or an equivalent designation.
- Cities and towns – which often pose special tourism problems, especially when they have numerous tourist attractions. These may be municipalities. Urban planning will normally designate certain tourism priority zones within a city or town. The planning needs of these zones may require very particularized solutions.

Work takes place at the various levels. At the national level policies and guidelines will be clearly established. At the other levels they will be interpreted and tested against the opportunities and constraints locally perceived. Local plans are then elaborated. Figure 10.2 shows the possible interaction between national and local planning levels.

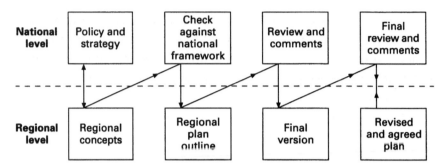

Figure 10.2 Interaction between national and regional planning levels

The components of a plan

The strategies in tourism development fall into three main and interdependent areas:

- *Markets*. What comparative advantages exist? The marketing opportunities to pursue; the image to project; the products to emphasize; the promotional strategies for each market; the sales networks to develop; the representation overseas. What joint public/private sector initiatives?
- *Product*. What to develop where? Infrastructural needs; the number of hotels and other installations; improvements and additions; in what regions, areas and locations? land use and zoning; forms of development; standards; legal and regulatory framework. What action programme? What investment promotion and investment?
- *Human resources*. The future workforce and training needs in accordance with the expected development of tourism. Strategies for the training of all levels of staff, in all specializations, in various parts of the country. Pre-employment training in training centres and institutions. Post employment training − in-service − in the industry itself. Various specialized training. Foreign language courses. Occupational skill standards and a national system of testing and certification.

Other components such as regulation and control or public awareness help to create the conditions for tourism development to be successful.

All of these areas will be set out in more detail in Part Three.

Allocating and using resources

In exercising leadership, the GTA can play an active role in the deployment of the three basic economic resources – capital, land and labour.

- *Capital* – the GTA can stimulate, promote and help to mobilize a variety of new investments. It can recommend incentive schemes designating particular development zones, particular types of development – in terms of location, size and category.

  It can possibly offer financial grants for certain types of project. It can actively promote investment, seeking out local and foreign investors. It may also choose to participate in investments either directly or through other government or quasi autonomous non-governmental organizations (QUANGOs).

  It can also invest in institutional marketing – designed to project the image of the destination, promote sales and develop the distribution system.
- *Land* – the GTA can participate actively in the formulation of national land use policies and planning and environmental management. It can help to designate zones for tourism, produce outline design schemes, and specify the way in which certain sites should be developed.

  Where the government owns land it may contribute it for certain projects or exchange it for equity.
- *Labour* – the GTA can participate actively in setting minimum conditions of work for tourism workers. It can play an active role in the promotion of careers in tourism and the recruitment of new personnel.

And as mentioned under human resources development, it can also be catalytic in the formulation of national standards, testing and certification.

These areas will also be covered further in Part Three.

Regulating the tourism sector

The main reason for regulations is to achieve and maintain the type and conduct of tourism described in the tourism policies. One should never regulate for the sake of regulation. Unnecessary government intervention may be caused by:

- Anti-business attitudes among the politicians (becoming less common in the 1990s).
- Over-zealous officials who want to expand the importance of their roles and responsibilities.

Some of the basic guidelines to follow are:

- Only regulate what really needs to be regulated.
- Be sure that self-regulatory efforts, by the people involved with a particular activity, will not work just as effectively.
- Do not choose regulation just because one or more other countries have done so. They may be wrong.
- Do not copy legislation blindly from one country to another.
- Ask the questions — what will regulation give us that we don't already have, or perhaps could have with private sector collaboration? Is regulation really the best way of achieving the objective?
- And — does the private sector agree with the need for regulation?
- And — what are the implications of regulation in terms of inspection and enforcement? Is effective government control feasible?

These various considerations return one to the question — Why regulate at all? Some of the principal reasons are as follows:

- To protect the consumer against abuses.
- To ensure minimum safety requirements.
- To safeguard life and limb.

- To ensure a minimum standard of quality.
- To protect the environment.
- To protect minors.
- Generally to protect society against unwelcome events and outcomes.

Regulations may sometimes be introduced wrongly as a way to add another source of government revenue, i.e. through application, licensing or other fees.

Tourism facilities classification systems

Licensing and registration alone should not be confused with classification. Licensing may require certain minimum requirements and authorizes whatever is specified by the licence.

Registration (often linked to licensing) requires that particular kinds of business register themselves, usually annually.

Classification or grading (incorporating licensing and registration) systems require that enterprises meet certain minimum standards of facilities and services to qualify for the particular rating or grade.

The GTA may decide to have systems of classifying tourism enterprises, the most common of which are hotel classification systems. These systems establish particular criteria for each category (usually from one to five stars) according to the range and quality of facilities and services.

Such classification systems usually have the following objectives:

- They provide a tool for government to take a direct role in controlling the quality and composition of the tourism product.
- They indicate to buyers (both individual consumers and the travel trade) the likely price/value relationships, and the standards and quality levels which can be expected.
- They provide guidelines to developers and investors about the standards of a particular category of hotel or other facility.
- They enable planners to designate particular sites for certain categories of hotel or other facility.

These objectives are valid, but one does not need government administered classification systems to pursue them.

The first purpose of quality control poses the question – Is this role for the government, or is it best left to the market – to the consumers and to their representative associations?

In many countries a government operated classification scheme, poorly administered and with poorly trained and lowly paid hotel inspectors serves no purpose at all. And even if well administered, it can be argued that these systems still represent unnecessary intervention.

A GTA can play an active role in quality control, without a formal classification system, by working closely with the private sector associations. It can collaborate in areas such as training, market research and visitor surveys and in providing assistance to private sector grading systems, consumer publications and guide books. Building codes and regulations can also be used to control quality. Minimum sizes of bedrooms and other facilities, together with other minimum specifications, can be among the criteria included.

The price/value relationships are a question for the free market, and should not require government intervention. However, government can collaborate with trade and professional associations in discussions on price as a part of the marketing mix. This might relate to special promotions, off-season periods, and marketing programmes in general.

As to guidelines for investors and planners, the GTA can provide these without having to have classification systems.

Developers can discuss the range of facilities, services and quality levels which they might choose to provide. Planners, if they wish to designate a site for a particular kind of development, can specify the facilities and services to be included.

In a number of countries governments have decided not to classify establishments since this is already done adequately by the private consumer associations, motoring organizations, guide books, etc., and sometimes by the trade associations themselves (the travel, hotel and restaurant associations).

Additionally, it may be argued that any qualitative assessment has subjective aspects and involves value judgments best left to private sector publishing.

Government should only establish a classification system, if the need is clearly justified; where, for example, the sector is in its infancy, standards are very low, operators are untrained, and there is little sensitivity to traveller's needs. Later, however, it is possible to hand it over to the trade associations.

Generally, government operated classification systems are complicated to implement and administer. The development of objective criteria and the recruitment and training of a body of competent and conscientious inspectors often proves difficult.

Critics also point out that classification systems do not assess the intangible product components, like warmth, friendliness, atmosphere and the appeal of the location and image. By contrast, these are the factors which a guide book will usually explore and discuss extensively.

Computer-assisted planning tools

There are a number of planning software packages on the market. These make it easy to plan activities, to allocate work among team members and to monitor progress.

The software presents workloads in an easy-to-follow format ready to distribute to team members. This also makes it easy for people to coordinate with one another. Activities can be delegated in an interrelated way, regular status updates distributed, to-do lists assigned and critical dates signalled.

The software can help to evaluate and improve the logic of a plan. It can also help to break up activities into manageable steps, balance workloads and spot bottlenecks. It can compare on a regular basis the current schedules to the original plan. It can also show how long activities can be delayed without altering final dates.

Plans will always experience some change. These tools help to see the effects of such change, keeping projects and planning on track.

Strengths, weaknesses, opportunities and threats

A straightforward technique commonly used in management (Cole, 1993) is known as a SWOT analysis, which stands for strengths, weaknesses, opportunities and threats. It lends itself well to tourism development and management.

Strengths

The strengths describe those parts of the operation which contribute notably to the success of the tourism sector. For example, strengths might consist of well trained staff, a variety of tourist attractions, a good airport with spare capacity, a well developed road system, friendly people, good three and four star hotels, excellent local produce, reasonable and competitive prices and an unspoilt environment.

Weaknesses

Weaknesses represent the other side of the coin; they are those characteristics of the tourism sector which detract from the quality of the product or hurt marketing efforts. Weaknesses have to be seen from the customer's viewpoint. For example, museums closed without reason, poor food, slow service, an interrupted electricity supply, bad telecommunications, a shortage of water, lack of clean beaches, insufficient recreational facilities, or rude immigration officers.

Opportunities

Having analysed the market and the product, it should be possible to identify those opportunities which can lead to substantial improvements and expansion, as well as the development of major new demand. Various changes and trends may open up a variety of new opportunities: recent political changes at home or in major markets; economic trends; social trends; opportunities opened up by new technology; new decisions on the environment; and the business climate for investment.

Threats

Threats are any trends, events or factors which could affect the future of tourism in a negative way. Such threats might comprise, for example, negative social attitudes, deteriorating air transportation services, the growing pollution of the sea or a river, various supply shortages, the loss of key staff, changes in foreign exchange rates, new competitors, or future inadequacies in the water supply.

A SWOT analysis can provide inputs for the tourism development planning process. SWOT is a good way of taking stock of the existing product and identifying the various ways in which it can be improved.

A technique which overlaps with SWOT is known as PEST – standing for political, economic, social and technological change. These criteria are normally incorporated in a SWOT analysis, under opportunities and threats.

References

Cole, G.A. (1993) *Management Theory and Practice*, 4th edn, DP Publications Ltd.

Drucker, P. (1954) *The Practice of Management*, Heinemann.

Krainer, S. (ed.) (1995) *Financial Times Handbook of Management*, Pitman.

Part Three
Planning and Management Strategies

11 Managing the GTA, regulation and research

This chapter marks the beginning of Part Three which deals with the planning and management of the sector. This is covered under seven areas, which could correspond to a GTA's departments; management of the GTA itself, regulation and control, research, marketing, product development, human resources development and public awareness. The chapter starts by summarizing overall strategy. It goes on to deal with the first three areas: GTA management itself, regulation and control and research. It then lists the objectives, results and activities for each of these areas. The chapter concludes with checklists for the tourism management information system (MIS) and tourism assets inventory.

The GTA's management role

The different areas of tourism management, used in Part Three, could correspond with a GTA's departments: the management itself, regulation and control, research, marketing, product development, human resources development, and public awareness.

These seven areas, when taken together, could also represent the content of an integrated plan, structured according to policy/strategies, objectives, results and activities. This is illustrated at Figure 11.1. They can also act as the basis for the seven GTA departmental work plans.

As indicated, the start of the plan and management framework is

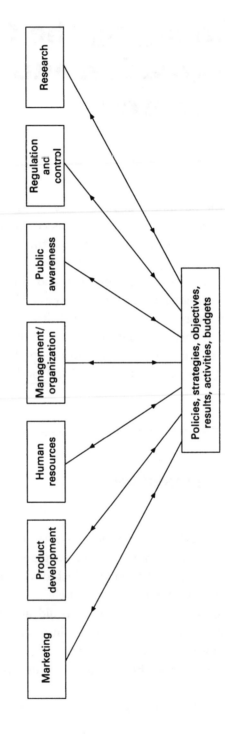

Figure 11.1 The integrated plan

formed by the policy and strategies. The strategies are kept under constant review, and adjusted in the light of changing conditions and opportunities.

Strategy

As noted in Chapter 1, strategies consist of the specific courses of action needed to meet the policy. Strategy establishes the basis for identifying objectives and results, and listing activities needed to achieve them.

The strategy should outline the actual shape which tourism will take. In doing so it should concentrate principally on marketing opportunities. These point to the tourism possibilities offered, and the likely scale and volume of tourism and its expected contribution to the economy.

It can also help to formulate what types of tourism should be developed and where, how many new hotels and other facilities and services should be added, of what types and where, and how many cultural and other attractions – of what types and where. It can also indicate the various improvements in facilities and services that need to be undertaken.

The strategy can be published as a short document. It can employ a framework similar to the following:

- The tourism development policies – a short statement of policies similar to the example at the end of Chapter 1.
- A summary of the country's macro-economic perspectives, showing the contribution of the tourism sector.
- International tourism growth – world and regional – showing the context in which tourism growth and development are expected.
- A current description of the sector describing the make-up and characteristics of both demand and supply.
- The marketing opportunities confronting the tourism sector – according to the purpose of travel and other market segmentation criteria.
- Tourism development areas – the division of the country into a

sensible system of tourism development areas — explaining the characteristics of each. These should be related to the organization of the government's administrative units — region, state, county, province, borough and township.

- The infrastructural situation covering airports, roads, railways, ports and inland waterways, energy and water supply — explaining new projects and development priorities.
- A description of the needed product development by tourism development area (or region, state, county, province, borough and township) — covering: improved access; additional resort areas; hotels, restaurants, shopping and tourism services; the development of cultural, scenic and heritage attractions; and the addition of other attractions such as sporting and recreational facilities.
- The expected development of tourism. An indication of the expected volume of tourists and tourism receipts, to accord with the macro-economic plans summarized earlier. An analysis of the investment climate and needed promotion.
- A regulatory framework for tourism to achieve the necessary standards and quality.
- The human resources development programmes, ensuring an adequate supply of trained staff.
- The public awareness programmes needed to give the general public an understanding about tourism and its benefits, and tourists an understanding of the culture of the country they are visiting.

This description of the strategy will establish the framework for the planning and management of the sector.

Management of the GTA itself

The management of the GTA itself corresponds to the office of the chief executive (Minister, Chairman or Director-General as the case may be) and the organization's executive secretary, depending on the precise form of organization which the GTA takes. The various types of GTA organization were described in Chapter 5.

There is obviously a difference between managing the GTA itself and managing the tourism sector. To manage the sector well, the GTA itself must first be managed effectively. This is the function of overall management. It will direct the response of the GTA to the tourism sector, maintaining up-to-date tourism development policies and strategies.

The GTA will also maintain an integrated sectoral planning and management process. It will be able to both speak for the tourism sector, and answer for the tourism sector.

The GTA should employ a management by objectives approach, assisted by:

- An annual plan — broken down by department — supported by a corresponding budget and a system of joint working groups set up between departments to tackle interdependent tasks.
- A satisfactory network of joint/standing committees, consultative groups, councils and other appropriate mechanisms, ensuring close coordination with all parts of the sector.

Management will also be helped by a legal adviser, whose responsibilities will cover:

- Reviewing, suggesting and outlining various legislative action as it applies to the different aspects of tourism development.
- Advising on the relevance and need for new types of legislation and the corresponding drafting of codes, regulations and licensing requirements.
- Advising on the interpretation and interrelationships with respect to various existing legislation.
- Advising on the legal basis for any Government involvement in projects, through lease agreements, management agreements or full joint ventures.
- Advising, if appropriate, on the acquisition of land or assets for tourism uses, and legal aspects of land tenure and land use planning.
- Representing and supporting applications for work permits when they are considered justified.

Management may also call on an auditing function, to monitor the proper financial management of its various affairs.

Management will be concerned in particular with the economic and social impacts of tourism and the achievement of overall policy objectives for the sector, and on tourism's contribution to government revenues.

It must also play a key role in lobbying on behalf of the sector, and bringing tourism and its needs to the constant attention of the policy-makers.

Another key part of management's role should concern the organizational development of the GTA. There should be a constant effort to improve the managerial capacity of the GTA and the skills and knowledge of its personnel. This will be reflected by an organizational development programme, formulated and executed through a human resources development and training department.

Management has to interact with the highest levels of government, up to the level of the head of government and the cabinet. It should also coordinate with all other ministries and government agencies. These are all likely to be involved with tourism, either directly or indirectly.

Administration

The administration of the GTA can be broken down between general administration, personnel, and financial management and accounting.

General Administration. Provision and control of administrative supplies. Maintenance and management of the GTA's motor vehicles and other assets. Secretarial Services. Transport and travel arrangements. Security.

Personnel. Personnel records. Labour relations and conditions. Recruitment and selection. Coordination of career development, performance appraisal and training.

Financial Management and Accounting. Financial planning and budgeting. Accounting and financial controls.

Matters of budgeting and finance will involve the Ministry of Finance, while questions of personnel may involve the Public Service Commission or equivalent agency.

Management information system (MIS)

Information systems monitor what is happening. They plug into the trends. It is critical to build up an accurate and total picture of the actual situation. An MIS is not feasible without the use of up-to-date information technology.

Where manual systems are maintained much of the data is found filed away in the various departments of the GTA. It is impossible to bring it together, and interrelate and analyse it in the necessary way.

A well designed and installed computer-based MIS will hold all the data together and allow for easy updating. It can be programmed to process the data in any particular way, providing for instant access; for example, it may be programmed (given the input of the necessary current data) to measure the economic impact of tourism.

When the MIS is designed, its precise scope and content can be agreed. In most cases, standard hardware and shelf software can be used to provide an adequate system.

A checklist of the usual data to include in the MIS (including a tourism assets inventory) is attached at the end of the chapter.

Close liaison should be maintained with the government agencies responsible for information, culture, the environment and natural resources. Also with libraries and documentation centres organized by other gvernment ministries and agencies, including the Central Bureau of Statistics or similar agency.

A documentation centre may also be attached to the MIS. The GTA needs good access to tourism texts, reference material, and teaching material. A full-time documentalist should maintain wide contacts with various international agencies and centres of learning, and attempt to maintain a flow of technical and other published and printed material relevant to the current needs of tourism development.

As time goes by more and more published information will be accessed through the information highway, and there will be less need to obtain hard copies through the conventional mail. At the new campus of California State University in Monterey Bay, a traditional library has been omitted. The University will rely on the Internet.

Close liaison needs to be maintained with the Government

Information Office, libraries and documentation centres organized by other government ministries and agencies, and the Central Bureau of Statistics or similar agency.

Regulation and control

A legal framework for tourism was discussed in Chapter 5, and mentioned the umbrella type of tourism act, which can define all the roles and powers of the GTA.

The degree of regulation and control by the government is a question of policy. All countries, however, tend to license many tourism enterprises at least against a minimum set of requirements. The reasons for regulating the tourism sector, and the basic guidelines to follow, were summarized in Chapter 10.

The following is the range of regulation and control with which a GTA will normally deal. This follows much the same list as included in Chapter 5.

Hotels/restaurants	Licensing
Bars/night clubs/discotheques	Minimum standards
	Hygiene regulations
	Fire regulations/safety
	Classification systems
Travel Agents	Licensing
Tour Operators	Minimum paid-up capital
	Bonding – indemnification
Tourist Guides	Occupational skill standard
	Licensing by examination
Ground transportation	Licensing
Buses, taxis	Minimum standards
	Meter control – taxis
	Approved tariffs – taxis
	Allocation of roles – tour operators and taxis

Marine transportation (including yachts)	Licensing Minimum standards Approved tariffs
Water sports (scuba diving, water skiing, parasailing, etc.)	Licensing Codes of practice
Gambling casinos	Licensing – standards

As noted, the GTA will work closely with the trade and professional associations on questions of licensing.

Various ministries and agencies are responsible for a variety of supporting legislation. For example, the Ministry of Trade or Interior Commerce may normally set minimum requirements for businesses. The Ministry of Health may set hygiene standards and the Ministry of Transport may handle all licensing for road and marine transport. If there are gambling casinos, one government agency or other may be designated to take care of the necessary supervision and control.

Air transport has not been mentioned. This is normally the domain of the Department of Civil Aviation, sometimes independently and sometimes under a Ministry of Transport. A GTA will need to maintain close liaison on all matters dealing with freedoms, rights and routes.

Wherever a GTA does not take the lead role in licensing and regulation, it should still be consulted to give the essential tourism criteria.

Research

Research as a separate department is linked with the major frontline departments – marketing, product development, regulation and control, human resources development and public awareness. Some research should concentrate on the social, environmental and economic impacts. Research should consist principally of intelligence and action or problem centred research.

As with management information, the research department should liaise with other government agencies acting as sources of social, environmental and economic data. The management information system and documentation centre can also be treated as a part of the research department and, as discussed, take advantage of the possibilities offered by the Internet.

A GTA should monitor international trends in product development, market preferences, regulation and control, sustainable development, training systems and other areas of interest. Through desk research, it will monitor various books, learned journals, studies, reports, and other published material.

It may undertake visitor surveys and surveys of the labour force. It should also update sectoral cost and revenue data, monitoring tourism's economic impact, and it will monitor the social impacts of tourism, and collaborate with other government agencies on questions of physical planning regulations and environmental protection.

As also noted, action or problem centred research is aimed at the product and the process. Product research looks at design, costs and feasibility. Process research examines how to do things in cheaper, quicker and better ways. This is illustrated in Figure 11.2. Some research projects and studies may be undertaken directly by GTA staff, others may be contracted out to the universities or consulting companies.

A GTA should certainly involve the universities. Staff and students can be used on survey work and studies. This links the universities with the sector, giving them valuable experience in tourism, developing

Figure 11.2   Research

their understanding of needs, and highlighting career opportunities. This involvement also increases the capacity of the universities to undertake research in the field. And it helps to focus their attention on tourism as an important area for research and academic study.

The GTA should seize all opportunities to collect data on the sector. For example as a part of the annual renewal of hotel licenses, each establishment can be required to submit a range of marketing and operational data. For example, occupancy figures, average length of stay, average room rates, and number of staff by occupation. This can be expanded into a comprehensive source of annual data.

Similarly a requirement for other types of establishment to renew licences annually not only provides for close control of standards, but also permits the collection of valuable data.

Management/organizational development, regulation and control and research objectives and results

Management/organizational development objective

This objective is to develop and improve the Government's capacity to manage tourism effectively through: tourism development policies and strategies; organizational development; management by objectives; and close collaboration within the sector.

The results planned are:

Result 1
Up-to-date tourism development policies and strategies.

Result 2
An improved organization achieved through better regional links, and the development of the knowledge and skills of personnel.

Result 3
An integrated planning process, implemented through a system of management by objectives and providing for interdepartmental collaboration to tackle interdependent tasks.

Result 4
A satisfactory network of joint/standing committees, consultative groups, councils and other appropriate mechanisms (at central and local levels) ensuring close collaboration between all parts of the sector.

Regulation and control objective

The objective is to ensure the enforcement of minimum standards for hygiene, fire prevention, safety and consumer protection (coordinating with the other ministries or agencies responsible) while further improving quality control standards for various tourist facilities and services. To also collaborate on the development and enforcement of physical planning standards, and measures for environmental protection and conservation.

The results planned are:

Result 1
The completion of a review of the current legislative framework for tourism, identifying any weaknesses, needs, bottlenecks or other problems, and preparing recommendations accordingly.

Result 2
The introduction of any changes or improvements from a legislative or regulatory standpoint.

Research objective

The objective is to maintain information systems and either conduct or commission research to monitor the performance of the sector, to investigate problem areas, and to provide research support for frontline departments; notably marketing, product development, regulation and control, human resources development and public awareness.

The results planned are:

Result 1
A well-designed and functioning computerized tourism information system (MIS) covering all aspects of the sector, and incorporating statistics based on WTO standards (see Chapter 1). A comprehensive documentation centre – hard copy but computer-administered (titles, subject area) and integrated with the MIS. Internet connections to access other databases. Dissemination of information through periodic publication and newsletters.

Result 2
A system of periodic visitor surveys to monitor nationalities, profiles, patterns of behaviour, preferences, complaints, expenditures, etc., and workforce surveys covering numbers, personnel profiles, productivity, shortages, levels of skill, occupations, and training.

Result 3
A system of surveys to update tourism sector cost structures, purchasing patterns, expenditures and revenues, and provide data inputs for the measurement of economic impacts.

Result 4
A system to monitor the environmental impact of tourism development (particularly through the analysis of environmental impact statements for new projects), identifying problem areas and preparing periodic reports.

Result 5
A system to monitor social impacts through surveys of selected communities and sections of society, linked to the implementation of public awareness programmes and activities.

Result 6
Special studies of the major markets (trends and competitiveness) and specific problem situations, to include such areas as facilities, transportation, infrastructure, and tourism services.

These three objectives — management/organizational development, regulation and control, and research are further examined in this chapter with lists of the necessary supporting activities.

Activities

The activities support the achievement of the objectives and results. As noted above, they are listed here for only three of the seven areas covered by a plan: management/organizational development, regulation and control, and research.

The other four areas — marketing, product development, human resources development and public awareness programmes — are explored in the book's remaining chapters. Each of these chapters conclude with the relevant list of activities.

Management/organizational development activities

The activities for the four results described are as follows:

Result 1 – Policy/strategies
- Review the tourism development policies and strategies. This is always the principal activity of the GTA's management. Policies may seldom require adjustment, but strategies need to accord with changing conditions and opportunities.
- Initiate steps to facilitate tourism, for example, to ease visa requirements.

Result 2 – Improved organization
- Keep under review the roles and functions of the GTA's regional offices. These offices have to play a part in the implementation of planning, and this requires clear definitions, instructions and resource allocation.
- Coordinate the planning activities in each of these regions, keeping in view the tourism potential for future development. Each regional office plan will contribute to the overall objectives and results.

- Ensure, at the regional level, that these offices have effective working relationships with the private sector, local government and other ministries and public sector agencies.
- Improve the GTA through the development of the skills, knowledge and experience of staff. This will be approached through participation in various courses or attachments.

Result 3 – Management by objectives

- Introduce management by objectives through training programmes. Seminars should work towards: an understanding of the needs; setting objectives and developing plans; developing participation, involvement and commitment; and monitoring the results achieved.
- Adopt a management by objectives approach for all GTA departments.
- Identify areas of overlap and needed inter-departmental collaboration. Set up working groups to tackle the corresponding tasks.
- Keep under review the whole tourism development planning organization and process; the description of functions and jobs, and the satisfaction of the necessary working interrelationships.

Result 4 – Sectoral collaboration

- Maintain the effectiveness of the working relationships established between the public and private sector – through any existing consultative or coordinating mechanisms.
- Make any improvements. Set up new or additional mechanisms (councils, committees, working groups), or eliminate or modify existing ones.

Regulation and control activities

The activities are as follows:

Result 1 – Identification of needs

- Compare industry-wide performance of the various tourism services and facilities against the established standards for hotels, restaurants,

catering and entertainment establishments, tour operators and travel agencies, identifying areas for any needed improvement.
- Monitor closely tourist complaints and the results of any GTA spot checks or investigations, identifying areas where improvements are needed.
- Monitor examples of tourism regulations and legislation at the international level, noting any improved approaches.
- Maintain close coordination with the private sector, developing joint recommendations on minimum quality standards.
- Review all customs, immigration and security procedures related to tourism, working with the government authorities responsible, and develop recommendations for any changes.
- Review the procedures for tourism project appraisals, environmental impact statements, investment and incentive approvals, and the granting of licences, and develop recommendations for any changes.
- Evaluate the needs and procedures related to physical planning controls – land use planning and zoning, and building regulations.

Result 2 – Improvements and changes
- Recommend and introduce changes or modifications to established regulations to better respond to identified needs.
- Develop changes in the minimum standards required for certain categories of establishment, to achieve improved quality standards.
- Recommend and introduce any new legislation or regulations to achieve the results listed in other parts of the plan.
- Consult closely with the private sector on all improvements, changes and new regulations.
- Collaborate with the regional authorities on the development and enforcement of zoning and planning regulations (working closely with the product development area).
- Provide any assistance to townships and municipalities on the development and introduction of any local regulations affecting tourism.

Research activities

The activities for the six results described are as follows:

Result 1 – Information system

- Review and improve as necessary the system for collecting and processing tourist arrivals and departure statistics.
- Review and improve as necessary the scope and accuracy of other tourism information currently accessible, paying particular attention to demand and market data, supply data and tourism assets, and recent sectoral performance.
- Assess the current information available on hotels and accommodation units, restaurants, travel agencies and tour operators, local ground transportation companies, banking, medical services, tourist guides, conference and meeting facilities, and identify the additional data needed.
- Check and develop the inventory of tourism assets (tourist attractions and existing and new tourist facilities), evaluating their characteristics, and recording all data in the MIS.
- Update the documentation centre – ensuring that it carries all key books, publications and other key documents needed. Disseminate information through periodic publications, newsletters, etc.
- Review and improve as necessary the hardware, software and systems currently in use. Develop the staffing and conduct the necessary training.
- Review and improve as necessary the methods and procedures for the collection and updating of data. Identify any additional sources of data, and develop the possibilities of an interface with other databanks.
- Review and improve as necessary the reporting needs, and the distribution of monthly and other periodic reports.

Result 2 – Visitor surveys

- Plan the programme of periodic visitor surveys to monitor nationalities, profiles, patterns of behaviour, preferences, complaints, expenditures, and workforce surveys covering numbers, personnel profiles, productivity, shortages, levels of skill, occupations, training.
- Determine the sampling method to be employed, the points where interviews will be conducted, the design of the questionnaire, and the selection and training of survey staff.

- Finalize and agree the budgets, ensuring that adequate funds exist to keep to the agreed survey methodology.
- Carry out the field work, liaising as necessary with the private sector and airport authorities.
- Process results and analyse. Prepare and distribute the survey reports. Participate in workshops to present and discuss the results.

Result 3 – Economic impact

- Design and conduct surveys to update and collect data on tourism sector cost structures, purchasing patterns, expenditures and revenues.
- Develop the models and methods to calculate the various indices: contribution to GDP, foreign exchange earnings; employment; and government revenues at the national and local levels; and the income multiplier effects.
- Measure, on a selective basis, the economic contribution to particular regional development.

Result 4 – Environmental impact

- Work with the Ministry of the Environment – or other responsible government agency – on the identification of needs, and implementation of appropriate action on environmental questions (liaising closely with the product development and regulation/control departments).
- Provide inputs, in particular, on environmental legislation affecting tourism and on procedures governing the preparation, review and approval of environmental impact statements for tourism projects.
- Collaborate on public awareness, proposing the messages that need to be sent, the target audiences and suggesting ways in which material can best be communicated.

Result 5 – Social impact

- Establish a system to monitor social impacts through surveys of selected communities and sections of society, linked to the implementation of public awareness programmes and activities.
- Liaise closely with the area of public awareness, to monitor audience

reaction and community feedback on radio, television programmes and other activities.

Result 6 – Special studies

- Undertake, as necessary, a variety of marketing surveys in the major markets to identify data related to tour operators programmes, consumer preferences, price competitiveness, competing destinations, and distribution/sales networks, etc. Such data should complement desk research and the MIS.
- Draw up a range of special studies related to various aspects of product improvement programmes. Plan and execute these studies, taking appropriate follow-up steps to review and discuss the recommendations made.
- Identify with the regional offices and the private sector, various problem areas requiring action. Structure the problems for investigation and study, produce recommendations, and follow up with the persons and organizations involved.
- Investigate, in particular, any problems in areas such as local transportation and infrastructure, and prepare and follow up recommendations accordingly.

Checklist – Management Information System (basic information to be included)

Basic data

Geographical description
Climate
Government
Population
Principal towns
History
Education and vocational training
Public health
Law enforcement and community services
Entry formalities and procedures

Economic data

Gross domestic product
Structure and description of the economy
Characteristics of the labour force
Impact of tourism
    Multipliers – income – employment/regional development/foreign
      exchange earnings/GDP, etc.

Access and transportation

Air transport
    Origin and frequency of services
    Capacity and arrivals
    Current characteristics and bottlenecks
Road
Maritime
Other

National development perspectives and projects

Overall plans and targets
Targets by sector

Current patterns of tourism

Arrivals
    International
    Domestic
    Market segment
      Mainstream
      Special interest
Origins of visitors/excursionists
Lengths of stay
Profiles of visitors
Average expenditures – foreign exchange earnings
Hotel occupancies
Hotel profitability
Other characteristics

Marketing information

Analysis of principal characteristics and trends by market
Characteristics of regional demand − by market
List of major tour operators by market
List of principal retailers by market
Details of tour operator packages currently offered − capacity and numbers sold
List of major travel writers by market
Consumer publications − circulation/readership
Travel trade publications − circulation/readership
Special interest publications − circulation/readership
Other data and trends.

New developments and future trends

Overall trends
New projects − planning stage
New projects − in construction
Expanded transportation and access
New tour programmes/packages
New marketing trends
Future perspectives

Tourism assets inventory

This inventory will normally include all assets contributing to the overall tourism product. A list, which may not be exhaustive, is as follows:

Natural resources

Climate
Beaches
Sea and coastline

Flora and fauna
Rivers
Lakes
Forests
Mountains
Caves
Waterfalls
Panoramas
Islands (islets)
Other characteristics of the landscape.

Cultural and historic attractions

Art galleries
Museums
Historical sites
Mosques, churches, temples
Handicrafts workshops
Artist, artist's groups and art galleries
Musical groups
Folkloric groups
Dance groups
Cultural centres
Festivals
Parades and special events

Other tourist attractions

National parks
Sea gardens
Aquariums/marine worlds
Zoological gardens
Botanical gardens
Fun fairs/leisure parks
Spectator sports
   Racetracks
   Boxing

Football
Other
Theatres and cinemas

Activities – sports, recreation and entertainment

Hunting
Fishing (rivers)
Fishing (deep sea)
Trekking
Horseriding
Mountain climbing
Canoeing
White water rafting
Water sports (shore-based)
Water ski, para-sailing, sailing, windsurfing, etc.
Yachting (charters)
Yachting (bareboat)
Scuba diving
Tennis
Golf
Squash
Archery
Clay pigeon shooting
Gymnasiums
Public swimming pools
Other

Services

Travel agencies
Tourist information services
Car rental agencies
Medical services
Shopping/handicrafts
Postal services
Telecommunications services

Banks/money changing
Hairdressers/beauty salons
Taxis
Buses
Religious services

Infrastructure

Airports
Ports
Road network
Telecommunications
Water
Electricity/power
Waste collection and disposal
Drainage

Accommodation, restaurants and allied facilities

Hotels and accommodation
   Hotels
   Other tourist accommodation
Restaurants/bars
Discotheques
Night clubs/cabarets
Convention centres/meeting facilities

12 Managing marketing

This chapter further develops the concept of the marketing strategy, examines the marketing role of GTAs, and discusses various aspects of market research. Promotional approaches and techniques are then discussed: advertising, printed and audiovisual material, direct mail, travel writing, travel agents' familiarization trips, travel trade shows and exhibitions, special promotions, representative offices abroad, and other public relations activities. The chapter then examines the evaluation of promotional effectiveness. It concludes with a summary of the marketing objectives, results and activities, representing the marketing part of the overall planning process.

Marketing strategy

Marketing strategies can also be published as a short document. This document can be drafted using the following framework:

- The relationship of the tourism development policies to marketing – a short statement describing their marketing applications.
- International tourism growth – world and regional – showing both the performance of competitors and overall trends.
- Past performance and results, market research findings and their relationship to future perspectives.
- The marketing opportunities offered by the tourism sector – according to the purpose of travel and other market segmentation criteria.
- The current tourism product – strengths, weaknesses, opportunities and threats (SWOT).
- A description of the needed product development and improvement

by tourism development area (or state, county, province, or region) – covering: improved access; additional resort areas; hotels, restaurants, shopping and tourism services; the development of cultural, scenic and heritage attractions; and the addition of other attractions such as sporting and recreational facilities.

- A description of any changes in the markets to be pursued. Details of the measures to be taken to achieve these changes.
- The expected development of tourism giving an indication of the expected volume of tourists and tourism receipts broken down by area/region.
- A promotional programme, developed and approved, covering advertising, sales, representation, public relations, and other promotional activities.
- The approach to sales in each of the principal markets, and the adequacy of distribution and sales networks.

This description of the strategy serves as the framework for the marketing plan. The overall approach is illustrated in Figure 12.1.

The GTA's marketing role

The private sector is extensively involved in all aspects of marketing. Normally, in established destinations, its marketing expenditures far exceed those of the public sector. It is obviously sensible for the public sector to tackle the destination's marketing programme in collaboration.

The GTA should retain the responsibilty for projecting the overall image of the country's tourism sector. And the GTA itself, in consultation with the private sector, should coordinate marketing policies and strategies.

The GTA also plays a key part in product development. It has important responsibilities in shaping and maintaining the overall tourism product to meet marketing objectives.

The promotional role is to position the destination in an overall manner; it differentiates it from competitors. The private sector will then sell it in a variety of ways, through a range of programmes, to a

Figure 12.1 Marketing plan

number of different markets. The difference between the public and private sector roles is sometimes dramatized by the statement – 'We promote the dream, they sell the package.'

A tour operator's catalogue may be printed in hundreds of thousands, with very clear marketing objectives. It may give a destination several full colour pages, promoting specific packages.

However, collaboration between the GTA and the private sector ensures that this kind of promotion fits with the overall marketing strategy.

The major tour operators and travel trade interests, the hotel and the airlines are the forces which make a marketing success of a destination. But the GTA helps them.

The GTA shows the country in the best light possible, enhancing its appeal as a holiday destination. Image building is a constant process.

The GTA and the private sector together may jointly fund some marketing activities. This may be done through a joint marketing committee or board, or may take place on an *ad hoc* basis only. The private sector is more likely to support activities which have visible and specific outcomes. For example, travel agency familiarization trips, travel trade shows and exhibitions and special promotions.

A GTA's product development and marketing departments may also collaborate on investment promotion. They may develop a promotional strategy covering both domestic and foreign investment.

Market research

Market research relies heavily on the management information system and the GTA's research department, the results and activities of which were discussed in Chapter 11.

There should be a regular flow of tourism statistics. In many countries these are frontier statistics, with the initial data processing undertaken by the immigration authorities often in collaboration with the government's department of statistics. Trends will be identified by the GTA and explained in periodic reports.

One should also follow the performance of competing destinations and make comparisons. It is important to note which destinations are doing better than others and why. It is easy to agree to share statistics with other countries, and to exchange data on a monthly basis. Desk research will monitor worldwide trends in tourism.

The GTA should receive constant intelligence on the behaviour of the markets, especially about tour operators and major intermediaries selling the destination. A lot of information can be picked up by maintaining frequent contact with the travel trade. Also by studying the trade press. One must also rely on the GTA managers of any representative tourism offices abroad.

Promotional activities

If a high proportion of tourism is sold through tour operators, and a low porportion through independent travel, this will influence the choice of GTA promotional support. Conversely a high proportion of independent travel will require different forms of support.

Business travel requires a different approach to promotion. So do health tourism and convention tourism.

Domestic tourism will often require a more active GTA role, using quite different media. For example, bill boards, radio and television, often less likely to be used in international tourism, may be used locally.

All promotion must have a clear objective. What is it setting out to achieve?

It has to have a clear message. What is it trying to say and to whom?

It has to use the right media. Is this how and where to give the message, and will it reach the right people?

In the following sections a number of marketing approaches and techniques are discussed: advertising, various printed and audiovisual material, direct mail, travel writing, travel agents' familiarization trips, travel trade shows and exhibitions, special promotions, representative offices abroad, other public relations activities.

Advertising

Advertising is any non-personal communication of ideas and messages, usually paid, intended to sell goods or services.

It is always advisable to use an advertising agency with previous experience, a good track record in tourism, and a close knowledge of the characteristics of the particular market. It should know the most appropriate media to use and, from previous experience and testing, the effectiveness of different copy, layout, segmentation, frequency and coverage. An agency will prepare the media plan in consultation with the client, and provide marketing justification for the proposals made.

The media's advertising tariffs are discounted to allow for the agency commissions. The agency costs to the client, therefore, may be mostly covered or alternatively negotiated on a fee basis. Any GTA advertising is likely to be mainly image building. It is always important to keep the image of the destination to the forefront.

Image building through advertising is an expensive proposition since it usually involves prestige newspapers, magazines and possibly television. It will therefore depend on the size of the promotional budget. This will generally depend on the size of the country, its level of development and the scale of the tourism sector.

Prestige advertising such as a full page in *Time* magazine or *Newsweek* is commonly used by a number of countries. Such advertisements may also feature the national airline.

Whether image building is effective or not is difficult to measure. If a country's tourism is successful, and growth rates are maintained, keeping up or doing better than competitors, it is judged to be effective. If tourism drops, then part of the blame is usually attributed to the advertising. There may be no sound basis for either conclusion.

Better methods of research have enabled researchers to establish a closer correlation between advertising and resulting sales. However, this is easier to do for consumer products than for tourism.

Small destinations with limited budgets may rely on other ways of strengthening the image; mainly through press coverage – notably travel writers – and public relations in general.

However, small destinations are often accused of spreading their budgets too thinly. It is often suggested that they should keep their resources together, concentrate their buying power and still buy a small quantity of image building advertising. This is mostly a question of judgement.

Much will depend on how well the destination is doing and how much spare capacity exists. If sales need to be boosted substantially then an approach using high profile advertising may be justified.

If a high proportion of tourism consists of independent travel, a GTA may place some advertising in the travel trade press. If there is a large market of business traffic this may also justify some travel trade advertising. A GTA may also link with tour operators and airlines to place some travel trade advertisements linked to a specific promotion or programme.

It is unlikely, except with some domestic promotion, for GTAs to advertise alone. They are more likely to act in collaboration with the private sector. Joint marketing initiatives usually include some advertising.

Television and radio are more likely to be used to promote domestic tourism. Some destinations, however, have made a point of using both radio and television in their major markets. Television advertising can have wide impact, but it is expensive both in production costs and air time. A number of Caribbean destinations, during their winter season, use television advertising in North America.

Printed and audiovisual material

Tourism printed and audiovisual material (principally video) is aimed at information, promotion or education. For example, a brochure is promotional, a city map provides information and a museum leaflet may be mainly educational.

However, all three purposes may be combined in a single item of printed material, for example, a brochure which is not only promotional; a city map which can promote tourist attractions and carry advertising; a museum leaflet which can recommend other things to do and see, and also carry some advertising.

People tend not to keep material which is purely promotional. However, if it contains useful information, or educational content for future reference, they may well keep it.

The purpose of any item has to be defined as closely as possible.

- What is the purpose?
- Who is it aimed at?
- To say what?
- With what result?
- Where will people obtain it? Where will it be available?
- Will it be mailed/distributed? If so how?
- How many will be printed?
- How will they be used or distributed?

A lot of promotional material is produced without going through these questions rigorously. Material with a vague purpose is a waste of money.

If an item is to be used for mailing, its size and weight are important considerations. Brochures are historically small to facilitate mailing. But a destination brochure may be intended primarily for a display rack. It can be bigger, bolder and more striking.

Brochures

As noted, one should define the exact purpose of the brochure and how it is to be used. This is essential in determining size, layout and design.

The brochure should not have too much text or too many photos. Essential information such as maps, addresses, agencies/reservations, telephone and fax numbers should also be included. Brochures should be concise, crisp, and reflect the style of the destination.

How many different types of brochures are produced depends on the destination; for example, one may have a general brochure, a sports brochure, and a cultural appeal brochure. It depends on the composition of the product and the market, including both mainstream and special interest segments. Separate brochures may be produced for certain segments such as diving or trekking. A special brochure might be jointly produced with a tour operator or airline to support a particular programme.

Posters

Posters are a popular and effective means of promotion. If they are good they will be displayed. They must portray strikingly the destination's image. Posters can also be sold to the general public to help defray costs.

Collateral material

Collateral material includes items such as lighters, pens, credit card wallets, writing cases, postcards, etc. This collateral material carries the GTA's logo and is used for public relations and promotional purposes, usually as giveaways. Again it is has to be of a design and quality compatible with the image.

Promotional videos

Promotional videos are the most common audiovisual material used.

Videos of this type are a major tool in projecting the image of a destination. A video conveys a strong overall message – this is the place, this is what we are, this is what you will find. The video should be about 15 to 20 minutes, not longer, and be fast moving, comprehensive and have immediate impact. It has to hold people's interest from start to finish.

For these reasons a video should be professionally produced. It is a good idea to invite bids. This enables an assessment of the creativity and originality of film-makers. It can also verify whether they have correctly interpreted the destination's image.

CD-Rom and multimedia applications will have many future possibilities for tourism promotion.

Travel agents' manual

This is often called a manual, but it could be called equally well a directory or guide. It is a well produced piece of printed material containing a comprehensive description of the destination. It should include all the inbound tour operators, travel agencies, hotels, restaurants, tourist attractions, sporting and recreational facilities, entertainment facilities and the complete range of tourism services on offer.

It provides agents with an important tool. It is the destination's visiting card and a valuable source of reference. It provides the necessary information to make bookings and do business with the destination.

Although an expensive item to produce, a substantial part of the cost, if not all of it, can be recovered from advertising.

Information on rates and tariffs should be printed on a separate sheet to facilitate reprinting and updating.

A manual of this kind is for retailers or small independent tour operators as opposed to the large companies. The major tour operators will negotiate their contracts directly, and sell through their own catalogues.

It will be of particular value to agents wishing to plan and book independent and small group travel.

Direct mail

Direct mail is an advertising medium. The costs of postage make it relatively expensive, but it is an effective way of communicating with the travel trade. It is good to link it with the distribution of a regular newsletter or information bulletin.

An up-to-date mailing list of tour operators and travel agencies can be held in the MIS. Sub-lists may also include the clubs and associations linked to any special interest markets. For example, diving clubs, golf clubs, historial associations, and cultural groups.

The database will allow mailing lists to be printed for any particular purpose; country, type of agency or organization, and geographical area.

It is not normally appropriate for a GTA to use direct mail for a narrow sales purpose. It uses it for general advertising and public relations; to provide updated information, stay in touch and keep the destination in the forefront of people's minds.

Travel writers

The market information system should carry the details of the major travel writers of potential importance to the destination. Files should be kept up-to-date, with details of articles published.

Some of these writers, on their own initiative, may choose to visit or write about the destination. They may do this independently or through the GTA. The GTA should evaluate any request based on the criteria it has assembled.

Apart from this, the GTA should prepare its own list of travel writers as a part of an annual programme. Chosen writers should then be invited to visit and write about the destination. The cost of transport and accommodation at the destination, should be arranged by the GTA. The GTA will coordinate with the private sector on these arrangements. Writers should be invited singly and never in a group.

Writers may contact the GTA asking for visits to be facilitated, and accommodation arranged. An editorial letter of introduction or appointment should be requested. The GTA may decide to collaborate if the magazine (circulation and readership) and the proposal appear acceptable. Or it may only offer to arrange a discount and help with a programme. Some types of proposal may not be worthwhile at all.

Some magazines may offer editorial space if advertising space is taken. Many work with a formula – so much advertising is worth so much editorial. Some of these arrangements may be worth considering, but one should be cautious. Advertising plus editorial should be seen together as one package. The purpose should be clear and the expenditure well justified.

Writers engaged on guide books or travel books should be judged on similar criteria to the above. Are they known? Do they have an editorial letter from the publishers? Is the piece of work worthwhile? If so, the GTA should offer its maximum collaboration.

A GTA may take initiative in promoting proposals for particular kinds of guide books or travel books. It should write to publishers, outline proposals and spell out the assistance which it is prepared to offer. The purpose, and exactly why a particular book is needed, should be clearly justified. The number of copies, the readership, the distribution, the expected impact – all these things need to be studied.

Travel agency familiarization trips

These trips should continue all the time. It is important to maintain successive waves of travel agency staff passing through and getting to know the destination. Staff with this kind of direct product knowledge play a key role in sales. Having seen a destination firsthand they will speak about it with more conviction and enthusiasm.

The agencies to be invited should be among the biggest producers of business. The tour operators selling a destination can certainly recommend agencies as can the airlines.

A GTA, through visitor surveys, and working closely with inbound operators, the airlines and the hotels, can build up its own files. The MIS should maintain files on all agencies, gradually building up a record of the various supporting networks of retailers. The GTA's representative offices abroad can also provide valuable advice on the agencies to include.

The programme while in the destination should be drawn up in collaboration with the private sector. This is one of the tasks which any

joint marketing committee or board can undertake. In most destinations, trips will normally be from three to five days in duration. Groups
may consist of up to 30 agency personnel and sometimes more. At
times a tour operator may dedicate one entire flight, at the beginning
of a programme, to agents' familiarization.

The agency personnel are shown the hotels and facilities, the tourist
attractions and other features of the destination. They lunch and dine in
a cross section of restaurants, and see the various entertainments
available. They should try out the destination and all that it has to
offer.

Travel trade shows and exhibitions

There are many reasons for destinations to be present at travel trade
shows and exhibitions:

- It is a chance to reinforce the image of the destination – to show
  clearly what it represents and what it offers.
- It enables collaboration with the tour operators already selling the
  destination, creating an opportunity to support their sales efforts.
- It enables some worthwhile public relations activities – receptions,
  press conferences, interviews, radio.
- It can include television appearances for any accompanying dancers,
  singers and musicians.
- It can enable some direct sales follow-ups with the travel trade in
  general.
- It may be instrumental in establishing a first contact with one or
  more tour operators, with a visit to the destination arranged as a
  follow-up.

It is usually thought that few new deals are done at trade shows.
How much selling is done depends on the inbound operators and
hotels accompanying the GTA team. These are the people who can
actually sell, put together a variety of new arrangemnts and packages
and negotiate a contract on the spot. In most cases, however, trade
shows are used to make first contacts or to follow up old contacts.

The stand should be of a standard and quality to reflect the image of
the destination. Specialist designers should be used to produce some-

thing imaginative and eye catching. It is a good idea to enlist the help of dance and musical groups, and any of the country's outstanding artists and performers already known internationally.

It is common for destinations to put on a special night, using a national theme, with dinner and entertainment. If this is done the budget should be adequate.

Some activities have to be undertaken merely for the purpose of general image building.

Special promotions

Special promotions abroad may sometimes be run in conjunction with participation at a travel show. A variety of activities may be planned within the same week: a food and gastronomic festival, fashion shows, folkloric/dance performances, music recitals and pop concerts. This would be part of a short campaign linked to a theme. One must focus, as always, on the results to be achieved. Effectiveness will depend mostly on the preparation, coverage, timing, support and budget.

Representative offices abroad

These offices were discussed in Chapter 5. They play an important marketing role. They are not there to work for the country's ambassador; to provide local reservations, travel and airport 'meet and greet' services for visiting government officials. They should be completely separate and independent from the local embassy.

An office plays an important part in identifying market information. It has to monitor what's happening in the market and make regular reports to the GTA.

An office will also work on public relations staying in close touch with travel writers, radio producers and other media people. It can also liaise with any local advertising agency employed by the destination.

Other public relations activities

The public relations section of the GTA's marketing department may take responsibility for a number of the areas already discussed. For example, travel agents' familiarization trips and travel writers. However, there are other important public relations activities.

A damage control system should exist to deal with any sudden and adverse publicity. For example, an earthquake or natural disaster, or civil disturbances, or the murder of a tourist. Rapid action is needed to try and lessen the impact of bad news coverage. It may consist of telephone calls to opinion makers, press releases, press conferences, emergency advertising or any other action depending on the type of occurrence and the market or markets affected.

The handling of complaints letters is another important area. Complaints should be followed up and investigated, and a detailed reply prepared for the signature of the GTA's chief executive. There should be close liaison with the regulation and control department, since enterprises may have contravened required minimum standards. Periodically the complaints should be analysed, and put into report form.

It may be desirable to organize press conferences from time to time. Led by the chief executive of the GTA, these can be an effective way of communicating with the media. A free wheeling question and answer session at the end can create a relaxed and open relationship. It will help to win positive media support for the implementation of plans, and future development of tourism.

Measuring promotional effectiveness

Rules of thumb are often cited about how many pieces of promotional material are needed to produce one tourist. There is no general rule. However, there is certainly a correlation in many people's minds between success and the promotional budget. A destination achieves a certain impressive growth rate and part of this success is attributed to the promotion. It is concluded that the promotional budget must have been right. As already pointed out, this does not follow.

There are rules of thumb about the proportion of tourist revenues that should be spent for promotion. These also tend to be misleading. The promotion needed is that which will achieve the planned results.

No more and no less. Promotion and its form and content are a question of judgement. There are so many variables at work that it is impossible to isolate the exact reasons for a sector's results.

The GTA's promotion sets the stage for, and supports, the private sector. It sows seeds in the market place which the private sector must follow up. This is image building. Once the private sector has followed up, the GTA undertakes other promotional activities which lend support; for example, travel writers, newsletters, travel trade shows, and familiarization trips.

A constant flow of feedback through the tour operators, the trade press, surveys, advertising agency studies and the hoteliers, is essential. This provides the basis to evaluate promotional effectiveness. As experience is built up, it becomes evident what works and what does not work, and what might work that has not been tried before.

If a GTA stopped spending money on promotion tomorrow, would it make any difference? This is the key question.

Private sector promotional effectiveness is often easier to measure. A tour operator's catalogue – the most important promotional tool in tourism – can be partly evaluated through the sales results achieved. However, there are many contributory factors in a person's buying decisions; promotion is just one.

Marketing objective and results

The objectives and results reflect the marketing strategy described at the start of this chapter.

Objective

To review and implement a marketing strategy, identifying the market segments to be attracted, the marketing criteria to guide product development, and including plans and programmes for all related advertising, sales, promotional and public relations activities.

Result 1

A review of the marketing opportunities and tourism product, the selection of market segments and the implementation of the marketing strategy.

Result 2
A marketing programme, developed and approved, detailing the promotion, printed material, direct mail, advertising, representation and public relations activities – together with the corresponding budget.

Marketing activities

In accordance with the results planned above, the first group of activities addresses the review and implementation of the marketing strategy. The second group tackles the planning and implementation of the promotional programme.

Result 1 – Marketing strategy
In its implementation the marketing strategy should include, where possible, targets for each market segment. These may include the number of tourists, length of stay, and (for international tourism) the value in foreign exchange earnings.

This breakdown may follow the purposes of travel already listed; leisure, recreation and holidays (mainstream, special interest and any alternative tourism), visiting friends and relatives, business and professional, health treatment, religion/pilgrimages and other.

Under each of these markets, the marketing strategy can be finalized and implemented according to the following activities:

- Review market research and intelligence findings (from surveys, desk research and the MIS) dealing with visitor satisfaction, needs, competitor's advantages etc, liaising with the research department. Identify and meet the needs for any further information.
- Prepare a background summary of past tourism performance, identifying trends.
- Identify the marketing opportunities by country of tourist origin, by

market segment, and assess the corresponding appeal and impact of the tourism product in marketing terms.

- Review and develop the marketing mix: product, price, image, promotion, distribution by province/area/region chosen – location, facilities, services, attractions: strengths, weaknesses, opportunities and threats (SWOT).
- Structure the product – disaggregate by province/area/region.
- Collaborate in the preparation of product development plans, and their implementation.
- Prepare an assessment of each market: profile, nationality, gender, stage of life, social grade, mode of transport/distance travelled. Identify any psychographic background – if data are available, and indicate any likely changes taking place.
- Plan the marketing results sought – numbers of tourists, length of stay, and expenditure, by area/region.
- Plan and implement the promotional programme (see separate activities).
- Integrate marketing activities with areas other than research and product development; notably, management and organizational development, regulation and control, human resources development and public awareness programmes.

Result 2 – Promotional activities
The following activities are needed to develop and implement the promotional programme (Result 2 of the marketing objective):

- Review the whole area of working relationships with retailers and tour operators, and ways of developing the sales network for each market.
- Set up marketing collaboration with the major airlines.
- Assess the image in these selected markets in terms of identity and appeal (negative and positive factors), and the right marketing mix.
- Consult with the private sector on any joint marketing initiatives and funding, and prepare and agree overall budget arrangements.
- Review the design and production of printed material – brochures, posters, folders and publications, and the production and distribution programme together with corresponding costings.
- Develop a schedule for the production of any audiovisual material.

- Develop mailing lists of both tour operators and retailers, planning the use to be made of direct mail and the production and distribution of a newsletter or similar publication.
- Plan any advertising to be developed and placed – by selected market.
- Develop annual plans working with each representative office abroad, and/or plan any other overseas representation.
- Plan travel agents' familiarization trips, and representation at major trade shows.
- Develop plans to work with travel writers and journalists, proposing who to invite and when.
- Plan and undertake other needed public relations activities.
- Collaborate on investment promotion strategies.
- Develop any special promotions. For example, a Tourism Week, in collaboration with the private sector, aimed at both tourism promotion and public awareness.
- Prepare and agree the marketing budget
- Implement the promotional programme, monitoring closely its effectiveness.

13 Managing product development

This chapter lists the product development strategies, and describes planning needs at different levels. It goes on to examine the concept of macroregional planning, the use of geographical information systems (GIS), a national development and land use planning agency, and microregional planning. It then describes the relationship of these approaches with regional tourism planning, and lists a number of minimum planning requirements. Coastal management plans are briefly described, as are urban tourism needs. The chapter then explains the content of the tourism development action programme, and the investment promotion and approval needs. The chapter concludes with the product development objectives, results and activities, representing the product development part of the overall management and planning process.

The product development strategy

The key sections of the overall strategy directly related to product development are as follows:

- The tourism marketing opportunities, according to the purpose of travel and other market segmentation criteria.
- The division of the country into a sensible system of tourism development areas. These should be related to the organization of the government's administrative units, e.g. region, state, county, province, borough, municipality and township.
- The infrastructural situation covering airports, roads, railways, ports and inland waterways, energy and water supply, explaining new projects and development priorities.

- A description of the needed product improvement and development by tourism development area, covering: improved access; additional resort areas; hotels, restaurants, shopping and tourism services; the development of cultural, scenic and heritage attractions; and the addition of other attractions such as sporting and recreational facilities.
- The expected development of tourism including a summary of the investment prospects. Also an indication of the expected volume of visitors and tourism receipts.

Planning at different levels

Figure 13.1 shows the inter-relationships in the planning of product development.

Tourism plans are needed, as discussed in Chapter 5 and Chapter 10, at national and regional levels, down to the various boroughs and townships. At the national level policies and guidelines are clearly established. At the regional and local levels these are reviewed against the opportunities and needs. Local plans are then elaborated following the guidelines established.

It is not a question of choosing between top-down and bottom-up approaches. One should combine these with a free flow of communication and exchange of criteria and opinions. This recognizes the relative role of each of the planning levels.

In most countries there is a degree of central approval and coordination. However, regional and local government authorities may be fairly autonomous to pursue local planning and development. In some aspects they may even be completely autonomous.

The division of a country accords with government needs. The various administrative units are used for planning, finance and budgets, and statistical analysis.

Decentralization, as also discussed in Chapter 10, recognizes that:

- As noted, regional and local government may be largely autono-

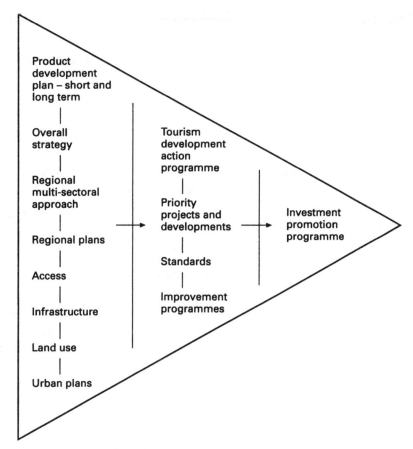

Figure 13.1 Product development plan

mous. They would involve key people and local interests, in planning and development decisions.

- They should develop their own capabilities, using their own specialists, to tackle management and planning.
- Tourism should be seen as one part of regional and local development. It has to be integrated with other local development.

Important interrelationships between regions can be made the subject of coordination. The GTA should be able to assist in this. It should recognize the value of getting different regions to talk together about their various problems and needs.

On an international scale, neighbouring countries may wish to coordinate various planning initiatives. For example, the development of transportation networks which link a group of countries together.

Macroplanning

Regional planning sets out patterns of future development – what to do, where and how. It concerns how human beings use land and other resources; how they choose to live, work and satisfy their needs. It studies a region in the following ways:

- It examines development realities and priorities within the region, identifying the preferred objectives and options.
- It looks at a region as a total area with varying geographical and physical characteristics. It breaks these down and lists them all: climatic conditions, coastline, topography and soils, vegetation, wildlife, rivers, lakes, reserves, protected areas, national parks and other features.
- It examines in detail the land. It asks how is it owned and used. What land remains free for new and further uses. What land should be reserved or protected.
- It identifies the spatial relationships which exist within the region and the contrasts and interactions between the different areas.
- It looks particularly at human settlement; where the population lives in what concentrations and with what kinds of problems.
- It examines ethnicity and demographic trends and how the population is changing.
- It identifies the various economic activities and trends: the kinds and extent of agriculture, forestry and fishing; industry and manufacturing; mining and quarrying; tourism and the services.
- It looks at the current supply, consumption and future availability of water.
- It examines the transportation networks.
- It studies the other existing infrastructure, notably the capacity and distribution of power supplies, and the systems of drainage and waste disposal.

- It identifies cultural resources, e.g. archeological and historical sites, and other attractions.
- Finally, it identifies current environmental, economic and social problems and their causes.

This creates a macro view of the region.

On the basis of the above criteria, a region can be seen as a system of zones each with its own characteristics.

Tourism development planning should be based on all of the above, plus the identification of all existing hotels, other accommodation facilities, major man-made tourist attractions, and current tourist traffic.

Tourism, in terms of diverse hotels, accommodation facilities and tourist attractions, might be scattered here and there throughout a region. Some concentrations of existing tourism facilities and attractions may also be found, together with areas for potential tourism development.

Clearly, the macroregional view is not created for only one sector of the economy. No single sector can be planned without reference to all the others. Yet isolated planning decisions are often made. This happens not only because of the lack of coordination between government departments, but also because of the complexity which integrated planning poses.

Geographical information system (GIS)

This is a computer mapping system. All the data relating to the various categories listed above are classified and coded, and entered in the computer.

- Natural resources – all information on the geographical features, climate, topography, soils, vegetation, wildlife, lakes, rivers, reserves, protected areas and national parks.
- Human settlement – water, power and other infrastructure, housing, urbanization, demographic data, economic data, transportation networks, mining, manufacturing, agriculture, forestry, fishing and other activities, etc.

If one were to adapt the GIS specifically for tourism purposes then a third category would be added:

- Cultural resources and tourism — following the content of the tourism assets inventory listed at the end of Chapter 11; hotels, restaurants, tourist attractions and cultural resources, recreational and sports facilities, and entertainment facilities etc.

It is then possible to print maps with any combination of the above data. One prints the maps as a series of overlays. This can show very clearly the existing spatial interrelationships.

One can see how the existing tourism facilities, attractions and services cluster together in given areas, forming tourism concentrations. One can also see how other activities may conflict with tourism.

Existing tourism zones become apparent, as do the opportunities for improvements. What also become evident are the considerations surrounding the carrying capacity of given zones, and whether there is still room for expansion.

Mapping will also point to new zones offering possibilities for future development.

Working with a GIS it is possible to illustrate a variety of alternative proposals. The GIS will also be used at a national level, bringing together the various regional data so that an overview of the country can be created.

A GTA depending on the size and complexity of the country, might maintain a GIS facility at both national and regional levels.

It would only input and update the tourism data. All other data would be accessed from a master system. In turn the master system would access the tourism data from the GTA.

A GIS installed to serve the complete national and regional government network, provides a very advanced tool.

As has been noted, the various sectors tend to compete for the same space. A GIS system can quickly identify these conflicting claims, can look at alternatives and resolve the problem in an integrated way.

A national development or land use planning agency

To formulate a land use plan, one has to decide what should take place. What will various land and zones be used for? This requires a multidisciplinary approach using economic, sociocultural,and environmental criteria. It also requires a multisectoral planning approach, involving a wide range of different government agencies.

As noted much of this planning will be decentralized and pushed out to the regions and local areas, so as to permit the maximum participation at the grassroots levels. Somebody from a central viewpoint, however, has to coordinate all of this planning activity. It should see that it follows a consistent approach, observes national policies and priorities, uses the same planning criteria and standards, and considers the same environmental safeguards and measures.

This government agency, often simply called planning, can handle responsibility for land use, urban planning and the environment. In many countries each government ministry designates a department responsible for coordinating with this planning agency.

Regional tourism planning

At the macrolevel one establishes zones; at the microlevel one deals with specific developments and projects, for example, a housing estate or residential area, a manufacturing estate, an airport, a national park, a theme park, a resort development, or a power plant.

The private sector will conduct firstly a feasibility study and, on this basis, will then produce a design scheme. The criteria they would follow were listed at the end of Chapter 3, and cover a marketing analysis, product definition, the marketing mix, the proposed design, and project justification.

While this approach illustrated a tourism project, it would need very little modification to be used for any development project. For example, a toy factory, a food processing plant, a brewery or a discount store. Any development project will require a similar approach to feasibility, design and environmental impact.

The criteria for evaluating a private sector project, from a government viewpoint were also listed at the end of Chapter 3. They indicated that proposed projects should conform with government policies and development needs, together with environmental, social and economic criteria. Similarly, these government criteria would not differ greatly from sector to sector. Using this as the starting point, an environmental impact statement (EIS) should be prepared, using the checklist at the end of Chapter 7.

The mapping of tourism assets will illustrate the cluster concept also discussed in Chapter 3. Mainstream tourism requires a complete range of facilities, services and attractions in the same location and area.

Regional planning is faced with the following product development options:

- Further development of already established tourism zones. Significant tourism development may already be in place.
- Upgrading and improvement of facilities and installations, including redevelopment and renovation.
- Further development of existing resorts.
- Improvement of the tourism zones in towns and cities.
- Initial development of undeveloped or relatively undeveloped zones.

The emphasis changes from the macro to the micro, from the identification and study of zones to the development of areas and sites.

Tourism zones can be ranked according to the potential which they offer. The ranking can assign points according to the merits which each one possesses. This helps to decide where to concentrate development efforts. In assessing a development zone for tourism potential one would examine the following criteria:

- Whether climatic conditions are good.
- Whether it has a variety of attractive natural resources – pleasant surroundings, good landscape, recreational attractions, and scenic attractions.

- Whether it has a variety of cultural attractions including historical and archaeological sites.
- Whether it has access to plentiful water supplies.

A more advanced stage will have been reached if mainstream tourism has already started to develop. In this case an evaluation of the zone or area will include:

- Whether it is well located in terms of regional transportation links, with easy access from other parts of the region and country, and serviced by an existing airport, or in the absence of an airport, if it has a good potential site for an airport.
- Whether it has a variety of sporting and recreational facilities or possibilities.
- Whether it has towns/cities or established resort areas already offering a range of entertainment and shopping facilities.
- Whether it has a mixed and already developed local economy able to supply and service the needs of tourism.
- Whether it has already well-developed infrastructure with spare capacity, or capacity for easy expansion.
- Whether well-developed community services already exist, e.g. police, fire brigade, health services, postal services, etc.
- Whether there is a local population able to supply a growing tourism labour force.

If these various requirements are already well satisfied, then the issue is one of expansion. To what extent can a zone expand its tourism, and whether this will change the product markedly? More importantly, will any changes result in an improvement?

In a zone with very little development but with mainstream tourism potential, one may decide to start from the beginning. If so, then the basic development and infrastructure cost will be such that a major tourism resort (in some thousands of rooms) may be contemplated. A large-scale project may be required to justify and cover the initial development costs.

A resort project of this size has to satisfy a rigorous market feasibility study, and win the commitment of the banking and financial community. Also needed are enough private sector interests willing to invest in various facilities and services.

Major new developments of this kind are often planned for islands. In the 1970s and 1980s major tourism resorts have been developed on Langkawi Island in Malaysia, on Margarita Island in Venezuela and on Batam Island in Indonesia. Batam is a mixed development which has combined tourism, commercial and industrial development together; its feasibility is based largely on its proximity to Singapore. In each case, these islands were previously only home to small agricultural and/or fishing communities.

Some minimum requirements

The precise planning and building regulations established may differ from country to country. The following are the principal types of minimum requirement which should normally be included:

- Easy access for people to reach public beach and resort areas should be maintained. These areas should not seem to be shut off, restricting use to resort and hotel guests only.
- Busy roads running directly along the coastline have usually cut off beach areas from the main resort facilities and areas. These lie on the other side of the road.

  Wherever possible, traffic should run along the back of coastal developments. Parking areas should keep most traffic on the perimeter. Only limited vehicular traffic should be permitted into the resort area itself, e.g. tourists on arrival and departure. If it is practical, mainly pedestrian access to the resort should be encouraged. However, depending on distances, some special forms of public transport may be employed, for example, a motorized mini-train system, open roofed vehicles, or horses and carriages.
- Environmental features on sites, particularly trees, may need to be conserved. Development may also need to conserve existing views.
- Setbacks should be adequate. It is important not to allow hotel and resort buildings to be developed too close to roads, other buildings and the shoreline or river banks. The exact setback may depend on where the building is to be located, and the site's surrounding physical characteristics. Setbacks are normally from about 10 to 60

metres. For shorelines, lakes and riversides they should be generous to conserve the beauty of the setting. Distances between buildings can also help to create a feeling of spaciousness. In all cases, the setback should be in keeping with the character and scale of the location.

- Floor area ratio is the ratio between the total floor area for all stories of the proposed buildings and installations and the total site area. This may be as low as 30 to 40 per cent for low density beach front developments, to a few hundred per cent in high density city centre developments.
- Site coverage ratio is the ratio between the total ground floor area of all buildings and installations and the total site area. It determines the feeling of spaciousness, influencing the extent of the landscaping and garden area.
- Height restrictions are partially controlled by the floor area ratio together with the site coverage ratio. However, the height limitation should be quite clear. In the Caribbean the height on many islands has been limited to 'no higher than the surrounding coconut trees.' Normally one, two or up to four storey buildings are allowed in many resort destinations, four to eight storeys in suburban environments, and up to twelve or considerably more in urban areas.

    Between 20 and 60 hotel or resort rooms per hectare might well be planned in resorts – 70 to 150 rooms in suburban areas and up to 300 rooms or more in urban areas. As noted in Chapter 7, this might cover development ranging from cottage or bungalow type projects to two to four storey blocks to high-rise buildings. In areas of high density resort development, 500 rooms or more may be planned for a five hectare resort site. Depending on the availability of land in resort areas, the yield in rooms per hectare should not be too low.

- Building regulations stipulate a wide range of standards. These cover the main building specifications, including hygiene and health, fire, safety and environmental requirements. They will specify minimum dimensions, window space and indicate standards for electricity and other installations.
- Parking requirements are usually specified in accordance with the

type of facility created, the particular location and the characteristics of the expected traffic.

- A particular style of architecture may be required to ensure that a building blends in with the surrounding environment.
- Requirements governing demolition may be included in the building regulations. These cover whether existing buildings may or may not be demolished. There should be certain procedures to follow to obtain the necessary approvals.

WTO has illustrated examples of different minimum requirements in a number of case studies (WTO, 1994).

Coastal management plans

Different public sector interests usually lay some claim over coastal waters and areas. There are also distinctive problems which coastal planning poses, and considerable interdependence between one coastal area and another. Because of this, long stretches of coastline should be studied together at the same time. It is often advisable, therefore, to treat the coast as a separate zone for planning purposes. This need not change the framework of working by regions, or any other established government administrative unit. However, coastal zones can then be considered together on an interregional basis.

Urban tourism

In towns and cities, tourism takes on many different aspects. Normally an urban environment already has a well-developed infrastructure. It may also have well-organized community services, e.g. police, fire, health and postal authorities.

Some cities or towns like Venice or Toledo, as already noted, have become dedicated to tourism. Other places, however, still have a busy commercial and industrial life apart from tourism.

The major issue in urban environments is usually the competition between vehicular and pedestrian traffic and the need to separate them.

The concept of zoning can also be introduced to urban areas. In most cities or towns it is the old part which contains most of the historical sites and main cultural attractions. Much of it can usually be pedestrianized, limiting the access of any vehicular traffic. Parking areas should be planned to catch and hold vehicles; they act in this way as a hub. Vehicles are channelled to park at the one point, and people then circulate by foot or public transport.

In other parts of a city there may also be concentrations of theatres, hotels, restaurants, shopping facilities and other attractions. Treated as tourism zones, these too can often be partly pedestrianized. Some downtown areas may be reserved for public transport only – buses and taxis – restricting access by private cars.

The renovation, conservation and beautification of old parts of the city also add to the enjoyment of the local population. The city administration may involve itself in many redevelopment schemes, converting some buildings to new purposes such as cafes, restaurants, shops, boutiques, artists' workshops and galleries.

Cities and towns, of course, are centres of business and convention tourism. They need to offer a range of facilities and services to satisfy these visitors. Increasingly new hotels are being clustered together, in composite developments, with shopping malls, cinemas, sports and health centres, and other entertainment and recreational facilities.

Product enhancement and improvement

Quite apart from the physical development of the product, through new facilities, there may be a number of other ways in which improvements can be made.

Opportunities will differ from place to place, depending on the particular local needs and problems. Generally they will fall into the following categories:

- Diversification and improvements in the various services and facilities.

- The creation of festivals and special events.
- The innovative linking together, or packaging, of various product elements.

For example:

- The organization of song or film festivals.
- The development of local ground transportation, particularly the availability of adequate taxi services.
- The availability and improvement of tourist information services.
- The beautification of the town environment and surroundings.
- The introduction of additional excursion circuits and itineraries.
- The setting up of better links between tourism and the local museums.
- The improvement of shopping facilities for tourism, including duty free shopping.
- The development of the production and retailing of handicrafts and arts.
- The addition of small and micro tourism enterprises.

Much of this product improvement can be achieved through the better linking of various facilities and services, for example, golf green fees and hotel tariffs, shopping discounts, theatre tickets, and entry to museums or historical sites.

A GTA can organize a number of product improvement workshops involving a wide range of private and public sector interests. It gives people a chance to participate, while harnessing their ideas and creativity to find a number of improvements.

A series of one-day tourism action workshops can be organized at the various levels – national, regional, local areas, cities and towns. The day can be divided between a morning session, followed by lunch and a short afternoon session. The morning session can consist of the GTA's presentation of problems, needs and ideas for product development. Following a lunch, the afternoon session can break the participants into work groups, to discuss specific ideas for improvements and new initiatives. A reporting back session and final discussion, possibly with a panel of four private sector representatives chaired by the GTA, can conclude the workshop on a results-oriented note.

The action programme

The action programme moves a plan into immediate implementation. It should be prepared based on the zones within each region and the improvements and developments proposed. It will need to cover: additions or improvements in infrastructure; improved access; additional resort areas and installations for all sections of the market; additional and improved hotels, restaurants, shopping and tourism services; the development of cultural, scenic and heritage attractions; the addition of other attractions, the introduction of special events and the development of all other aspects of the product.

It will also include any proposed changes in the minimum standards required by the regulations, and any incentive schemes and/or loan and grant schemes.

The government may decide to play a catalytic role in the development of a major project or projects. These should be fully described with drawings and artists' impressions.

The government may also decide to lease land for a specific tourism project on a design, build, operate and transfer basis. To this end it may decide to invite competitive bids. If so, it should describe the time frame, the lease conditions, and the prime objectives.

As part of the action programme, the support of the private sector can be enlisted in any overall product improvement programme.

Investment promotion and approvals

Projects cannot be implemented without the necessary capital funds. Depending on the projects included in the action programme, investment from both private and public sectors may be required. An investment promotion programme should be drawn up for the same five-year period.

Promotional trips and visits may be made in collaboration with any investment board (or equivalent government agency). There will be joint agreement of any advertising and other promotion. Investment promotion should be narrowly targeted at potential investors, once they are identified.

An investor's interest may be captured not by general ideas so much as specific project proposals. Design concepts can be developed with cost estimates. Marketing and financial screening criteria should also be outlined. A GTA should be able to present and illustrate a project, indicating the likely returns and benefits.

Investment promotional material should be developed. For foreign investors, an investment pack should be put together. It will contain all information on investing in a country, the tax and commercial laws and other key regulations. It should also include information covering, for example, typical construction costs, the local availability of furniture, fittings and equipment and operating supplies, and details of training programmes and the local labour market.

The GTA should also agree the criteria used to evaluate licensing applications for new projects, and to grant approvals on environmental impact statements (in collaboration with the government agency responsible).

Similarly it should also agree the approval criteria for foreign investment in tourism projects (in collaboration with the investment board or equivalent government agency).

Product development objectives and results

Objective

To establish a planning framework and process, and to formulate and maintain a plan for improving and developing the tourism product. This will meet the needs of international and domestic tourism, in each of the country's regions during the short, medium and longer term periods (5, 10 and 15 years).

Result 1

A fully formulated product development plan (5, 10 and 15 years), by region and forming a part of a continuing management and planning process.

Result 2

A tourism product development action programme by region for the first phase – five-year period.

Result 3

An effective promotional programme for domestic and foreign investment in tourism.

Product development activities

The activities of the product development department are expected to arrive at the three results above.

Result 1 – Product development plan

The review and refinement of the tourism development policies and strategies represent the starting point for product development. They include: the policies themselves; macro-economic perspectives; international tourism growth – world and regional; the current state of the sector; the marketing opportunities; the division of the country into a system of regions or other tourism development areas; the infrastructural situation; and the expected development of tourism.

One should also coordinate on the updating of national conservation plans and strategies, with the other government agencies responsible.

The rest of the activities are as follows:

- Keep the development strategy under review, updating, improving and adding to it, so that there is always a clear idea of how, by how much and where tourism is to develop.
- Evaluate the trends in tourism demand and the principal short,

medium and long term marketing opportunities. Formulate the appropriate marketing strategies.
- Join forces with the integrated multisectoral planning initiatives for each region, developing needs and proposals for the regional tourism sectors.
- Describe the product development plan for each region (or state, county, province, etc.) and zone, covering all aspects of the product including the particular types and size of resort and tourist centre.
- Review access to zones, areas and cities and the corresponding transportation systems, including all plans and proposals: airports, the road network, railways, inland waterways, and harbours.
- Assess the civil aviation policies, as they respond to tourism development needs and strategies.
- Check the necessary additions and improvements in the remaining infrastructural development, particularly water and power supplies.
- Review coastal development (if there is a coast), and formulate a coastal management plan – coordinated on an interregional basis.
- Finalize, in accordance with the above activities (in particular the regional plans), the various development proposals together with their land use and urban planning needs. Review with the appropriate government agencies.
- Coordinate overall product development proposals for each region, and finalize the updated national product development plan for the short, medium and longer term periods.

Result 2 – Action programme
This describes the activities for the tourism product development action programme for each region, consolidating the various regions into a national programme (result 2 of the product development objective).

- Justify the action programme on the basis of marketing assumptions and the expected development of tourism.
- List all new projects either planned or under consideration, evaluating their contribution to overall sectoral performance.
- Identify the projects which will form a part of the action programme,

scheduling their implementation over the five-year period in question.

- Agree with the relevant government agencies the realization of any priority infrastructural projects, providing detailed justification.
- Propose any projects, on government owned land, for development by the public or private sectors. Develop well-defined terms of reference for development, design, construction and operation.
- Agree any changes in the minimum standards required by the regulations and any special development incentives and/or loan and grant schemes.
- Maintain close coordination with the appropriate government agencies in the evaluation of environmental impact studies and statements.
- Develop various project ideas expressed through preliminary design concepts, drawings and artist impressions, accompanied by outline market and financial feasibility evaluations.
- Launch an improvement and development programme, to include various aspects of the tourism product.
- Add any other tourism-related projects due for execution by the private sector, e.g. any new tourist attractions or tourism services.
- Discuss and agree the action programme, on a regional basis, with a cross-section of government and private sector interests and publish and disseminate it accordingly.
- Integrate the proposed action programme with the plans for other areas; namely, regulation and control, research, marketing, human resources development and public awareness programmes.

Result 3 – Investment promotion and approvals
The following are the activities which need to be undertaken.

- Prepare an investment promotion plan for an initial period of five years (in accordance with the action programme). This should include a selection of tourism projects, with the promotional strategies to attract the necessary investment.
- Develop investment promotional material (printed items and promotional aids).

- Collect market information on potential investors and sources of investment.
- Develop advertising and direct mail activities, and any other investment promotion initiatives.
- Decide the approach for project evaluation reports, as a part of licensing and approvals of any grants or incentives.
- Use the specific conceptual designs and outlines (see the action programme activities) to attract the necessary investment.
- Set up a system to check the implementation of foreign investment projects, ensuring that all requirements are satisfactorily fulfilled.
- Promote domestic investment in the projects identified, and in the broader range of tourism services and facilities.
- Identify and develop links with the banking community.

Reference

World Tourism Organisation (1994) *National and Regional Tourism Planning, Methodologies and Case Studies*, Routledge.

14 Managing human resources development

This chapter discusses the importance of human resources development and the corresponding GTA role. It goes on to describe the steps taken in seeking to establish internationally agreed minimum working conditions. The chapter then explains the interrelationship between education and training, and discusses the role of a national committee or council for tourism education and training, and the links which should be established between different types of course. Surveys of the workforce are explained together with the estimation of future workforce needs, the assessment of existing education and training programmes, and the projection of future training needs. The chapter then describes the human resources part of the information system, occupational skill standards, trade testing and certification and minimum requirements for training institutions. It then covers both pre-employment and post-employment education and training, and describes other types of specialized training. The chapter concludes with a summary of the human resources development objectives, results and activities, representing the human resources part of the overall planning process.

The importance of human resources

The need to develop human capital is the starting point for all development. Nothing is possible without trained and skilled people.

A human resources development policy can be split into two parts:

- To offer competitive employment conditions and career opportunities to ensure the adequate recruitment of all levels of personnel.
- To provide educational and training opportunities for all occupations and specializations, at agreed and specified levels of skill wherever necessary in the country.

The responsibility for human resources development at the GTA is normally assigned to a separate department. This department should coordinate all aspects of a national tourism human resources development strategy.

Developed countries tend to have more money to spend on training initiatives. However, they often spend money on expensive training at the tertiary level; training which might be provided more cheaply in secondary schools or through on-the-job/work-based training schemes.

They may also develop adult training schemes which only seem to compensate for inadequacies in earlier education and training, or are merely a response to high rates of unemployment. Governments may also assume other training responsibilities (adding, many would say, to the costs of an already burdensome bureaucracy), which are best left to the private sector.

The relative roles of the public and private sectors do differ from country to country. Much will depend on the stage of development of the private sector, and its capacity and willingness to tackle training effectively. This, in turn, may depend on the level of organization of the professional and trade associations.

A human resources development strategy, covering education and training at all levels addresses these questions.

The human resources development strategy

The human resources development strategy can also be published as a short document. It should cover the following main areas:

- The relationship of the tourism development policies to human resources.
- The current tourism product and the existing labour force – this will

summarize characteristics such as numbers of staff, geographical distribution, age, gender, educational level, staff turnover, length of employment, seasonal employment, training background and experience, occupation, and levels of skill. It will also assess the level of technology, operational standards, and occupational skill standards.

- The expected development of tourism and future workforce and training needs indicating the expansion in the number and category of hotels and other tourism enterprises.
- The current situation in the development of all training and education for tourism – both for pre-employment and post employment levels. This will assess the adequacy of existing courses and programmes, location, capacity and output. As a result it will identify existing and future training gaps.
- The future development of all levels and types of education and training, located where it is needed and including the establishment of any new public and/or private sector tourism training institutions. It may also propose measures to encourage the development of other new private sector training initiatives.

Working conditions

Tourism has developed steadily but conditions of work, worldwide, have not kept up. Workers, in many countries, have been forced to tolerate poor conditions. This has been mainly true of hotels, catering and similar establishments.

The International Labour Organization's (ILO) Hotel, Catering and Tourism Committee is of fairly recent origin. The first meeting was held at the ILO in Geneva in December, 1989. A convention concerning working conditions in hotels, restaurants and similar establishments, ILO Convention 172, was not adopted until 1991. This convention applies to hotels and similar establishments which provide lodging, and restaurants and similar establishments providing food, beverages or both.

The convention, which is rather general in content, states that workers should be entitled to reasonable working hours, overtime provisions, and daily and weekly rest periods, according to national law and practice. They should also be given sufficient advanced notice of work schedules.

Workers should be compensated in time or pay, if they work on public holidays, as determined by collective bargaining or in accordance with national law or practice. They should also receive annual leave with pay also as determined by collective bargaining or in accordance with national law or practice. If not entitled to full annual leave, they should receive leave proportionate to the length of service or payment of wages in lieu.

Regardless of any tips, the workers concerned should receive a basic remuneration that is paid at regular intervals. The sale and purchase of employment are prohibited. Although this is all the convention covers, it represents a step forward. However, such a belated and limited starting point gives an idea of the backward nature of the sector on a worldwide basis.

Many of the more developed countries have already legislated far more comprehensive conditions for their tourism workers. Also the travel trade may often be more advanced in this area than the hotels, restaurants and similar establishments.

At the same time as the convention, the ILO also adopted a recommendation (ILO Recommendation 179) which goes further but lacks the teeth of a convention. It states that measures fixing hours of work and overtime should be the subject of consultations between the employer and workers or their representatives.

Overtime work should be compensated by a higher rate of pay than normal. Working hours and overtime should be properly recorded, and each worker should have access to the records. Split shifts should be progressively eliminated.

The number and length of meal breaks should accord with local customs and traditions, and with whether the meal is taken in the establishment itself or elsewhere.

Weekly rest should be not less than 36 hours which, wherever practicable, should be an uninterrupted period. The average daily rest period should be 10 consecutive hours. If the length of paid annual holidays is not four weeks for one year of service, it should be brought progressively to this level.

Programmes of vocational education and training, and management development, should exist. They should be aimed at improving skills and the quality of job performance, and enhancing career prospects.

A GTA should encourage consultations between workers and employers to arrive at sound, fair and mutually acceptable working conditions. These are fundamental to the successful development of the sector.

Education and training

There are various definitions of the terms education and training. Education is about teaching ideas and knowledge; it's about understanding the world better. Training teaches specific skills; it's about how to do a job effectively.

In most cases students need some of both. This is particularly true when studying vocational subjects at an advanced level, for example, medicine, engineering, business, tourism and hotel management. The exact mix and balance between skill and educationally slanted subjects are questions of judgement.

The dividing line between education and training is often very fuzzy. The usage of each term also tends to differ from country to country. To avoid such difficulties, it is often best to link the two terms together – education and training.

Sometimes there is an aspect of elitism in the rejection of training. Superficial values often judge education as superior. As a result students are taught too few skills, and may be poorly qualified to take up many jobs.

A national council for tourism education and training

The GTA will look for ways to achieve the best possible coordination between the various agencies and organizations involved in human resources development. It is possible to establish either a national committee or council for tourism education and training.

This committee or council can be advisory and consultative, aimed at bringing together all the various interests: the government agencies responsible for tourism, labour and education; the worker's organizations (unions); and the professional and trade associations (employers). Also the association of the country's hotel and tourism schools, if it or a similar organization exists.

The committee or council provides for the active participation of the tourism sector itself, in setting standards and reviewing policies, objectives and results. It also monitors educational and training activities, watching for adjustments and improvements as they become necessary.

The committee or council will be required to:

- Monitor labour market conditions, and all related trends.
- Keep under review the existing and future needs for management, supervisory, skilled and unskilled staff.
- Keep under review the existing education and training institutions and centres and their relevance to the identified needs. Liaise closely with the appropriate authorities and recommend any changes or modifications as considered appropriate.
- Recommend, based on the above, the development of any new centres or programmes listing their proposed objectives and programmes.
- Liaise with the university system so as to promote the development of appropriate programmes and activities.
- Encourage the private sector to take initiatives in the provision of training facilities and programmes, and to recommend any tax and fiscal incentives.
- Advise, in particular, and encourage the sector in the development of in-service training programmes, establishing guidelines and organizing workshops.
- Keep under review a current database on the numbers and backgrounds of lecturers, instructors and trainers needed to meet existing and future needs.
- Set out guidelines as to the career development of vocational

educators and trainers, and their recommended participation in intermediate and advanced programmes of further study.

- Promote the organization of seminars and workshops in management and supervisory techniques, and teaching and training techniques for trainers (train the trainers).
- Liaise with the relevant authorities in the development of occupational skill standards, and the testing and certification for agreed occupations.
- Enhance the image of the sector as an employer, and improve recruitment.
- Promote the effective teaching of foreign languages for tourism.
- Undertake all other activities which will assist in the development of education and training for the sector, and the general improvement of standards.

Linking types and levels of training

Training should last a lifetime. One should build on what has gone before, adjust training to changing demands, and develop and upgrade people's skills. The links should exist between various stages and types of training. Each successive type of training should open up a further stage of personal advancement.

These links are important. Training and education should not be categorized, and then sealed off within tight compartments. People should be able to transfer between different levels and types of course. The chef, for example, should be free to study management. The university graduate in management should be free to study cooking.

Surveys of the workforce

The first step in formulating a human resources development strategy is the study of the workforce. If adequate data do not already exist, surveys of the personnel currently employed in the tourism sector should be carried out. These will identify their characteristics (e.g. age, gender, educational level, staff turnover, length of employment, seasonal employment, training background and experience, occupation, and level of skill), and training needs. They will also assess the level of technology, operational standards, and review the development of occupational skill standards for the sector.

Surveys start by identifying the number of hotels, tourist facilities and services in the country by size, category and geographical distribution. The methodology used to collect and analyse data should be discussed and agreed with the private sector itself.

Estimates of future workforce needs

The various employment ratios from the survey, adjusting for trends, can be applied to the expected development of tourism to estimate future workforce requirements by occupation and level of skill.

The expected development of the tourism sector will cover growth of tourism traffic, number and location of new hotels and tourist facilities, and other future perspectives.

These requirements for new staff should be reconciled against labour market conditions and the sector's current recruitment and selection policies.

The adequacy of existing education and training

The current situation in the development of all training and education for tourism – both for pre-employment and post-employment levels, also needs to be surveyed. As a result the adequacy of existing courses and programmes, location, quality, capacity and output, should be evaluated.

All educational institutions, centres, and training programmes should be identified and their curriculum, training materials and standards assessed for their current relevance and effectiveness.

Post-employment training, including all in-service training, and train-the-trainer courses should also be assessed.

Future training needs

Future workforce needs should be translated into future training needs. These can be compared to the capacity of the existing educational and training facilities and programmes. As a result, shortfalls in this capacity to meet future needs can be identified. These are termed training gaps. They are gaps which will need to be filled.

One should develop a strategy to respond to all future training needs. It has to be developed according to all levels, all specializations and all parts of the country. It should cover, as appropriate, universities, tertiary level vocational training institutions, and secondary schools. It will also cover a framework of minimum standards, in-service training, supervisory and management short course programmes, and foreign language training.

It will also recommend, if justified, the establishment of any new public and/or private sector tourism training institutions – to interrelate appropriately with the national educational and vocational training framework. And it may also propose measures to encourage the development of other new private sector training initiatives.

Human resources information system

The human resources information system will form a part of the GTA's MIS, normally coordinated through the research department. It will monitor trends in employment, the profile of the labour force and labour market, the continuing trends in sectoral growth and development, future manpower and training needs and the capacity of existing education and training systems to respond to them.

To do this, it should input the results of the surveys described above. As a requirement in the annual licensing of hotels and other tourism enterprises, applicants may be asked to supply specific human resources data.

From time to time, other special surveys may be conducted to complement the information system. These may cover certain sections of the sector, or particular questions, or specific locations and provinces.

A framework of minimum standards

Occupational skill standards, trade testing and certification

Occupational skill standards are the minimum standards of knowledge and skills that a worker in a particular occupation, at a particular level, should possess. These are minimum acceptable standards – staff can do better than the standards but nobody should fall short of them.

The emphasis of these standards is on employable skills. There is also a certain amount of knowledge needed with each skill. Standards for different occupations are agreed, and trade testing and certification are developed according to basic, intermediate and final levels of skill. Corresponding curriculum development and skills testing follow on. There are three steps:

- The standard specifies what people have to be able to do, where, when, how and under what conditions. It indicates both the skills and knowledge they should possess.
- Curriculum and teaching material which reflect the standard enable the trainee to reach the correct level of performance.
- The test validates that the trainee can reach satisfactorily this level of performance.

Skill standards help support sector-wide quality targets. They also assist employers in performance appraisal, career planning, recruitment and selection, and the development of training plans and targets. They create a basis for inter-company comparison, and they enable skills development to be monitored for the whole sector.

National certification enables the quick recognition of levels of skill as well as the outputs of training institutions. Through the system of testing, all personnel can gain recognition for their level of skill.

Where classification schemes exist for hotels and other tourism enterprises, minimum training requirements (the number and categories of staff certified according to the skill standards) may also be included.

At first glance, it may seem that industry-wide occupational skill standards are very production oriented rather than market oriented. One starts by asking – what do workers do? One then asks what skills and knowledge they should possess to be able to do it. A marketing approach would start with what staff should be doing to meet the needs of the customers.

Skill standards, however, are usually influenced by the major hotels and tourism enterprises, many of which are operated by multinational companies. Usually these enterprises have already attuned their product to the mainstream market demands.

Minimum requirements for training institutions

Regardless of which government agency is authorized to approve and license training institutions, minimum standards should also be established. Applications and submissions should include:

- A plan covering a period of at least five years. It will describe the needs and justification for the courses offered, and give details of student recruitment and links with the hotels and other tourism enterprises.
- Standards and curriculum describing their interrelationship with the relevant national skill standards and curriculum. Examples of teaching materials and methods should also be included.
- The number of instructors and teachers, their qualifications and experience, and teacher/student ratios.
- The numbers of students enrolled or targeted, and the capacity of the programmes and their annual outputs.

- The financial structure including capitalization, projected operating results and sources of funds; government or any other grants and any proposed student fees.
- The facilities: land area, floor area ratio, range of facilities, planning ratios, classrooms, offices, laboratories, library, student facilities, and other areas.
- The organization and the administrative staffing and systems.
- The employment expected to be obtained by students, on the completion of their education and training.

Pre-employment education and training

Vocational secondary schools

Some secondary schools may have, or should have, courses specializing in hotel, catering and travel subjects. This will keep this type of basic pre-employment course at the secondary level of education, leaving the tertiary level to concentrate on higher level courses. These basic courses will prepare school leavers for careers in the sector. Courses may cover accommodation-related subjects, travel and tour operations, and food preparation.

Government-funded tertiary level hotel and tourism educational and training institutions

Tertiary level institutions of this kind are usually costly to build and equip and expensive to operate. Some countries have attempted to leave this level of training to the private sector. However, the private sector may not be sufficiently well developed to make this feasible. In such cases, the public sector will need to play a catalytic role setting up one or two key institutions to:

- Teach and develop management and supervisory level courses and programmes.
- Conduct research on employment trends, manpower and training

needs, acting as a resource for the GTA, and assisting in the upkeep of the human resources section of the MIS.

- Maintain well-developed libraries, centres of documentation, and possibly computer Internet access.
- Act as a key resource in the development of national vocational skills standards and curriculum, and a system of trade testing and certification.
- Develop training material for all levels of tourism education and training.
- Train future vocational teachers for the country's secondary schools, as well as for private tertiary level hotel and tourism schools.
- Act as a major resource in the development of government tourism officials in tourism management and tourism development planning.
- Act as resource centres in certain specialized areas of tourism development, for example, in acting as custodian of the culinary heritage, or in acting as a resource centre in the promotion of small enterprise development in tourism.

In developed countries, without limitations of resources, there may be numerous tertiary level institutions offering hotel and tourism courses. Their contribution should be monitored by the GTA and any national committee or council.

Private sector tertiary level hotel and tourism educational and training institutions

Government, in close collaboration with the private sector, should encourage private enterprise to take appropriate training initiatives. Existing private sector schools should be encouraged to improve their physical facilities, teaching materials and equipment, as well as the standards of their teaching.

If there is a shortage of training programmes, the government may wish to encourage the creation of new institutions. It may therefore provide some guidelines for the location, size and student capacity for any new hotel training centre or centres, specifying the categories and levels of personnel to be trained. It may also offer incentives to set up such new institutions.

Universities

Universities generally have not all recognized tourism as a serious field for academic study and research and for assistance to the local community. Yet the universities play a key leadership role in the formulation of values related to overall socio-economic development. In this sense they not only educate the future generation of technocrats, but condition attitudes to development options.

For tourism to be viewed favourably, and for a wide range of graduates to have developed an awareness of its needs and potential contribution, the study of tourism should be included across a wide range of university programmes. This means not only full-time courses in various tourism specializations, but the inclusion of tourism in the social sciences, business studies, architectural, environmental and physical planning studies, and language and communications studies.

The role of the universities in relation to tourism should be studied to:

- Identify and review current university programmes and activities, in support of the tourism sector.
- Identify ways in which the universities can develop or improve this support.

Universities should be surveyed to review the following questions:

- University perspectives in developing postgraduate programmes related to various aspects of tourism, and particularly tourism development planning.
- The development of tourism options within the social sciences curriculum (particularly economics, social studies, geography and business). Any MBA programme might have a tourism option, and even the possibility of a major in tourism.
- The intention and capacity to develop tourism as a subject for research, relating this to the specific university faculties and departments. The integration of tourism in any current university research programmes.
- Involvement with local government in studies related to the monitoring and development of the tourism sector, for example,

the economic and employment impacts of tourism, the physical planning aspects, and the management and marketing aspects.
- The range of short courses in tourism-related subjects which a university might feel able to organize, related to the needs of a particular region.
- The links with community development and public awareness programmes, and the role of the university in these areas.
- The development of any programmes for small enterprises.
- The possibilities of using university resources in the training and upgrading of tourist guides.
- Any role that universities are able to play in foreign language teaching programmes, directed specifically at the needs of tourism.

University activities base themselves on the link between teaching, research and documentation and the concept of service to the community.

Post-employment education and training

A supervisory and management development programme

The public and private sector training institutions should offer, often in collaboration with the trade associations, a variety of upgrading and re-cycling courses particularly for supervisors. However, these are often fragmented, and of varying standards, certification and scope.

A national committee or council, as described, can play an important part in identifying the precise needs for these types of course. It can then encourage their organization.

There may be a case for one centrally coordinated and controlled sector-wide management and supervisory development programme, endorsed by the appropriate government bodies. Such a scheme might best be organized by the professional and trade associations, under the auspices of any national committee or council.

In-service or in-house training programmes at the local level

A GTA should want to improve the operational standards of the sector. In-service training will contribute significantly to this objective. The professional and trade associations should be encouraged to help organize this training working closely with its members.

Large enterprises should be encouraged to appoint specialized training personnel and develop in-house training departments and programmes.

In many countries there is a need to cover basic skills training in the more remote parts of the country, and mobile training teams can be used. These teams will journey from area to area, organizing basic level training courses.

Specialized clubs and societies

The formulation of specialized clubs and societies among different hotel and tourism specialists, can greatly assist the objectives of human resources development. These may include, for example, one for marketing specialists, one for financial management specialists, and one for food and beverage specialists. Of particular importance will be one for the sector's personnel and training specialists, creating an additional forum for the discussion of all human resources development issues.

Training for small hotel and tourism enterprises

As noted in Chapter 9, small and medium-sized tourism enterprises offer an important source for new jobs and income generation in rural areas. New business activity of this kind can also create more opportunities for the employment of women.

Assistance will focus on those areas considered essential for successful business establishment and growth, namely:

- The identification of business opportunities.
- Technical assistance in project formulation and feasibility studies.
- Training in the basic skills and knowledge necessary for starting and

running a business enterprise (management, financial, entrepreneur ial, social and technical skills).

- Assistance in obtaining appropriate loan finance.
- Ongoing technical assistance and advice.
- Development of support networks for small businesses.

Cooperatives

The development of cooperatives also relates to the area of small and micro-tourism enterprises. There is a strong case for the creation of cooperatives among these operations, particularly small hotels, with a focus on marketing and training.

Other educational and training courses and programmes

Tourism documentation and publications

The tourism sector needs access to tourism texts, reference material, and teaching material. These needs may be met by private sector initiatives. If not, the GTA may promote and assist the production of various texts and material.

Vocational teachers

In many countries there is a shortage of qualified vocational teachers for hotel and tourism studies in both the private sector and public sector.

Some teachers can be drawn from senior personnel working in the sector, interested in becoming teachers. They can be given the teaching skills through specially organized intensive courses. However, where the sector is not as yet highly developed, this source of recruitment may be limited.

Alternatively a number of hotel and tourism school graduates may be interested, after a few years of appropriate experience, in a teaching career. They will just need to acquire the necessary teaching skills.

Another course of action is to offer three-year courses at the tertiary level, designed to produce vocational teachers in tourism specializations.

Government tourism officials

Highly skilled technicians are essential to the effectiveness of a GTA. It is important that these personnel be kept up-to-date on various tourism management techniques and approaches.

Tourist guides

Many visitors form their impressions of a country through the tourist guide. The skills of these personnel are therefore a major influence on the quality of the overall tourism product.

Tourist guide standards may be developed for general tourist guides and tour leaders, with a separate category for various special interest guides. This latter category represents a guide specialized in one aspect of tourism or one tourism attraction. To designate the different categories, a system of badges can be introduced.

A major problem affecting the standards of guides is the level of foreign language proficiency, and the proportion of guides available in each particular language. While English has become the major international language, its importance and widespread use has not replaced the need for proficiency in other languages; for example, in Japanese or Korean.

Tourist guide should be included among the occupational skill standards and national system of trade testing and certification.

Language training

The ability to communicate effectively with tourists is fundamental to a successful tourism sector. The introduction of specified standards for foreign language competence is essential, together with a range of comprehensive courses and programmes. A number of occupational skill standards for tourism should include a foreign language component.

Human resources development objective and results

Objective

Identify future manpower needs, and review and develop all human resources development policies and strategies for tourism.

Result 1
In accordance with the expected tourism development and growth, forecasts of the future tourism sector workforce together with existing and future training needs.

Result 2
An integrated human resources development strategy for the sector, covering all levels of personnel in all occupations.

Human resources development activities

Many of the activities have already been discussed and explained during the course of this chapter. The following summary can therefore act as a checklist.

In accordance with the results planned, the first group of activities addresses the identification of existing workforce characteristics and future needs. It also assesses existing and future training needs. The second group tackles the planning and implementation of a programme to respond to these needs.

The objectives, results and activities are illustrated together in Figure 14.1.

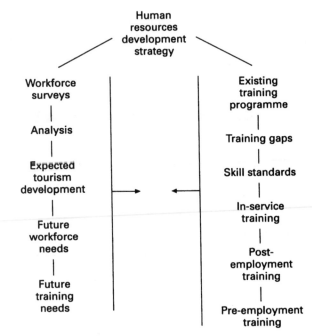

Figure 14.1   Human resources development planning

Result 1 – Future workforce and training needs

The following activities, described earlier in the chapter, enable estimates of future workforce and training needs:

- Design surveys of the existing workforce; questionnaires, interviewing and survey methods.
- Conduct surveys of the existing workforce including employee profiles and characteristics, occupations held, levels of skill, and any training received.
- Analyse data and process the results.
- Incorporate survey results, on a continuing basis, within the MIS.
- Institute a system for the regular collection and updating of workforce statistics.
- Review the expected development and expansion of the sector, the number of hotels under construction and the addition of other tourism facilities and services.
- Prepare, on the basis of the above, forecasts for future workforce needs.

- Review the future workforce needs by occupation, level of skill, and area of the country and identify future training needs.
- Discuss the workforce characteristics, and future workforce and training needs with any national committee or council, or similar consultative body.

Result 2 – Human resources development strategy

The following activities reflect the various components of the strategy discussed earlier in the chapter:

- Survey the existing education and training institutions and evaluate their contribution to human resources development; the quality of programmes and the capacity and output of trainees and students.
- Assess the capacity and quality of the existing education and training system and identify any training gaps.
- Prepare proposals for the improvement, expansion and development of the network of educational and training institutions and centres to meet future needs.
- Review in-service training programmes, and other post-employment training, in relation to the identified needs.
- Identify future needs for specialized teachers and training staff, and formulate proposals for the necessary teacher training programmes.
- Formulate programmes for all specialized training, including, for example, government tourism officials, tourist guides, and planning and marketing specialists.
- Outline the proposals for the development of a comprehensive set of occupational skill standards for the sector.
- Consult with the universities on the development of their role in relation to both tourism studies and research.
- Review with the educational authorities the introduction of tourism-related education and training in existing educational institutions.
- Develop initiatives to assist the private sector in playing a more active part in training, including the development of more and/or better in-service training programmes.
- Integrate all proposals with other areas of the plan, namely, GTA management and organizational development, regulation and con-

trol, research, marketing, product development and public awareness programmes.

- Draft, review and finalize, or update and finalize as the case may be, the tourism human resources development strategy.
- Consult extensively with any national committee or council, or similar body, on all aspects of the strategy.

15 Managing public awareness programmes

This chapter completes Part III by examining the management of public awareness programmes. It starts by describing their role in relation to the tourism development policies and strategies. It then explains that a public awareness programme answers four fundamental questions for the local community. The chapter goes on to examine local community involvement and the role of a local community tourism action group. It continues by explaining relations with the press, press releases and press conferences, advertising, tourist newspapers, television and radio, competitions, schools, a host programme, workshops and seminars and public awareness campaigns. The chapter then describes approaches to making tourists aware of the local culture. It concludes with the objectives, results and activities, representing the public awareness part of the overall management and planning process.

The role of public awareness

Listed among the tourism development policies in Chapter 1 was the need to keep the general public closely informed about the growth of tourism. This included giving explanations about its development and its contribution to the country's social and economic well-being. It also included the need to encourage the general public to support the development of both international and domestic tourism.

The overall strategy described in Chapter 11 reflected these policies by including the need for public awareness programmes.

Public opinion has to be informed and led. It has to respond to people's concerns. At the same time people themselves are a part of the tourism product, and should be able to make a commitment towards its success. The job of mobilizing public support on the side of tourism is first the GTA's. However, it is also the job of everybody who works in tourism.

For any local community a public awareness programme answers four fundamental questions:

- What is there positive to say about inbound tourism?
- About which issues should the local community be consulted?
- What help should be offered and to whom?
- Who are the inbound tourists and what are they like?

In answering these four questions a public awareness programme:

- Explains and signals.
- Explains, consults and involves.
- Explains and provides help.
- Explains and interprets.

A public awareness programme also explains to tourists important aspects of the local culture and how best to behave to get the most benefit from their visit.

Public awareness has many similarities to marketing. It is about communicating ideas, values and plans, and uses many of the same public relations, promotional, sales and advertising tools as marketing. It is trying to get across a point of view, to involve people, to inform them, to educate them, to benefit from their ideas and to win their support.

A public awareness programme will be coordinated at the national level by the GTA itself. It should cover mainly the contribution of tourism to national economic and social development and the perspectives for its future development. Other elements of public awareness should be organized at the local community level.

The GTA, however, should provide guidance, suggestions, resources and materials to local community action groups and visitor bureaus. The GTA may also coordinate nationally some other activities, for example country-wide competitions.

An important part of public awareness addresses the concept of sustainable development. Not as an abstract idea but in concrete and practical ways. This involves a commitment to maintaining high environmental standards through sensible controls.

Figure 15.1 illustrates the overall scope and content of a public awareness programme.

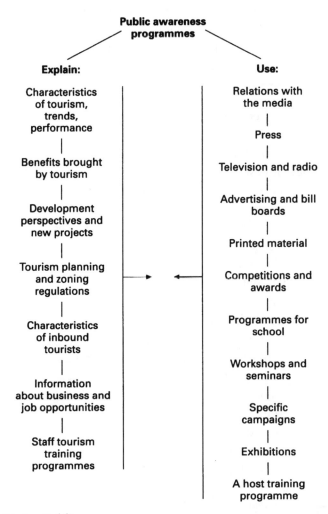

Figure 15.1   Public awareness programmes

What is there positive to say about inbound tourism?

This is a good question to pose to different groups, for example to groups of schoolchildren or groups from local clubs, societies and organizations. The question and the range of answers are exactly what public awareness programmes are designed to communicate. It is essential, as a starting point, to agree the message.

Ideas which people, given time to think and discuss the question, are likely to call out or list are as follows. These are some of the positive aspects (all highlighted in past chapters) which a public awareness programme should signal.

Inbound tourism:

- stimulates local economic development
- generates income
- creates new jobs and career opportunities
- creates new investment possibilities
- opens up chances for small enterprises
- earns foreign exchange
- creates an audience for local cultural performances
- stirs an interest in the local cuisine
- creates a market for local handicrafts and arts
- brings contacts with different cultures
- promotes an interest in foreign languages
- helps to improve the local environment
- triggers new infrastructural development
- enables the provision of new community services
- generates government revenue
- enhances the country's and the destination's image
- strengthens the sense of cultural identity
- assists local agriculture and manufacturing
- stimulates investment
- brings in students for educational programmes
- helps to make it a nicer place to live.

Nearly all of the above answers may involve both international and domestic tourism, and can serve as the basis for more detailed explanation and discussion. All of them can serve as the basis for news items and press releases.

About which issues should the local community be consulted?

The above list covers points about which people should be made more aware. They consist of the information which will expand people's understanding of tourism. There are a number of these issues which are not just a question of awareness and understanding, but of consultation. Many people may also have serious concerns and objections. They need a chance to voice these and to make their points of view known.

Tourism development plans, associated physical plans, and planning and zoning regulations need to be publicly aired, with sessions dedicated to public comments, questions, objectives and open discussion. Individuals and action groups should be aware of any rights they may have to register objections and appeals against particular developments.

In the presentation of new plans, the rationale, policies, strategies and objectives should be carefully explained. Objections and concerns often arise from misunderstandings.

Major issues are usually as follows:

- What are the perspectives for the development of tourism? How many tourists will be accommodated at any one time? Is this in keeping with the destination's carrying capacity?
- In land use planning and zoning, which areas are designated for what purpose? Where and how will tourism be allowed to develop and in what form?
- Where will new roads run, over what land, and to what purpose?
- Are there any new airports or extensions to existing airports planned? If so, where and on what scale?
- Is basic infrastructure adequate and will it be expanded, for example, water, power supplies and waste disposal?

- What specific planning regulations are to be applied to hotels and other tourism buildings – building setbacks, height restrictions, floor area and site coverage ratios?
- How do these interrelate with other types of building and proposed zoning plans?
- In which areas will hotel and other types of tourist facilities not be allowed and why?
- Are there new plans to add car parking facilities, pedestrianize certain streets and control vehicular traffic?

People should be told where they can view the detailed plans involved, and what further meetings may be held to review the details of these plans. They should know where and how to ask their questions.

What help needs to be offered to the local community?

Many people will want to be informed about tourism not only to learn about it, but also to take particular action. For example, they may want to know how a son can train for a tourism career; or how they can rent a spare room to accommodate a visiting student; or how they can start a guest house.

People will need answers to the following types of question:

- Where to go to learn more about tourism? Details of the following items should be provided: foundation and awareness courses; lectures and conferences; leaflets and publications.
- How to meet tourists? A possible programme might be organized by the visitors bureau whereby visitors and local citizens, with similar hobbies or professional interests, are introduced so as to meet and spend a little time together.
- What jobs are available and careers open? The prospects, opportunities and training available, including details of courses and educational programmes.
- How to start a small tourism business? Details should be provided

about the development of initial concepts and ideas. How to estimate capital costs, develop a business plan, and obtain loan finance.

- How to rent a room in one's house, for visiting students and members of youth groups? One should tell people where to find information about groups, times, prices, requirements and listings.
- How to clarify questions of planning permission? One should also tell people where they can view plans and future schemes, and obtain information and advice.
- Where to study foreign languages? Opportunities of using foreign language competence in tourism, including part-time jobs and training as a tourist guide. Details of language institutes, courses and programmes should also be given.
- How to design the products which visitors would like to buy? This may involve advice on menus and the choices to include. It may also include advice on handicrafts, souvenirs, or fashion items and jewellery design.

All of these answers will require liaison between the GTA or local visitors bureau and other agencies and organizations; for example, the educational authorities and secondary schools, the educational and training institutions, the planning authority, the local enterprise agency, the town hall or local government authorities themselves, the chamber of commerce and the local trade and professional associations.

Who are the inbound tourists and what are they like?

Most people have only a stereotyped image of visitors from abroad. This is true even in Europe where one country's understanding of another is still sketchy and full of mistaken ideas. One should explain the following principal characteristics of the culture which each major market represents:

- The country and its geography, climate, population, constitution, government and economy.
- Language and culture, ethnic and tribal origins, historical influences, educational and social development.
- The arts: literature, theatre, music, painting, sculpture, architecture, handicrafts, etc. The impact of contemporary arts.
- Food and drink. National holidays. Religious practices. Codes of dress. Customs and traditions. Minorities and subcultures.
- The way of life. Lifestyles, values and attitudes. Behavioural characteristics and social norms. Regional differences. Sexual behaviour and consumption of alcohol and tobacco. Drugs and drug abuse.

These five areas sketch out the comprehensive profile of a given country and nationality. This profile provides for valuable under-standing and insight when dealing with tourists from different countries.

Local community involvement

In every community there are groups of people with an interest in tourism and its development. They may be disparate groups representing different aspects of tourism; the local historical or archaeological society, for example, or an environmental group or the local hotel owners and travel agencies. Some may be directly involved with tourism, others less directly.

From these groups leaders will spring up; people with well-defined viewpoints prepared to give their time to prepare background notes and papers, call meetings, organize agendas, and contact other individuals, groups and organizations. These people will start to become aware of other people who share the same ideas. Eventually they will all come together, possibly through the chamber of commerce or similar body, as a committee or subcommittee set up for the purpose. Gradually a public forum on tourism is created, which may include tourism professionals, tourism businessmen, and people working on the fringes of tourism together with ordinary concerned citizens.

This may take time and the leaders may change, but the initiative is maintained. It is often more likely to happen at the local level involving villages, townships, small resort areas and perhaps some cities. It represents the typical action of a small community anxious to influence future development.

The GTA should be sensitive to any local initiatives and assist in any way possible to get people working together. If, however, there are dynamic private sector people leading such initiatives, then the GTA should let them get on with it – playing a supportive role only.

If the leaders and catalysts do not emerge and tourism is important, then the GTA should take the initiative. It can convene workshops or seminars to get people together for the first time and stimulate their interest. Local individuals and organizations are then likely to continue by themselves.

The role of a local community tourism action group

As noted at the beginning of the chapter, the GTA should spearhead public awareness at the national level. It should maintain excellent relations with the press keeping it well informed on sectoral performance, tourism statistics, expansion in supply and other major trends and developments. There may be some other activities best undertaken by the GTA at the national level. For example, some radio and television programmes, the production of audiovisual and other material, and national competitions.

Some activities may also be undertaken at the regional and local levels. It is here that the close involvement of the community can be built up. A local community tourism action group can organize many activities.

Depending on the community, different organizations may take the lead in organizing a group. This may also depend on the local GTA, or if the municipality has a tourism office or department, or whether an initiative to set up a visitor's bureau has been taken. Generally speaking, the role of the local community action groups is as follows:

- Maintain close links with the GTA receiving from it a newsletter, a constant flow of other current information on tourism, printed and audiovisual material, and notes, suggestions and guidelines on the development of the public awareness of tourism.
- Maintain close links with the sector's trade and professional associations, and any consultative organizations on tourism such as a council or committee on tourism education and training, or a joint marketing board or similar body.
- Organize a host programme providing basic foundation courses for tourism-related workers.
- Make the public aware of both the benefits and responsibilities brought by tourism.
- Make the public aware of the background and culture of the tourists.
- Stimulate public interest in the characteristics and requirements of tourism.
- Inform the public about new proposals and developments, reviewing their desirability and impact.
- Gain the commitment of both tourism workers and the population at large to the successful development of tourism.
- Provide education and training for all workers in direct contact with tourists.
- Develop on the part of visitors, some awareness of local cultural norms, practices and expectations.
- Maintain close relationships with the media enlisting their help and support in pursuing the above objectives.
- Organize a wide range of activities in pursuit of the above objectives including workshops, seminars, exhibitions, festivals, competitions and other special events.
- Advertise tourism public awareness messages through selected media.

If the local community action group is able to fulfil this role satisfactorily, the GTA may decide to offer financial support. For example the GTA may offer a fixed financial grant, or it may offer to match the funds provided through the local private sector and local government.

It is obviously in the interests of the GTA and tourism in general to build up effective and extensive local involvement.

Relations with the press

It is critical to maintain good relations with the press. This is a responsibility of the GTA's public relations staff. It is important not to fragment this activity, not to have different people talking to the press in an uncoordinated manner. The press should go through one centralized public relations office. Some flexibility has to exist on press contacts but people should always obey clearly established guidelines.

In public awareness the GTA should see that the press is kept informed:

- About trends in the growth of tourism, the numbers of tourists, the average length of stay, the foreign exchange earnings, the jobs created, and the impact on GDP and government revenues.
- About the government involvement in shaping tourism – new public sector projects, improvements to community services, particularly health and education, and new infrastructural projects.
- About tourism's support for the arts and contemporary culture, e.g. film festivals, song festivals, successes of local bands and pop groups, singers, other musicians, writers, poets and artists.
- About the perspectives for improvement and expansion. What the sector is doing to try and maintain and improve quality levels. What new projects are to be developed; where, in what form and with what impact.

Press releases and press conferences

The fax machine now offers an excellent way of distributing press releases. They should be written on all items of interest and sent out immediately. It is better to give the media too much material than not enough. Although still designated as press releases they should be distributed to radio and television as well.

Personnel who write press releases should be trained accordingly, and write in the correct journalistic style. It is essential that releases are impeccable – well written and with no spelling mistakes or errors of syntax.

Press releases have to be newsworthy It is pointless to send out weak stories which have no interest. It is also important to follow stories up. Press releases need to provide updates on what happened or what is going to happen.

All of the media should be given information. It is shortsighted to start to work with only one or two favourite publications while neglecting the others. However, this does not prevent the selective distribution of some releases. Not everything interests everybody. A well-organized public relations office should know where to send and where not to send particular items.

Press conferences need to be worthy of the occasion. The news to be announced should be of some import, with the head of the GTA acting as spokesperson. For example, the sector's performance for the last year with a complete set of results. Or major new tourism developments or projects.

The press conference should be held in a suitable place with comfortable seating and good audiovisual equipment. The press should be given every facility, and coffee and refreshments should be served. It is a good idea for the GTA, depending on the topics to be discussed, to invite the participation of the trade and professional associations. The sector then presents a united front demonstrating that it is working in a well coordinated manner.

Advertising

The use of billboards can be effective in promoting public awareness. They represent a very direct form of advertising having both immediacy and impact. And they are seen by a large and random cross-section of society. The different space and locations have to be planned to form a network of coverage across a given city or area, for example, billboards might carry the following sorts of messages:

Courtesy Pays
(Smile a little – bring a little pleasure)

Keep the Place Beautiful
(Making it beautiful – keeping it beautiful)

Tourism Helps Us All
(Tourism bring benefits – new hospitals, new schools, new roads – help us to help the tourists)

It's Nice to Come Back
(When people leave happy they want to come back)

Many different themes can be developed and used. Large billboards lend themselves to strong images and powerful messages.

Some local newspaper and magazine advertising can also be used. This need not be at the expense of the GTA. Tourism's private sector interests can be encouraged to sponsor some public awareness advertising. Radio and television stations can be encouraged to do the same.

Tourist newspapers

Tourist newspapers around the world are usually published in English on a weekly basis. English has now become the universally preferred second language. While 400 million people have English as a mother tongue, it is estimated that another 400 million speak it as a second language. Several hundred million more have some knowledge of the language, and are able to communicate at the basic level.

It was noted in Chapter 12 that most printed material used in marketing tended to mix three purposes – information, education and promotion. This is also true of a newspaper although much of the information can obviously be categorized as news.

The newspaper is likely to feature the highlights of local news, items about tourism, about places, people and attractions of interest. Also about events, entertainment, where to eat and what to see, and about the characteristics of the country. It may carry a map of the town and the area. It may also run a lively letters to the editor section, and any number of other features. Editors should maintain close contact with the GTA. In turn the GTA should support and assist these newspapers in whatever way possible.

Television and radio

The use of television and radio will depend on the particular country and culture. There are many types of programmes that can use tourism as a theme. Radio lends itself particularly to discussions on tourism and call-in programmes, with listeners able to comment and ask questions.

The local stations in tourist destinations can find many opportunities to support tourism. Programmes can be broadcast live from the hotels and resorts. Interviews with tourists and tourism workers can be featured, together with various types of quiz programme. A visitors of the week programme can be produced in which a tourist couple will talk about their holiday and choose favourite pieces of music. Programmes on the background and culture of various nationalities can also be produced.

Television also offers a variety of opportunities. A series of tourist dance competitions or talent competitions may make good viewing. Discussion programmes, tourist profiles, foreign language courses may all give wide exposure to various aspects of tourism. This all helps to build and develop public awareness.

Competitions

Skills competitions are preferable to competitions based on luck. Professionals may be invited to demonstrate their skills and knowledge. Or competitions may be based on ideas and insights about tourism in general. For example:

- Barman of the year, waiter of the year, chef of the year, etc.
- Hotel of the year, restaurant, travel agency of the year, etc.
- A national essay competition for tourist guides.
- Tourism essay competitions for schoolchildren.
- Most beautiful garden and most beautiful house.
- Best short story on tourism.
- A cookery festival, exhibition and competition.
- The most courteous police officer, immigration officer, customs officer, etc.
- Taxi driver of the year.
- Best newspaper article published on tourism.
- Best public awareness poster.

There are any number of other competitions which are possible. They should be tailored to the particular characteristics of the country's tourism. Some can be organized at the national level, others at the local level.

Prizes should be organized with the collaboration of the sector itself, particularly with the help of the airlines and multinational companies. Some winning personnel can be sent on short study trips abroad with arrangements made to meet their counterparts in other countries. Other prizes may be more conventional.

Maximum media coverage should be arranged for all competitions. Their objective is to focus attention on tourism and to promote the opportunities which the sector offers. A number of tourism companies may be willing to sponsor selected competitions.

Schools

A special introductory text on tourism should be prepared for use in the secondary schools. It should cover tourism's overall characteristics; the product, the demand, tourism development planning and the environmental, economic and sociocultural impacts. It should describe the opportunities offered by tourism.

There are different possibilities as to where and how to slot tourism into school curriculum. For example, it could be a part of social studies, geography or current affairs.

Additionally the local community action group or GTA can organize talks and presentations on tourism, particularly related to careers. Students should be told about jobs, prospects and training courses. As already noted, one can organize essays and other competitions designed to stimulate interest in tourism.

Posters can be displayed in the schools. For example the GTA might commission a 'Tourism – a Part of Our Future' series of posters or an 'Our Tourism' series. One can also distribute leaflets describing the sector and the career prospects which it offers.

A host programme

The participants for a host programme should be drawn from all occupations which have direct contact with tourism: for example, hotel and restaurant employees, shop assistants, taxi drivers, customs and immigration officials, travel and airline personnel and bank personnel. This programme can consist of a training module – of perhaps 30 hours contact time – which can be taught through either a full time or part-time course.

The curriculum can be developed and tried with some test groups before being finalized. However, the programme will probably cover the following subjects.

- General knowledge about tourism. Of what does it consist? What makes it a success?
- Main aspects of the national cultural heritage. What is there to interest tourists? What can they see and visit?
- Other aspects of the tourist product. What else is there to see and do?
- Culture and background of visitors. Where do they come from? What are they like?
- Motivational and behavioural aspects of tourism. What do people want? What are their needs?

- Standards, environment and quality. Upkeep and conservation.
- Crime and the tourist. Warning and protecting tourists.
- Social and communications skills; how to deal with tourists. Making holidays memorable.

At the end there should be a test. On satisfactory completion of the course participants can be awarded a badge and a certificate. They become accredited hosts. They should be encouraged to feel proud of this achievement.

The adoption of a host programme of this kind can produce rapid improvements in the quality of the tourism product.

Workshops and seminars

The major objectives of public awareness conferences, workshops and seminars are to educate people, to involve them, to listen to them, and to join with them in the discussion of policies and future plans. One seeks a common understanding, a consensus of opinion, and a commitment to certain courses of action.

These activities call for well-illustrated presentations about the existing situation, the needs and opportunities, and the proposed sectoral expansion and development. Ideas about policies and strategies should be carefully explained. People should be split up into discussion groups. Panels should be used for the final feedback and discussion sessions. Workshops or conferences should allow the maximum possible participation, and use an ample cross section of speakers and panelists.

Campaigns

Some advertising may be best linked to a number of other activities to form a campaign. A campaign can include conferences, television and radio programmes, competitions and contests, and exhibitions and festivals. It should be an intensive programme organized around a theme and running for a given period of time, for example, it can take the form of a tourism week.

A tourism week can be planned as an integrated programme highlighting all aspects of tourism. It can be opened perhaps by the head of the government and feature other prominent personalities during the course of the week. Activities should be designed to attract wide press coverage.

Making the tourists aware

People need help in the discovery and enjoyment of a new culture. They should be advised as to what to expect, how best to behave and what to watch out for; for example, in Chapter 8 situations were described where visitors of one cultural and religious background encountered strong religious beliefs of a different kind. The world's religions tend to know little about each other. One should explain to visitors the basic beliefs and practices of the principal local religions.

Most tourists, particularly when visits to religious sites are made, are interested to learn more. Printed material can help. Booklets and leaflets can summarize a religion's most important aspects. Books of a more substantial nature should be on sale. Posters can be used to alert tourists on how to dress and behave.

In general tourists should be advised on how to dress. Tourist guides should do this. The use of posters can also be effective. Some destinations are very open and permissive, others are sensitive to dress judged as improper.

Hotels and resorts can organize a lecture programme on aspects of the country and its culture, although this is seldom done. Tourists generally welcome the opportunity, in relaxed and pleasant circumstances, to listen and learn about the country they are visiting. The GTA should encourage hoteliers to take more initiatives of this kind.

All one can do is make tourists aware of local norms. It is impossible to restrain them completely. People on holiday are out to enjoy themselves. Some may drink too much. Some may be a little too noisy. Let groups enjoy themselves, it is seldom that behaviour will get out of hand.

Public awareness objectives and results

Objective

Develop and execute integrated public awareness programmes, designed to improve the general public's involvement with tourism, as well as its general perception and understanding of it.

Result 1
An integrated public awareness programme using:

- A range of media: for example, newspapers and magazines, television and radio, advertising and bill boards, and printed material.
- A range of complementary activities: competitions and awards, programmes for the schools, workshops and seminars.

Result 2
A tourism host training programme offered on both a full time and part-time basis for personnel having some contact with tourists, for example, hotel and restaurant employees, shop assistants, taxi drivers, customs and immigration officials, and travel and airline personnel.

Public awareness activities

Result 1 – An integrated programme
The following are the activities needed to formulate and execute a public awareness programme:

- Frame the precise objectives and content of the proposed public awareness programme.
- Assist in the development of any local community action groups or other local initiatives.
- Specify the various target audiences to be addressed – the public in general, the business community, special interest groups, and schoolchildren.
- Plan the messages to be communicated and the media to be used.
- Integrate proposals with other areas of the plan; namely, management and organizational development, regulation and control, research, marketing, product development and human resources development.
- Develop relations with the national and local press, and outline the use of press conferences, editorial, and advertising.
- Formulate ideas for the use of television and radio, call-in programmes, discussion panels, special programmes, advertising, etc. and implement.
- Plan and implement the placement of other types of advertising, including the use of bill boards.
- Plan the use of various printed material, design and prepare the items, and produce and distribute or display.
- Develop and organize various competitions, and decide the participation and prizes. Organize any exhibitions and other surrounding events.
- Organize a specific programme for schools; career talks, talks on tourism, special days and events, and special projects.
- Organize a programme of workshops and seminars, developing objectives, targeting audiences, and organizing venues and speakers.
- Develop any comprehensive public awareness campaigns to run in connection with a tourism week or other similar special event.
- Lobby on behalf of tourism, to mobilize the support of both public and private sector organizations and agencies.

Result 2 – A tourism host training programme

The following are the activities to be undertaken:

- Liaise with the various trade and professional associations at the national, regional and local levels, reviewing the needs for the host training course.

- Agree the duration of the course and its content.
- Draft the curriculum in modular style specifying and preparing the teaching materials.
- Agree the form of certification and any accompanying badge or other form of designation.
- Recruit and select part-time teachers for the course, and train and certify them accordingly.
- Agree the organization, venues, enrolment, fees, etc. for each particular location.
- Organize, advertise and implement the programme.

Bibliography

Ashworth, G. J. and Dietvorst, A. J. G. (1995) *Tourism and Spatial Transformations; Implications for Policy and Planning*, CAB International,

Ashworth, G. J. and Goodall, B. C. (eds) (1990) *Marketing Tourism Places*, Routledge.

Ashworth, G. J. and Tunbridge, J. E. (1990) *The Tourist — Historic City*, Bellhaven/Wiley.

Baum, Tom (ed.) (1993) *Human Resource Issues in International Tourism*, Butterworth-Heinemann.

Boniface, B. and Cooper, C. P. (1994) *The Geography of Travel and Tourism*, Butterworth-Heinemann.

Brent Richie, J. R. and Goeldner, C. R. (1994) *Travel, Tourism and Hospitality Research — A Handbook for Managers and Researchers*, 2nd edn, Wiley.

Burkart, J. and Medlik, S. (1981) *Tourism — Past, Present and Future*, 2nd edn, Butterworth-Heinemann.

Burns, P. and Holden, A. (1995) *Tourism — A New Perspective*, Prentice Hall.

Buttle, Francis (1986) *Hotel and Foodservice Marketing*, Cassell.

Cairncross, Frances (1995) *Green Inc: A Guide to Business and the Environment*, Earthscan.

Cater, E. and Lowman, G. (eds) (1994) *Ecotourism — A Sustainable Option*, Wiley.

Cole, G. A. (1993) *Management Theory and Practice*, 4th edn, DP Publications Ltd.

Coltman, Michael M. (1989) *An Introduction to Travel and Tourism: An International Approach*, Van Nostrand Reinhold.

Coltman, Michael M. (1989) *Tourism Marketing*, Van Nostrand Reinhold.

Cooper, C., Fletcher, J., Gilbert, D. and Wanhill, S. (1993) *Tourism; Principles and Practice*, Pitman.

De Kadt, E. (ed.) (1979) *Tourism — Passport to Development?* Oxford University Press.

Donaldson, Peter (1984) *Economics of the Real World*, 3rd edn, Penguin.

Downes, John and Paton, Tricia (1993) *Travel Agency Law*, Pitman.

Edgell, D. L. (1990) *International Tourism Policy*, Van Nostrand Reinhold.

Fewell, Arnold and Wills, Neville (1992) *Marketing*, Butterworth-Heinemann.

Fudfeld, Daniel R. (1994) *The Age of the Economist*, 7th edn, Harper Collins.

Fuster Lareu, Juan (1992) *Turismo de Masas y Calidad de Servicios*, 2nd edn, Grafica Planisi, Spain.

Frechtling, Douglas C. (1995) *Practical Tourism Forecasting*, Butterworth-Heinemann.

Geertz, Clifford (1993) *The Interpretation of Cultures*, Fontana.

Getz, Donald (1990) *Festivals, Special Events and Tourism*, Van Nostrand Reinhold.

Gold, J. R. and Ward, S. (1994) *Place Promotion – The Use of Publicity and Public Relations to Sell Cities and Regions*, Wiley.

Hall, C. M. (1992) *Hallmark Tourist Events – Impacts, Management and Planning*, Bellhaven/Wiley.

Hall, C. M. (1994) *Tourism and Politics – Policy, Power and Place*, Wiley.

Hall, D. (1991) *Tourism and Economic Development in Eastern Europe and the Soviet Union*, Bellhaven/Wiley.

Harrison, D. (ed.) (1992) *Tourism and the Less Developed Countries*, Bellhaven/Wiley.

Harrison, Richard (1994) *Manual of Heritage Management*, Butterworth-Heinemann.

Hartley, John (1982) *Understanding News*, Routledge.

Hawken, Paul (1995) *The Ecology of Commerce*, Phoenix.

Haywood, Les, Butcher, Hugh, Mullard, Maurice, Capenerhurst, John and Bramham, Peter (1994) *Community Leisure and Recreation – Theory and Practice*, Butterworth-Heinemann.

Haywood, Les, Kew, F. C., Bramham, Peter, Spink, J., Capenerhurst, John and Henry, I. (1989) *Understanding Leisure*, Stanley Thornes.

Heath, E. and Wall, G. (1994) *Marketing Tourism Destinations – A Strategic Planning Approach*, Wiley.

Hodgson, A. (1987) *The Travel and Tourism Industry – Strategies for the Future*, Butterworth-Heinemann.

Hofstede, Geert (1994) *Cultures and Organisations*, Harper Collins.

Hogue, Rod, Harrop, Martin and Breslin, Shaun (1992) *Comparative Government and Politics*, 3rd edn, Macmillan.

Holleman, Gary (1996) *Travel and Hospitality On Line*, Van Nostrand Reinhold, 1996.

Holloway, J. C. (1994) *The Business of Tourism*, 4th edn, Pitman.

Holloway, J. C. and Plant, R. V. (1992) *Marketing for Tourism*, 2nd edn, Pitman.

Hulmes, Edward (1989) *Education and Cultural Diversity*, Longman.

Inskeep, E. (1991) *Tourism Planning*, Van Nostrand Reinhold.

Jenks, Chris (1993) *Culture*, Routledge.

Johnson, Peter and Thomas, Barry (eds) (1993) *Perspectives on Tourism Policy*, Mansell.

Johnson, Peter and Thomas, Barry (eds) (1993) *Choice and Demand in Tourism*, Mansell.

Kinnaird, V. H. and Hall, D. (eds) (1994) *Tourism – A Gender Analysis*, Wiley.

Kingdom, John (1991) *Government and Politics in Britain*, Polity Press.

Krippendorf, J. (1989) *The Holiday Makers – Understanding the Impact of Leisure and Travel*, Butterworth-Heinemann.

Law, Christopher M. (1994) *Urban Tourism – Attracting Visitors to Large Cities*, Cassell.

Laws, Eric (1991) *Tourism Marketing*, Stanley Thornes.

Lawson, Fred (1987) *Restaurants, Clubs and Bars – Planning, Design and Investment*, Butterworth-Heinemann.

Lawson, Fred (1995) *Hotels and Resorts – Planning, Design and Refurbishment*, Butterworth-Heinemann.

Lickorish, Leonard and Jenkins, Kit (1995) *An Introduction to Tourism*, Butterworth-Heinemann.

Lobley, Derek (1989) *Success in Economics*, 3rd edn, John Murray.

Lockwood, A. L. and Jones, P. (1989) *Management of Hotel Operations*, Cassell.

Lundberg, D. E. and Lundberg, C. B. (1993) *International Travel and Tourism*, 2nd edn, Wiley.

Lundberg, D. E. Stavenga, M. H. and Krishnamoorthy, M. (1994) *Tourism Economics*, Wiley.

Mathieson, A. and Wall, G. (1982) *Tourism: Economic, Physical and Social Impacts*, Longman.

McIntosh, R. W. Goeldner, C. R. and Brent Richie, J. R. (1994) *Tourism – Principles, Practices, Philosophies*, 7th edn, Wiley.

Medlik, S. (ed.) (1991) *Managing Tourism*, Butterworth-Heinemann.

Medlik, S, (1993) *Dictionary of Travel, Tourism and Hospitality*, Butterworth-Heinemann.

Medlik, S. (1994) *The Business of Hotels*, 3rd edn, Butterworth-Heinemann.

Middleton, V. (1994) *Marketing in Travel and Tourism*, 2nd edn, Butterworth-Heinemann.

Middleton, V. (1995) *Sustainable Tourism: A Marketing Perspective*, Butterworth-Heinemann.

Mill, R. C. (1990) *Tourism: The International Business*, Prentice Hall.

Mill, R. C. and Morrison, A. (1991) *The Tourism System: An Introductory Text*, 2nd edn, Prentice Hall.

Murphy, P. E. (1985) *Tourism: A Community Approach*, Routledge.

Ormerod, Paul (1994) *The Death of Economics*, Faber & Faber.

Pat Hanlon, J. (1995) *Global Airlines – Competition in a Transnational Industry*, Butterworth-Heinemann.

Pearce, David, Markandya, Anil and Barbier, Edward, B. (1992) *Blueprint for a Green Economy*, Earthscan Publications.

Pearce, Douglas (1989) *Tourist Development*, 2nd edn, Longman.

Pearce, Douglas (1992) *Tourist Organisations*, Longman.

Pepper, Allan, D. (1992) *Managing the Training and Development Function*, 2nd edn, Gower Publishing Company.

Pompl, W. and Lavery, P. (eds) (1993) *Tourism in Europe: Structures and Development*, CAB International.

Prokopenko, Joseph (1987) *Productivity Management*, International Labour Office.

Quest, M. (ed) (1990) *Horwath Book of Tourism*, Macmillan.

Riley, Michael (1995) *Managing People*, Butterworth-Heinemann.

Said, Edward (1995) *Orientalism*, 2nd edn, Penguin.

Sloman, Martyn (1994) *A Handbook for Training Strategy*, Gower Publishing Company.

Smith, S. L. J. (1989) *Tourism Analysis – A Handbook*, Longman/Wiley.

Smith, V. L. and Eadington, W. R. (eds) (1994) *Tourism Alternatives – Potential Problems in the Development of Tourism*, Wiley.

Spink, John (1994) *Leisure and the Environment*, Butterworth-Heinemann.

Stanlake, G. R. (1989) *Macro Economics – An Introduction*, 4th edn, Longman.

Swarbrooke, John (1995) *The Development and Management of Visitor Attractions*, Butterworth-Heinemann.

Syratt, G. (1992) *Manual of Travel Agency Practice*, Butterworth-Heinemann.

Tack, Alfred (1992) *Profitable Customer Care*, Butterworth-Heinemann.

Teare, R. and Boer, A. (eds) (1991) *Strategic Hospitality Management*, Cassell.

Teare, R., Calver, S., Mazanec, J. A. and Crawford-Welch, S. (1994) *Marketing in Hospitality and Tourism: A Consumer Focus*, Cassell.

Theobald, William (1995) *Global Tourism*, Butterworth-Heinemann.

Thurley, Keith and Wirdenius, Hans (1989) *Towards European Management*, Pitman.

Tribe, John (1995) *The Economics of Leisure and Tourism*, Butterworth-Heinemann.

Trompenaars, Fons (1993) *Riding the Waves of Culture*, Nicholas Brealey.

Uysal, Muzaffer (1993) *Global Tourist Behaviour*, The Haworth Press.

Ward, John (1991) *Tourism in Action*, Stanley Thornes.

Webster, Katherine (1995) *Environmental Management for the Hospitality Industry*, Cassell.

Weiler, B. and Hall, C. M. (eds) (1992) *Special Interest Tourism*, Bellhaven/ Wiley.

Weinstein, Art (1994) *Market Segmentation*, Probus Publishing Company.

Williams, A. M. and Shaw, G. (eds) (1991) *Tourism and Economic Development – Western European Experiences*, 2nd edn, Wiley.

Williams, Raymond (1981) *Culture*, Fontana.

Wilson, Graham, K. (1990) *Business and Politics*, 2nd edn, Macmillan.

Winch, Peter (1987) *Understanding a Primitive Society*, Basil Blackwell.

Witt, S. F. and Moutinho, L. (eds) (1989) *Tourism Marketing and Management Handbook*, Prentice Hall.

World Tourism Organisation (1994) *Compendium of Tourism Statistics*, 14th edn, WTO.

World Tourism Organisation (1994) *National and Regional Tourism Planning*, Routledge.

Index

marketing role, 228–30
National Tourist Offices, 82–3
regulations, 194–5, 210–11
  objective, 214
research, 211–13
  objective, 214–16
role and scope of, 90–2
tourism facilities classification systems,
  195–7
see also Management; Planning; Public
  administration
Growth, constraints to, 113–14

Heritage royalties, 136–7
Host programme, 302–3
Hotels:
  multiplier effect, 119–20
  price integrity, 74–5
  small hotels, 167
    training for, 280–1
Human behaviour, complexity of, 42–3
Human resources:
  development of:
    activities, 283–6
    objective, 283
    strategy, 266–7, 285–6
  education and training, 269, 271
    adequacy of, 272–3
    future needs, 273, 284–5
    national council for, 269–71
    see also Training
  estimates of future workforce needs, 272,
    284–5
  human resources information system,
    273–4
  importance of, 265–6
  minimum requirements, 274–6
    occupational skill standards, 274–5
    training institutions, 275–6
  workforce surveys, 271–2
  working conditions, 267–9

Image, 47, 51–3
In-service training, 280
Inbound tourism, 8, 290–1
  expenditure, 14

Information systems:
  geographical, 249–50
  human resources, 273–4
  management, 209–10, 219, 221–6
  market, 45–6, 219
Information technology, 79–80
Infrastructure, 49
Input-output approach, 121–2
Internal tourism, 9
International Air Transportation Association
  (IATA), 72, 102
International Hotel Association (IHA), 102
International organizations, 101–3
International tourism, 5, 9
International visitors, 9–12
Investment, 171–2
  foreign investment, 114–16
  promotion of, 259–60, 263–4

Land tenure, 137–8
Land transport, 13
  railways, 60
  roads, 60–1
Land use, 132–5
  planning, 251
Language training, 282–3
Latin American Confederation of Tourism
  Organizations, 103
Leakages, 123–4
  reduction of, 124–5

Mainstream tourism, 28
Management:
  management by objectives (MBO), 188–
    90
  management/organizational development
    objective, 213–16
  planning role, 181–2
  private sector involvement, 190–1
  public sector, 185–8
    coordination, 187
    direction, 186
    monitoring, 187
    organization, 186
    planning, 186
    regulations, 194–5
      objective, 214